MEDIA IMPERIALISM

SAGE | 50 YEARS

SAGE was founded in 1965 by Sara Miller McCune to support the dissemination of usable knowledge by publishing innovative and high-quality research and teaching content. Today, we publish more than 750 journals, including those of more than 300 learned societies, more than 800 new books per year, and a growing range of library products including archives, data, case studies, reports, conference highlights, and video. SAGE remains majority-owned by our founder, and on her passing will become owned by a charitable trust that secures our continued independence.

Los Angeles | London | Washington DC | New Delhi | Singapore

MEDIA IMPERIALISM
OLIVER BOYD-BARRETT

SAGE

Los Angeles | London | New Delhi
Singapore | Washington DC

Los Angeles | London | New Delhi
Singapore | Washington DC

SAGE Publications Ltd
1 Oliver's Yard
55 City Road
London EC1Y 1SP

SAGE Publications Inc.
2455 Teller Road
Thousand Oaks, California 91320

SAGE Publications India Pvt Ltd
B 1/I 1 Mohan Cooperative Industrial Area
Mathura Road
New Delhi 110 044

SAGE Publications Asia-Pacific Pte Ltd
3 Church Street
#10-04 Samsung Hub
Singapore 049483

© Oliver Boyd-Barrett 2015

First published 2015

Editor: Mila Steele
Assistant editor: James Piper
Production editor: Imogen Roome
Copyeditor: Audrey Scriven
Proofreader: Rosemary Morelin
Indexer: Judith Lavender
Marketing manager: Michael Ainsley
Cover design: Jen Crisp
Typeset by: C&M Digitals (P) Ltd, Chennai, India
Printed in Great Britain by Henry Ling Limited at
The Dorset Press, Dorchester, DT1 1HD

Library of Congress Control Number: 2014940477

British Library Cataloguing in Publication data

A catalogue record for this book is available from the British Library

ISBN 978-1-4462-6870-4
ISBN 978-1-4462-6871-1 (pbk)

MIX
Paper from
responsible sources
FSC
www.fsc.org   FSC™ C013985

Table of Contents

Preface

I first wrote about media imperialism in the 1970s, from a variety of perspectives. In my study of international news agencies (Boyd-Barrett, 1980) I dealt with media that sometimes are considered illustrative of the concept of media imperialism, media that originated in the major centers of nineteenth century imperialism and expanded with it. My focus was principally on their history, ownership, economy and operations. Broader ranging publications (Boyd-Barrett, 1977a) examined inequalities of media power and influence between nations, and also the history of media as instruments of resistance to empire (Boyd-Barrett, 1977b). While I continued to publish in media studies during the 1980s and into the 1990s my time was largely taken up with other preoccupations, including a newly acquired interest in educational communications in the UK and Spain, university administration, and, not least, raising a family of four children with my wife and partner, Leah. By the time I returned to media studies in the early 1990s it seemed that much had happened both in the world and in the field, where a slew of new theories and concepts – including that of globalization and its progeny – seemed to have eclipsed earlier ideas of media imperialism. More sustained reflection followed upon my move to the USA in 1998, the WTO protests in Seattle of 1999, the elevation of George W. Bush to the US presidency in 2000, the events of 9/11 and the ensuing "war on terror," including the invasions and occupations of Afghanistan and Iraq. The phenomenon of imperialism that I had thought was disappearing in the 1970s, despite troubling residues, had re-appeared in partially new and virulent guise. Western and many non-western mainstream media appeared to act in complicity with it. I concluded that the narrative that I had helped in some modest way to establish in the 1970s had not been satisfactorily completed and that it was now imperative to try. I leave it to my readers to judge the extent to which this volume achieves its purpose.

Acknowledgments

This book is a product of my professional lifetime and of my disicipline. I owe an incalculable debt to an entire generation of scholarship. Relative to its size, I have had woefully insufficient opportunity in a book of modest length to acknowledge all the scholars that could and should belong here. Scholarship that has been of greatest foundational influence includes but is in no way limited to the books of my early mentor, Jeremy Tunstall, and those of Noam Chomsky, Peter Golding, Stuart Hall, Edward Herman, Vincent Mosco, Graham Murdock, Edward Said, Herbert Schiller, Raymond Williams, and Howard Zinn. I am particularly grateful to John Downing for his sage counsel on earlier drafts of the manuscript and to Daya Thussu for his collaboration in its earliest planning.

I thank Colin Sparks and faculty of the School of Communication at Hong Kong Baptist University, and Anthony Fung, Joseph Chan, Clement So, and Jack Qiu of the School of Journalism and Communication at the Chinese University of Hong Kong for pleasant and productive semester-long stays, 2013–2014. These provided me a wonderful opportunity to advance this book. Additionally, I thank faculty and students of the School of Media and Communication at Bowling Green State University (BGSU) for sustaining me with an exciting intellectual environment and motivating me to complete several books, 2005–2013. I am also grateful for the support of Richard Kallan, chair of the Department of Communication at California State Polytechnic University, Pomona (CPP). I am proud to be Emeritus Professor both of BGSU and CPP.

The calm professionalism of Sage editors Mila Steele, James Piper, Imogen Roome and Audrey Scriven has been the absolutely indispensable steady hand navigating the volume to safe harbor. My gratitude is profound. My heart, of course, belongs to Leah, my wife, friend and advisor of over forty years, and to my children Claudia, Francesca, Jonathan and Daniel, their spouses and partners, and to my grand-daughter, Sofia. You are each my life's meaning and purpose.

Ojai, California
June 2014

Redefining the Field

MEDIA IMPERIALISM

What does it mean to talk of "media imperialism?" The expression implies that certain forms of imperialism are directly related with the media in some way. At least three forms of relationship are implicated. Firstly, processes of imperialism are in various senses executed, promoted, transformed or undermined and resisted by and through media. Secondly, the media themselves, the meanings they produce and distribute and the political-economic processes that sustain them are sculpted by and through ongoing processes of empire building and maintenance, and they carry the residues of empires that once were. Thirdly, there are media behaviors that in and of themselves and without reference to broader or more encompassing frameworks may be considered imperialistic. These may be international (as in the unequal news exchange relationships imposed by western international news agencies on national agencies throughout much of the nineteenth and twentieth centuries) or national (as in the case of powerful entertainment and news media that exercise inordinate commercial and political influence in given national markets – the influence of Rupert Murdoch in the United Kingdom comes to mind). In the literature on media imperialism, all these inflections and others are to be found. Sometimes the term is ascribed a theoretical status, as one or more theories within a much broader range of existing theories about international communication. The literature that specifically addresses media imperialism represents a relatively small body of work when compared with broader literatures that, while they are relevant in important ways to the topic of media imperialism, do not invoke the term itself.

In this book I propose as a starting point that the term "media imperialism" designates, first and foremost, an area of study, an area that deals with the range of relationships and interconnections between phenomena that scholars label "imperialism" and those that they label "media," an area that is available for empirical investigation. Within this area of study, previous and surely future scholarship proposes research questions or hypotheses that manifest characteristics of "theory" in social science. For example, drawing on primary or secondary data, or both, they may hypothesize that the interactions of two or more phenomena, dimensions, factors or variables that connect imperialism and media demonstrate consistency over time or place, yielding predictive value. While any such finding might be thought of as contributing, whether in endorsement or refutation, to a theory of media imperialism, I prefer to avoid the presumption that within the empirical field of media imperialism study there should be only one theory as opposed to an open-ended range or chain of such theories.

Within the field of media imperialism study one may identify quite different theories about the nature of this relationship. This is not the place for a substantive or exhaustive exegesis, but for the purposes of illustration and introduction we can identify four separate theories that were current from the 1940s to the 1970s. Harold Innis (2007 [1950]) identified what he believed were distinctive relationships between the physical properties of communication systems (e.g. stone, papyrus or paper) and the structures and capabilities of power in ancient civilizations. Herbert Schiller (1992 [1969]) called attention to what he considered to be an intensifying dependence of media political economy on new, transnational methods of electronic communication (notably the satellite). These embedded the media ever more closely within a regulatory system that served the US military industrial complex, first and foremost, while wedding them to business models that coincidentally also facilitated the global extension of US economic and political power. Extension of US power occurred as a result both of the direct sale of US commodities through advertising and, less directly, of the demonstration – through entertainment – of enviable consumerist modernity. Together, these forces helped shape popular consciousness by means of a hegemonic, ideological frame that was at least consonant with the role of the USA as superpower. Like Schiller, Jeremy Tunstall (1977) was also intrigued by the role of media in sustaining and extending US power but thought of this largely in terms of comparative market advantages. The USA was a large and prosperous media market. By recovering the costs of production at home US media could easily compete with local communication products in what were generally much smaller overseas markets: they could afford to tailor their prices in any way necessary to ensure market dominance, except where local regulations restricted foreign imports. Oliver Boyd-Barrett (1977a) extrapolated from three media phenomena of the 1970s, each supported by ample empirical evidence. First was Anglo-Franco-American dominance of an international or systemic network of global, regional and national news agencies. Second was the dominance of Hollywood studios in the international supply of movies and television entertainment production such that in many developed and emergent markets during the 1960s and 1970s local cinema and television were heavily dependent on US imports. And third, from his observations of post-independence Ireland he noticed the continuing influence if not market dominance of the UK over national Irish broadcasting and printed media. These led him towards a theory of media imperialism that centered on the inequalities of media power between countries, sometimes involving the direct exercise of market supremacy by media of powerful countries on media of less powerful countries, as in the case of Hollywood intervention on local movie markets (e.g. by imposing deals on local theatre chains to ensure that they continued to favor Hollywood product) and its suppressive consequences for local movie production. But in a separate work (Boyd-Barrett, 1977b) he also traced the role of media as agents of colonial resistance to British, French and Spanish imperialism in the long run-up to the achievement of the formal (but problematic) political independence of these territories.

MEDIA

I will not assume that the principal terms of my subject are everywhere comprehended in the same way, so some discussion of basic terms is in order. Let me start with the somewhat plainer term "media." While this term also has significations that lie outside of the study of technology-mediated communications it is with this arena that we are principally concerned. Several generations of research lend confidence to the observation that in this field it has generally been understood that the term was intended to refer to technology-enabled means of communication from the few to the many. These included books, newspapers, recorded music, film, radio and television. More recently, it has become universally appreciated that to this classic list of media should be added computer or digitally-enabled Internet and the World Wide Web. These fuse traditional few-to-many media with the one-to-one communication capabilities of telephony or radiophony and introduce facilities or forms of communication that did not previously exist (e.g. Internet browsers and portals, search engines, social network media) and are carriers of digital versions of all previous media forms. Particularly through the development of social network media, the Internet has considerably extended and enriched the scope for all kinds of communications among groups and networks, from very small to very large.

I see no particular merit, therefore, in limiting the discussion only to the so-called classic mass media or mass communication. A principal characteristic of mass communication is that communication content is formulated by the few for delivery to the many. A characteristic of both mass communication and technology-enabled interpersonal communication is that governance and operation of the technological, administrative and business infrastructures that give shape to and set the conditions for both these forms of communication are controlled by the few, with limited active involvement, if any, by the many.

Previous media scholarship centered predominantly on content – the production of content and the consumption or use of content by audiences, receivers or even interpretive communities. I propose in this book that in addition to an interest in point-of-consumption content (seen in previous research in terms of either the decoding of messages or collaborative meaning-making) we must also be concerned with the technological, administrative and business infrastructures that enable the production and dissemination of point-of-consumption content, including the range of devices through which that content is produced, delivered and received (hardware) and the protocols and operating systems they incorporate ("software"). Naturally, the relationship between software and hardware is symbiotic: hardware shapes and gives tone and texture to software, while software inspires the design of hardware. The onset of digital communication, which enables the delivery of a vast range of communication activity and content through the same device or range of devices, has highlighted the increasing significance of media concentration, the process whereby single media corporations acquire interests across all major forms of communication in processes of vertical and horizontal integration and extra-media conglomeration. Digital technology and the infrastructures that enable it (including cable, satellite and wireless networks) massively enhance communications activity across local, national, regional, international and even global markets, and compel us to understand the term "media" as encompassing all technology-enabled forms of communication, irrespective of time or space.

In approaching media with an outlook that emphasizes the importance of technology I shall try to avoid the attendant seductions of technological determinacy – the fallacy of attributing to technology some of the consequences of media that should more appropriately be attributed to the people, interests and social formations that gave rise to the technology. Certainly, once formulated, a technology may have highly significant consequences for determining who gets access to the means of communication for the creation, dissemination or reception of communications and the kinds of communication that are possible. Some of these consequences may be different from or go beyond what was initially intended by the originators and developers of the technology.

I cannot do justice in one volume to all the relevant issues of media and technology that relate to broader concerns of imperialism and resistance to it. Issues that deserve further treatment, but for reasons of space I have not developed, include but are not limited to those of Internet governance and the Internet Governance Forum, intellectual property legislation and issues of "piracy," the politics and weaponization of "surveillance," and the significance of the World Summit on the Information Society meetings of 2003 and 2005.

If I limited the discussion only to technology-enhanced communication, however, I would not do justice to the importance of more fundamental aspects of communication. These have to do with the always context-suffused processes of the generating, sharing, storing and retrieving of meaning, with or without the aid of technologies that go beyond the human body. This includes, of course, all aspects of human language, verbal and non-verbal, upon which almost the entirety of all media processes are dependent and which are every bit as accessible to discourses about imperialism as are the media. More broadly one can say that this realm of consideration invokes and is inseparable from an appreciation of culture(s) understood in the Raymond Williams' sense as way(s) of being (Williams, 1958). There is nothing about media that we can or should say that is not in some way or another embedded in a broader and deeper context of culture.

IMPERIALISM

While the term "media" must assuredly have a range of normative and other associations for any who would use it, it is a concept that readily lends itself to a working separation, in the hands of scholars, of its sense of media-as-empirical-tool from normative precepts or prescriptions as to how those tools should be used. This is less true, by an order of magnitude, of this volume's second key term, "imperialism," which presents itself with an even heavier weight of historical and ideological baggage. I surmise that the term is more often used with negative than with positive connotation, although certainly there are some who regard at least certain manifestations of imperialism as being benign or having long-term benign effects (a view that is likely more common among agents of imperialism, the imperialists, than those they colonize).

This problem notwithstanding, I choose to retain the term with all of its baggage and imprecisions. First of all, it usefully invokes the idea of power and unequal relations of power, particularly in the context of power exercised by some tribes, communities, and nations over others. Secondly, it is a term that in the study of media has now acquired a heritage of at least half a century's thinking, research and debate. Thirdly, it is incontestably the case that virtually all scholarship recognizes the phenomenon of "empire" as a long-established historical and institutional reality, and the term tends to be least controversially applied in the case of geographically identified centers of power such as Carthage, Crete, Athens or Rome that have extended political and military influence and control over wide swathes of territory for appreciably long periods of time in a process that is invariably accompanied by profound changes in commercial, social and cultural activity. Any inquiry into the role of media, albeit in the form of stone, papyrus or paper in relation, say, to the supply of armies, records of administration and trade, propagation of imperial edicts, ideology and religion, not unreasonably may be considered aspects of media imperialism (Thussu [2006] cites several such examples from antiquity in his textbook on international communication).

Western scholarship has had no difficulty in recognizing the existence of ancient empires whether in the west or in the east; nor has it scrupled in recognizing as empires the far-flung territories acquired, for various periods of time within the last few hundred years up to and beyond the Second World War, by ruling elites of countries as diverse as Austria, Belgium, Britain, Denmark, France, Germany, Holland, Hungary, Italy, Japan, Portugal, Russia, Spain, Sweden, Ottoman Turkey. European land-acquisition extended to the far Atlantic coast, igniting a process that led to the formation of the USA – which quickly joined the imperial club – and to vast regions of the Gulf, Africa, Asia and South America. The relinquishing of colonies (in Africa, the Middle East, Pacific and Far East) by Britain (in particular), Belgium, France and Portugal within the two decades following the Second World War – even if in most cases the imperialist's apparent departure was hastened by highly motivated local movements of independence or liberation – has created considerable confusion in many minds, scholars' included. Whether the motives for "giving up" colonies were idealistic (in altruistic celebration of the principle of national self-determination), diplomatic (e.g. comprising part of the settlement of "peace" terms by the victorious powers at Yalta towards the end of the Second World War in 1945), propagandistic (presented as representative of western liberal "civilization" and intended to stand in stark contrast to communist or fascist "totalitarianism" and barbarism) or in other ways self-interested (as in: dispensing with the pain, costs and other "burdens" of empire in the face of liberation movements and/or in order to better sustain political and capitalist "stability" at home), it seemed indisputable at the time that the "winds of change" heralded by British Prime Minister Harold Macmillan in Cape Town, 1960, did indeed portend the passing of the age of empires. The Soviet bloc or what we may call the empire of State communist Russia (originally conceived as a kind of imperial anti-empire) survived several more decades. Its implosion, starting in 1989, was the consequence of a mixture of internal contradictions (heavy investment in infrastructure yet an inability to respond to the growth of consumer expectations and the clamor for greater regional autonomy) and external pressures (including the 1980s occupation of Afghanistan). It was also a voluntary policy choice, one undertaken by a section of the Russian elite, under the leadership of President Mikhail Gorbachev, with a view to unblocking the systemic sclerosis of Soviet bureaucracy.

Throughout the Cold War (but also, long before and persisting long after the Cold War) there were many superpower and particularly US interventions (my interest is primarily in the USA in this book) in the supposedly sovereign affairs of other nations and territories that did not involve their territorial incorporation within the formal political apparatus of the hegemon. I shall argue that these kinds of intervention are best understood as a continuation of classic imperialism in relatively new (but also some quite old) forms. Their goals are not always to do with territorial acquisition; they are to do with securing – by any means possible, including violent coercion, provocation, bribery, threat, subterfuge – the foreign policy goals of the USA and of those parties or interests that have had most access to the shaping of these goals. The latter often, if not usually, include large multinational corporations based or originated in the USA or among the most powerful allies of the USA. Given the wide discrepancies between the declared motivations that are proffered by governments in justification for intervention (especially in the context of a supposedly "post-imperial" world), and "real" aims (typically representing a consensus of convenience struck between otherwise diverse interests), interventions require significant manipulation of public opinion through control of or influence over the media. Superpower interventions are therefore of critical importance to scholars of media imperialism. Later chapters will trace some of the key forms of imperialist intervention and its justification not only in the period since World War Two but since the emergence of the USA as a world power which is to say, almost from its very birth as a nation in 1776. Frequent objectives at play have included territorial acquisition but even more routinely involve discourses of national security and, behind or through such discourses, consolidation of political leverage in international relations and favorable terms of access to raw materials and to all kinds of markets, from the sale of debt to the provision of arms.

CRITIQUE AND COUNTER-CRITIQUE

While never disappearing from the research literature, the media imperialism tradition fell out of favor among those who criticized it for being either over-simplistic or out of date (e.g. see Straubhaar, 1991). The actual phenomenon of media imperialism, on the other hand, has never disappeared or ceased to be important. I shall propose that this field of study is sustainable, has evolved, and has never been more relevant than in the current, so-called digital age. It is central to considerations of media and power and although questions of power do not by any means exhaust the questions we may have about the media, there is a critical urgency for issues of power to be returned to center place in the field. In outlining reasons for the reinstallation of a concern for media imperialism, I prefer the term "media" to "cultural" imperialism. Although there are clearly many important and dialectical interrelationships between media and culture, I use the idea of "media imperialism" to focus attention on the political economy of the communications industries which is where I propose the analysis of media and power in a global context should begin.

Several critics, and even some who work within the tradition of media imperialism studies, confine their attention mainly or solely to manifest media content. Content tends to be judged by such considerations as whether or to what extent it is locally produced or imported (or the degree to which it is "hybridized") and its generic status, often in the context of fears of cultural homogenization and what that might mean. This may be to the exclusion of other vitally important variables including transnational transfers of media-related capital, ownership, advertising, expertise, technology, formats, patents and royalties. Even at the level of content, analysis is too often unsophisticated, with little work expended on how issues are framed, the ideological premises (with respect, for example, to the neoliberal agenda that has been promoted by the USA and its major allies), sources cited, degrees of consonance with domestic or foreign state policies and corporate interests. Some of the original models of media imperialism (e.g. Schiller, 1992 [1969]; Boyd-Barrett, 1977a) specifically emphasized components that went beyond manifest content. Some more recent work (e.g. McChesney and Schiller, 2003; Boyd-Barrett, 2006) has tried to broaden the field of relevant media in the era of technology convergence, embracing not simply "old" and "new" media, but consumer electronics, telephony and computing. These media are important both in and of themselves and also because, increasingly, electronic access to both "old" and "new" media forms is determined by electronic hardware (including cable, satellite and telephony, wired or cellular wireless operators) and software gatekeepers (including operating systems, internet service providers, browsers and appliance applications).

Misleadingly, some critics have conflated ideas of media imperialism with the historically specific, still enduring, but inevitably finite phenomenon of US global hegemony (notice of whose death, nonetheless, has been much exaggerated, as I shall argue in Chapter 7, due in part to a relative neglect of the roles of advertising and capital accumulation). Some of the earlier literature (e.g. Boyd-Barrett, 1977a, 1982; Tunstall, 1977) specifically identified different and competing centers of media production, insisting that media imperialism is exercised by media, corporate and political powers of many different nation states, not only the biggest, across different time-periods. More recent literature (e.g. Boyd-Barrett, 1998b) argues that media imperialism should be understood not only as a transnational but also as an intra-national phenomenon. This extension is supported by voluminous evidence of media concentration and conglomeration at local, national, regional and transnational levels, involving as it does the commandeering of available communications space by small numbers of giant, highly commercialized, media conglomerates (e.g. Arsenault and Castells, 2008; Noam, 2009). A good example is *Rede Globo* of Brazil, associated with the Marinho brothers whose family founded the group. Despite some vigorous competition, it controls the country's most prestigious daily newspaper, *O Globo*, as well as three other dailies, accounting for some 40 per cent of daily newspaper sales, and operates 27 magazines, while its broadcast television network, including a separate news channel, is available throughout all of Brazil and accounts for well over half of primetime viewing (and snagging 75 per cent of total expenditure on television advertising), in collaboration with 122 owned or affiliate stations, plus 26 pay channels (Sinclair, 1999). Its domestic television audience declined in the 2000s. Sinclair and Straubhaar (2013) consider that Mexico's Televisa has a stronger history of near monopoly.

Writing his classic *The Media are American* close to 40 years ago, Jeremy Tunstall (1977) modified the thrust of his own argument by drawing attention to the importance of regional centers of media production. When he revisited his argument in 2007 with *The Media were American* it appeared as though the profusion of both national and regional centers of production throughout the world had significantly eclipsed older traces of empire. Features of the so-called Korean Wave that emerged in the 1990s together make a good example among several of precisely the kind of phenomenon that led the older Tunstall to revise his argument: the development of a robust national economy, with strong local media production activity across most of the old and some of the new media forms, together with substantial export activity to other areas of its geopolitical region and beyond.

I question the basic premise of those who might leverage the Korean Wave and comparable phenomena as demonstration of the declining significance of media imperialism in the early decades of the twenty-first century. I will examine the Korean Wave in greater depth in Chapter 9. Here I want merely to question the premise that its very existence refutes broader claims as to the very existence of media imperialism. Such a premise, first of all, is ahistorical. It invites us to ascribe particular significance to present trends at the expense of trends in the past even though what has occurred in the past may be fundamental to the present and our understanding of it. Secondly, the argument entertains a narrow conception of media imperialism, focusing principally on the phenomenon of US media imperialism as though other forms of media imperialism whether in the past (stretching back, as we have seen, to ancient civilizations) or present – including, say, that of South Korea itself and the considerable popularity of Korean Wave products in China, throughout East Asia and further afield – are unremarkable. Further, it is narrow because it tends to focus, as did Tunstall's own original approach, on media economics and, in particular, on international trade in media products in preference to aspects of corporate concentration within and control over media markets and the interrelationships of media enterprises with the agendas of political, corporate and other elites, local and global. Among other considerations, Tunstall's emphasis on national media markets would invite the conclusion that so long as a media market is not controlled by foreign media there is no media imperialism. In any nation that exercises imperial control, whether regionally or globally, the usual pattern is for the mainstream media of that country to frame its imperialism as benign or cloak it in a language that negates the possibility of imperialism or aggression. The possibility of imperialism rests just as much or even more on the complicity of media within the imperial center as on media complicity in the countries that are imperialized. Domestic populations often do not favor the aggressive actions of their own governments and need to be educated or misled into accepting elite interests as compatible with their own. Emphasis on national media markets unreasonably ascribes to the nation state the status of being the only building block in the development of media theory. This fails to take into account the always fluid and porous character of national and other forms of territorial boundary, especially when considered in relation to the twin forces of globalization and digitization. Analysis that prioritizes relations between national media markets tends to downplay media imperialism within domestic markets wherever a small number of large media behemoths have captured the available communications space, in all its forms, for the production and supply of information and entertainment products for large audiences.

A further limitation to the argument of those who would use phenomena such as that of the Korean Wave to downplay the significance of media imperialism does call attention to differentials of power and the hierarchical relations between nation states. Making sense of media activity in any part of the world invites consideration of the broader context of international relations. Assessment of the nature and significance of nation states, whether as single entities or in clusters, should be inclusive of those other nations states to which they owe allegiance or with whom they are allies, or of any given power or power-alliance within a geo-political or geo-cultural zone of influence. Considering South Korea as a significant center of media activity and export, we need also inquire into the relevance of its status as a US client state. South Korea would not exist as a nation state were it not for US military intervention on the Korean peninsula in the 1950s and the US role since that time in helping police the border between North and South Korea. How might this history influence the form and the limits of the Korean Wave? This in turn leads to what may be an overriding critique of what I call the ideological "weaponization" of the Korean Wave phenomenon. Those who are determined to celebrate a world of media pluralism tend to avoid paying sustained attention to political coverage and other forms of media representation of the events that, within any given era or area, are open to interpretation as imperialism, neo-imperialism or neo-liberal imperialism. If it is to mean anything, the expression "media imperialism" and its derivatives must go beyond mere questions of market and embrace phenomena of media support for, antagonism to, or relationships with the acts or agents of imperialism and imperialistic aggression.

MEDIA AGENTS *FOR* IMPERIALISM: MEDIA *AS* IMPERIALISTS

The broad field of media studies has not been shy of critical or even radical thinking. In particular, a great deal of attention has been given to the phenomena of media corporatization, conglomeration, consolidation and globalization (e.g. Herman and McChesney, 1998; Croteau and Hoynes, 2005; Mosco, 2009). These phenomena are often deemed highly problematic for the survival of a system of news and entertainment provision that can dependably provide information and perspectives that (1) hold power-holders to account; (2) are inclusive with respect to their representation of both the majority and minority demographic and ethnic divisions common to any society; and (3) provide their publics with information and understanding that enhance their capabilities as citizens and inspire them as human beings (Habermas, 1991). Issues of bigness extend just as much or even more to telephony, computing and Internet giants such as Apple, China Mobile, Google, Microsoft, or Samsung, and these will be my specific focus in Chapter 8.

Bigness in itself is not always problematic: a large news media conglomerate may be able to pool its resources to achieve a more comprehensive or more investigative report than, say, a single and independent news outlet. Smallness is not always good either. A newspaper owned by a local, wealthy tycoon may have little interest in providing coverage that is critical of local elites and their economic interests. But the owners and chief executives of big media, which may themselves be components of larger and possibly global conglomerates that own both non-media and media companies, have acquired membership of a corporate elite whose business interests likely override their responsibilities to the "public sphere." Media do not simply cover the political system; they should be seen as constituting a part of it (Cook, 1998). In return for creating access for politicians and executive agencies to address their publics on favorable terms for the purposes of information and propaganda, media owners expect a regulatory environment for communications that does not interfere with their ability to do business. As part of the deal, large mainstream media work with power: I shall argue that this is especially evident in coverage of foreign policy and the military-industrial-security Establishment.

The influence of big media was dramatically exposed in the Newscorp scandals from 2011 onwards. The founding chairman of Newscorp is Rupert Murdoch whose media empire in 2000 already stretched to more than 800 companies in over 50 countries. In the USA, among other media properties, Murdoch owns the *Wall Street Journal*, Dow Jones Financial Information Services, *New York Post*, Fox Broadcasting (which includes the Fox News channel), Fox Entertainment (which includes 21st Century Fox) and HarperCollins Publishing. In Britain, his empire (including *The Times*, *The Sun*, and BSkyB) had become so powerful an influence on news agendas through his ownership of substantial shares of print, broadcast and satellite news audiences that he was able to exercise considerable influence over politicians. For over three decades politicians in Britain considered that in order to win elections they had to deal with Murdoch. Part of that deal was to adjust the regulatory environment to his advantage so that he grew even more powerful. An ex-Newscorp editor, Andrew Coulson, was even appointed spokesperson for Prime Minister David Cameron and continued to hold shares in Newscorp. Perhaps even more alarming was the scope that this influence provided Newscorp – in effect, to blackmail politicians or to punish them through negative coverage or the threat of it. This trend was supported by the development in some Murdoch properties of a journalistic culture of impunity with regard to the use of illegal wiretaps on potential targets, some of them celebrities or other people "in the news" for one reason or another. Even more serious was evidence of illegal payments to officers of law enforcement in return for information and for their assistance in covering up or failing to follow through on investigations into illegal wiretaps (Channel 4, 2011).

Bigness in media tends to be associated with a diminution of competition and usually results from the ambition of owners and executives to earn more money on behalf of themselves and their shareholders. The compulsion to increase profit demonstrably leads in many cases to a diminution of quality, as in the rise of "infotainment" in the news business, and the "dumbing down" of many entertainment genres. Bigness often involves the seizure of a larger market share and the formation of cross-media enterprises whose bid to achieve economies of scale reduces competition within and between market sectors. Bigness has typically involved the raising of large sums of money either from the stock market or from financiers for the purpose of expanding operations and buying out other companies: either way, either large public corporations or private financial institutions end up on the boards of big companies. Their presence has two important consequences for this discussion. They increase the pressure for short-term returns, often at the expense of longer-term quality or sustainability. Financial institutions, whose business is to advance money and earn interest, are motivated to lend more money and to encourage their client companies towards further mergers and acquisitions. In the process the financiers acquire more influence over the companies they support and the decisions these companies make. This also reduces the incentive for news media to provide critical coverage of the financial sector (Almiron, 2010).

The world's largest media groups can boast a substantial global imprint in terms of turnover, profits and audiences or clients. The top-tier companies tend to be concentrated in the wealthiest economies of the world, particularly those of the USA, Japan and the UK. Some especially powerful groups have appeared in emerging economies, notably Samsung in South Korea and Huawei, Alibaba and CCTV in China. Generally speaking the largest of the media groups outside of the USA, Japan and the UK tend to belong to the "second tier" of global companies and there are numerous networking alliances, joint ventures and other connections between first- and second-tier companies. One list, which appears to have excluded telephone networks such as AT&T and Verizon, includes among the top-tier Time Warner, Disney, NewsCorp, Bertelsman, Comast-NBC Universal, CBS & Viacom, Microsoft, Google, Yahoo! and Apple (Arsenault and Castells, 2008).

Some if not all large media conglomerates may be regarded as agents of imperialism where they exercise business practices in ways that suppress the viability of media in countries other than their own, or suppress the viability of smaller media in their own countries of origin so that the diversity and inclusiveness of creative voices and expression in the media are diminished or that access to those voices is reduced. A strong indication of this form of media imperialism is the presence of an oligopoly of media businesses (typically three or four) controlling a substantial share, usually 50% or more, of any given media market between them and whose business activities are closely intertwined with those of second- or third-tier players in the market.

In this book, however, greater attention is given to the role of media not as agents of imperialism on their own behalf but as agents *for* imperialism, whether that takes the form of classic territorial imperialism, "free trade" or "neoliberal" imperialism, and whose hallmarks are coercive interventions in the affairs of sovereign nations, usually with the purpose to secure territory, political leverage, raw materials, trading advantages and markets. Media become agents for imperialism when they frame their narratives in a manner that presents imperialistic activity in a positive or benign light, when they prioritize the voices, justifications and discourses of imperial actors over the voices of victims, dissidents and alternatives, and when they omit or marginalize details and perspectives that would serve to critique imperial power.

CONCLUSION

In this chapter I have proposed that there are many different kinds of relationship between forms of communication and forms of empire, and that the vectored forces between media and empire are bidirectional. The term "media imperialism," therefore, should not be thought of as a single theory but as a field of study which incorporates different theories about the relationships between media and empire, as well as theories that address the exercise of forms of imperial power by media institutions themselves. By way of illustration of this point, I have identified four among many such theories, each one distinctive: those of Innis, Schiller, Tunstall and Boyd-Barrett. I note that the term "media imperialism" had fallen increasingly out of favor after the 1970s, but many of the criticisms of the term were not well substantiated. While many other terms have subsequently come into vogue, some of them addressing similar themes (for example, globalization, media "scapes," media hybridization, asymmetrical interdependence), most

of these lose sight of or interest in the actual historical phenomena of imperialism that is the main focus of this book. The book applies a broadly
inclusive approach to what we mean by "media," a term that incorporates
both the "old" and "new," that is about content, yes, but about a lot more
besides, including infrastructures of communication, production, dissemination and reception, and the interests that control them. All technology-
enabled forms of communication are here covered by the term "media,"
always with the important proviso that these are analyzed through broader
perspectives of history, power relations and culture. In introducing the term
"imperialism," I note that it has a taken-for-granted status within a great
deal of scholarship, but it is a status that privileges the feature of territorial
acquisition. This is a problem when dealing with periods in which indigenous classes retain nominal ownership of territory or retrieve territory that
was taken from them, yet remain vulnerable to other forms of depredation
exercised through the greater power of wealthier nations, communities or
tribes. In this book, therefore, I am equally interested in territorial and non-
territorial forms of imperialism and I find many examples of both throughout the "classic" period of European imperialism from the sixteenth
through to the twentieth centuries, and in the imperialism of the USA and
its major allies from the nineteenth through to the twenty-first centuries.

2 Territorial and "Free Trade" Empire Building: War by Media-Sanctioned Pretext

NOT ALWAYS ABOUT TERRITORY

Territorial acquisition was sometimes the preferred *choice* of imperialistic strategy, but it was not imperialism *per se*. While the seizure of territory may conform to popular ideas of imperialism, there are other modes of the practice that are as old as, often run concurrent with, and may be related to territorial aggrandizement. To insist on imperialism as necessarily having to do with the formal annexation of territory by a stronger over a weaker power is to somewhat miss the point of the exercise. British economists of the late nineteenth century lauded the benefits of what they called "free trade imperialism," a phenomenon not so different from its neoliberal re-versioning in the 2000s: in both cases, the "freedom" in question is the freedom for a more powerful economy to do what it wants in the confines of external markets, with the minimum of accountability and for the primary benefit of the aggressor. Communications and media play a highly significant role mainly in facilitating but sometimes in resisting the exercise of both territorial and non-territorial practices of imperialism.

Formal annexation typically was not the most significant element of empire building. Galeano (2003) describes Spanish and Portuguese empires, for example, as feudal rather than capitalist. They extracted enormous quantities of silver and gold from their respective South American possessions, for example, at a barely calculable cost in terms of the loss of indigenous lives (whose numbers fell from 70 million to one and a half million in the space of 150 years from the arrival of the *conquistadores*) and the lives of imported slaves, together with all manner of brutal cruelties. Much of the extracted gold and silver, however, was used either to repay foreign bankers such as the Fuggers, Welsers, Shetz or Grimaldi whose loans financed the expeditions and mines, or to pay for industrialized goods from the Dutch and, increasingly, the British, to service the consumption needs of rapidly increasing numbers of colonists in the Americas.

Silver and wool that had been exported from South America were reworked not by the Spanish or the Portuguese but by the Dutch, British and others who exported the finished products back to South America. In this way Holland and later Britain succeeded in acquiring the gold and silver that had been expropriated so cruelly from the indigenous peoples, effectively conquering Latin empires without the inconvenience, Galeano notes, of invasion and conquest. For reasons that have sometimes been ascribed to a "Protestant ethic" (Weber, 2012 [1904–1905]), these nations encouraged innovation and trade. The gold and silver that they earned from commerce with the Spanish and Portuguese were reinvested in further innovations, of which the steam engine was among the most significant. Spanish and Portuguese distaste for industry, either in their own countries or in the colonies, created South American economies that were deeply dependent on the vagaries of external or global markets, disadvantaging them to this day. In Brazil, the British supplied two-thirds of Portuguese necessities. The Portuguese obsession with mineral extraction and later, the mono-cultivation of sugar, rubber, cotton, coffee and other such crops depreciated the fertility and value of the land, thereby rendering these colonies highly vulnerable to new sources of competition and fluctuations in world prices. Such vices and mistakes, inherited by succeeding imperial regimes, have proven difficult to remedy, as even revolutionary Cuba discovered.

Both territorial and non-territorial imperialism may be discerned throughout the expansion of the USA in the eighteenth and nineteenth centuries, in the context of US conquests of the continents of North and South America, by means of a variety of tactics that included:

- vast land purchases on terms highly favorable to the USA;
- capitalist exploitation by US corporations: Gonzalez describes the region as an "incubator for the multinational American corporation" (2000: 58), particularly in such fields as cotton, fruit, horses and cattle, the mining of gold, silver and copper, oil, timber and wool: even while still a Spanish possession, for example, Cuba became an economic colony, in part, of the USA, accounting for one fourth of US world commerce (Gonzalez, 2000: 53);
- military interventions of brief or long duration (sometimes at the behest of US corporations that found themselves at loggerheads with local political elites, and alleging a concern to protect American lives). These allowed US banks and corporations to gain control over key industries in every country. They also sometimes provided cover for personal economic gains by military leaders and for generous trading and tax concessions to corporations. US troops intervened more than a dozen times before 1900 to

protect the Panama Railroad from Colombian factions (Gonzalez, 2000: 51). In 1902 Panama was simply seized by Theodore Roosevelt who orchestrated a revolution and then boosted Panamanian demands for independence from Colombia. Between 1900 and 1925 the USA intervened militarily in Honduras (1903, 1907, 1911, 1912, 1919, 1924, 1925); Cuba (1906, 1912, 1917); Nicaragua (1907, 1910, 1912); Dominican Republic (1903, 1914, 1916); Haiti (1914); Panama (1908, 1912, 1918, 1921, 1925); Mexico (1914); and Guatemala (1920). Some of these interventions involved extended occupations: Nicaragua 1912–1933; Haiti 1914–1933; Dominican Republic 1916–1924; Cuba 1917–1922; Panama 1918–1920 (Stone and Kuznick, 2012);

- strategic migration of US populations into adjacent territories belonging to Spain or to Mexico, eventually outnumbering locals in many cases;
- "*filibustero*" buccaneers who invaded or populated select cities in areas owned by Spain or Mexico, then quickly declared these to be "independent," gambling that their declarations would be supported by US federal troops and the territories later inscribed within the USA. Celebrated *filibusteros* included US heroes Sam Houston and Davy Crockett. Among the most notorious was ex-journalist William Walker, his exploits widely lauded by the US press and who, with the support of an army financed by Cornelius Vanderbilt, proclaimed himself President of Nicaragua in 1856;
- debt-slavery foisted by US banks on nominally independent countries such as Nicaragua or the Dominican Republic; debt repayments were enforced when necessary by US marines;
- provocations, leading to war and ending with the acquisition of territories ceded by the vanquished regimes against whom the provocations had been perpetrated;
- strategic marriage into Spanish-Mexican elites with a view to acquiring land-use entitlements through the family-based *mayorazgo* system of land ownership;
- imposition of policies of land ownership, customs revenues and tax policies (and concessions) by the US government on debt-enslaved countries;
- the crafting of hegemonic ideologies such as those of "manifest destiny," a term coined by publisher and Democratic Party publicist John O'Sullivan in 1848, or of the eugenics movement that was initiated by figures such as Dr George Caldwell or Dr Josiah C. Nott, or of the doctrine of "American exceptionalism";
- financing by US banks or corporations of the forces of one or another local contender in civil wars, in order to assure whatever outcome was preferred by US interests;

- sheer treachery: for example, the US Congress assured anti-Spanish Cuban rebels that US troops would depart from Cuba after they had helped effect the revolution, and anti-Spanish Filipino rebels were lulled by similar false promises. In both cases the USA became an occupying power for many decades. The Treaty of Paris that formally ended the Spanish-American war gave the USA direct control over Cuba, Puerto Rico, Guam and the Philippines. Under US control, Puerto Ricans enjoyed less self-government than they had enjoyed under Spain.

The corruption or further corruption of nascent Latin entities as a result of US depredations, occurring long before the USA could conjure the threat of communism as the *pretext-du-jour*, was attributed by US media to the regimes that the USA had helped install and maintain, many of them dictatorships or soon to become such with US support. In one example, US emissary Sumner Welles encouraged Fulgencio Batista, commander of the Cuban army, to stage a coup in 1933 against the progressive regime of Ramón Grau San Martín. In Panama in 1903 Theodore Roosevelt supplied marines in support of a coup staged by canal investors Manuel Amador and Bunau-Varilla. In the Dominican Republic, US emissary Sumner Welles (the same) prepared the way for withdrawal of the US marines and the accession to dictatorial power of Rafael Leonidas Trujillo in 1924; after World War Two, US marines helped prevent the return to power of democratically elected Juan Bosch. In Nicaragua, US companies financed the overthrow of progressive nationalist leader José Santos Zelaya in 1910. Progressive president Juan Sacasa was overthrown by Anastasio Somoza García, with secret backing from US Ambassador Arthur Bliss Lane, in 1934. Other dictators propelled into power with US help in the 1930s included Guatemala's Jorge Ubico Castaneda, El Salvador's Maximiliano Hernández Martínez, and Honduras's Tiburcio Carias Andino.

Gonzalez (2000: 55, 59) writes:

The pattern in US-Latin American relations by now was unmistakable. During the first seventy-five years of their independence, Latin America's leaders had watched incredulously as their northern neighbor annexed first the Floridas, then Texas, then another huge chunk of Mexico. They followed with consternation the exploits of Walker in Nicaragua, of Lopez and his mercenaries in Cuba; they were aghast at the arrogant way North American leaders treated them in diplomatic circles, at the racist labels those leaders used to describe Latin Americans in the US popular press; they watched fearfully as annexation schemes gave way to massive economic penetration, so that by century's end, the Dominican Republic, Mexico, Spain's Cuban and Puerto Rican colonies, and much of Central America had become economic satellites of an expanding US empire ...

Journalists, novelists, and film producers reinforced that message. They fashioned and perpetuated the image of *El Jefe*, the swarthy, ruthless dictator with slick black hair, scarcely literate broken-English accent, dark sun-glasses and sadistic personality, who ruled by fiat over a corrupt banana republic. Yet, even as they propagated that image, our bankers and politicians kept peddling unsound loans at usurious rates to those very dictators.

"FREE TRADE" IMPERIALISM AND MEXICO

Consider the relationship of the USA and Britain to Mexico in the early 1900s. Mexico had already by this time lost half of its territory and three quarters of its mineral resources to the USA (Gonzalez, 2000: 28). US petro-capitalists provided the necessary financial means, armaments, cross-border protections and White House support for the termination by forces loyal to democratic reformer Francisco Madero of Mexico's 35-year presidency of Porfirio Diaz in 1911. Certainly no saint, Diaz shrewdly appraised the benefits to Mexican "sovereignty" of spreading his risks and, at least for a time, privileging Europeans over Americans in land, extraction and tax concessions. By 1911 North American capitalists controlled all of the country's oil, 76% of its corporations, and 96% of its agriculture. They included famed publisher William Randolph Hearst, who owned a ranch with a million cattle in Chihuahua, and whose newspapers had previously supported Diaz. In retaliation against the privileging of Europeans, US petro-capitalists – above all Standard Oil – manipulated the end of Diaz and his replacement by the reformer Francisco Madero. Although the popular choice, US capitalists assumed that Madero, to compensate his sponsors for their confidence in him, would prioritize the demands of US oil interests. But Madero calculated that to maintain popularity and protect Mexico's nascent democracy he needed to cap the greed of petro-capitalists by taxation and, in the event of a violent reaction, expropriation. US petro-capitalists, led by their fanatical representative – the US ambassador in Mexico City, Henry Lane Wilson – conspired, in effect, to murder Madero and have him replaced by a military dictator, Victoriano Huerta.

The British Crown, on behalf of British oil interests, spared no time in recognizing Huerta, the murderer and usurper, helping him raise capital from British banks in return for his granting sizzling new oil concessions to the British. Britain had learned that the new US President, Woodrow Wilson, much to the disgust of his country's petro-capitalists, would refuse, on principal, to recognize Huerta. Wilson's idealistic stance was a cause for British celebration – until Wilson began to direct money and arms to the cause of the Constitutionalists who, under the leadership of Venustiano

Carranza, formed an unsteady but vigorous coalition of which Pancho Villa and Emilio Zapata represented different wings. Wilson's purpose was to bring down Huerta (whom his predecessor, William Howard Taft, had helped install). His objective achieved, Wilson conspired to secure the British Crown's compliance with American power in Mexico – and in Latin America more generally. He threatened the banks that might otherwise have agreed finance for the restoration of Huerta while maneuvering a mysterious switch in the choice of oil supplier by the British Admiralty from a British to an American company (Standard Oil). The approaching war between Britain and Germany would be won by whomsoever had access to the cheapest oil. Forced to choose between pursuing their oil interests in Mexico and incurring the overarching enmity of the USA at this sensitive time, Britain withdrew its support of Huerta. British ambassador to Mexico City, Lionel Carden, caustically observed that political power in Mexico derived from the US White House and that if a US president should disapprove of how his Mexican counterpart starched his shirts then the whole of Mexico would know of his displeasure (Moreno, 1986).

All of these examples deserve incorporation within discourses of imperialism, then and now. How are they "imperialism?" Let us count the ways. First and foremost these are stories about dispossession and expropriation. The US and British oil companies used their concessions to buy up or lease, for pathetically small sums, large and small *fincas* from mostly dirt-poor farmers who had next to no understanding of the satanic desolation that would be visited upon their lands, livestock and produce. Secondly, the opulent rewards garnered by the large oil companies were repatriated to their owners and shareholders in the USA or Great Britain. Thirdly, the national economies that were subject to petro-capitalist violation were no longer remotely in control of their own destinies. The possibility of meaningful democracy was smothered at birth in favor of rule by bought-out despots, crony capitalism and the politics of banana republics – notwithstanding the success of President Lazaro Cardenas, who took advantage of the deteriorating international economic and political climate of the 1930s to effectively nationalize Mexico's oil (Moreno, 1986). Fourthly, and by extension of the foregoing, the market necessities of petro-capitalism were to require a constant cycle of new exploration and expropriation and the generation of new markets for the oil that was produced and refined, notably in the field of oil-dependent transportation and industry. The high negative externalities of the production of oil, fifthly, including heavy pollution, were paid for not by the companies themselves but by the peoples of the countries that they exploited – a process that has now after several decades reached such levels of production and consumption of carbon-based fuel, leading to ever higher average global temperatures, that the very survival of the human species is in doubt.

THE IMPERIAL STATUS OF THE USA

The three most important indicators of the imperial status of the USA as the world's remaining superpower in the second decade of the twenty-first century are its global network of military bases, its disproportionate military expenditure, and the deceitful nature of many if not most of its pretexts for aggression towards and intervention in the affairs of other nations. The vast network of American bases may be thought of as constituting a new form of empire, an empire of bases (Johnson, 2004). In 2010 the Pentagon listed 716 military bases outside of the USA, principally in the Middle East, Europe and Asia. The real total significantly exceeded 1,000 to include the 500 bases established in Iraq at that time and the 400 US and coalition bases in Afghanistan, together with another 300 bases of the Afghan national army and Afghan national police, most of which had been built, maintained or supported by the USA (Turse, 2010).

By 2012 many of the bases in Iraq had closed, and many were likely to close in Afghanistan, in alignment with the downsizing (but not the disappearance) of the American presence. Included among bases that did not appear on the Pentagon list was a one billion dollar construction, Al-Udeid, in Qatar, its function to oversee unmanned drone wars. The USA maintained some form of troop presence in 150 countries and spent $250 billion annually on maintaining bases and troops overseas. In recent years there has been an increasing number of relatively small bases, sometimes nicknamed "lily pads," scattered across regions in which the USA had previously not maintained a military presence (Vine, 2012). Despite planned troop drawdowns in Iraq and Afghanistan and the closure of some large bases in Germany, the Pentagon has expanded its base infrastructure dramatically, relative to pre-2001 levels, including a stepped-up presence in East Asia, East and Central Asia, and Africa (ibid.). About a dozen air-bases for drones and surveillance were added in the period 2007 to 2010.

A new strategy for bases has evolved, its principal features including special operations forces, proxy armies, the militarization of spying and intelligence, drones, cyber-attacks, and joint Pentagon operations with increasingly militarized "civilian" government agencies. These are in addition to unparalleled long-range air and naval power; arms sales besting those of any nation; humanitarian and disaster relief missions that clearly serve the functions of military intelligence, patrol, and winning "hearts and minds"; the rotational deployment of regular US forces globally; port visits and an expanding array of joint military exercises and training missions that give the US military a de facto "presence" worldwide and help turn foreign militaries into proxy forces (Turse, 2010; Vine, 2012). Vine (2012) has identified four concerns with the lily-pad strategy: small bases can too easily grow into big ones; the military are often content to establish such bases in countries with noxious regimes; the strategy represents a creeping militarization of the world; and bases of any kind typically foment local hostility over time and may actually provoke either cold or hot wars with stronger powers.

Global military spending was $1,738 billion in 2011. Of this, the USA accounted for 40% or $711 billion, close to 5% of the country's GDP. Totals have continued to increase even through the so-called years of austerity following the economic crisis of 2008. The USA spent five times more on military expenditure than China (the world's second largest military power), whose expenditure was just over 2% of its GDP, accounting for 8.2% of the world total; and ten times more than Russia (the number three, which spent over 4% of its GDP). When Britain, France, Germany, Japan, India and Saudi Arabia are factored in, it is apparent that the USA and its military allies account for a vast majority (60%) of all military expenditure (SIPRI Yearbook, 2012; Wittner, 2012).

During the Cold War, US interventions were most frequently justified as necessary to prevent the spread of communism or communist influences. The neo-conservatives of the Reagan regime, resisting the more balanced counsels of the CIA, deliberately sought to inflate the size of the Soviet "threat" to the USA, setting up their own intelligence cells within the Department of Defense and protesting that the absence of evidence for their estimations of the Soviet threat was not evidence of absence but proof of the cunning of the Soviet empire. The narrative of this Cold War resurgence is related by Scott Noble in the second part of his documentary trilogy *The Power Principle*. Media representations of these events in the USA, among US allies and further afield, were strongly impregnated by the disinformation campaigns of Operation Mockingbird, a CIA brainwave that co-opted senior publishers such as William Paley, President of CBS; Henry Luce, the founder of the Time-Life empire; and the general manager of that empire, Michael Jackson. The CIA planted over 400 agents or coopted journalists in the newsrooms of most major mainstream news media (Noble, 2012). Evidence of a continuation of such strategies came to light in congressional investigations of the 1970s and, more recently, in exposure of the "TV pundit generals" (Pentagon "surrogates" or "message multipliers") in the 2000s, continuing unabated into the 2010s.

The term refers to retired generals who are used by mainstream television as "independent" experts on US wars. They are briefed by the Pentagon, and many are salesmen for defense companies (Tugend, 2003).

US INTERVENTION AND THE DEATH OF DEMOCRACY

US interventions have frequently involved the deliberate destabilization of regimes, sometimes democratic ones, in favor of leaders or interests that were more favorably disposed to the USA. Some entailed prolonged periods of combat, as in the Korean War 1950–1953 and the Vietnam War 1955–1975 where, in addition to the Soviet Union, a principal threat was represented as the growing influence of communist China. Other interventions involved the unseating of governments, or governments-in-the-making, that the USA simply did not like. These were usually considered too "leftist." Policies of nationalization and wealth redistribution – in particular land redistribution – were seen as a threat to US economic (i.e. *corporate*) interests. Many interventions occurred in covert partnership with local or neighboring forces or movements that in some cases the USA and/or other western intelligence forces had revived or kindled into existence. Many campaigns entailed the overthrow (even the assassination) of democratically elected leaders and their substitution by right-wing dictators. Overthrows of and impediments to democratic regimes that took place with direct or indirect US involvement included:

- plots in support of the military coup of 1949 in Syria that brought an end to civilian rule and its replacement by the regime of Army Chief of Staff al-Za'im;
- a coup against the government of Mohammed Mossadegh in Iran in 1953 (Muhammad Reza Pahlavi, Shah of Iran began a period of personal rule);
- the overthrow of Jacobo Arbenz in Guatemala in 1954 (replaced by a military junta led by Carlos Castillo Armaz);
- the assassination of Patrice Lumumba of the Republic of the Congo in 1961 (replaced by the government of Mobutu Sese Seko);
- the removal of João Goulart of Brazil (succeeded by a military dictatorship under General Humberto Castello Blanco) in 1964;
- the prevention of a return to power of Juan Bosch, the first democratically elected President of the Dominican Republic, in 1965;
- the removal of President of Ghana, Kwame Nkrumah, in 1966 (replaced in a military coup d'état by Emmanuel Kwasi Kotoka and the National Liberation Council);

- the removal of President Sukarno of Indonesia in 1967 (replaced by the military-dominated government of Suharto);
- the derailing of Georgios Papendreou's Center Union party that would likely have taken power in Greece in 1967 (a move that paved the way for the dictatorship of a military Junta); the USA had previously played a major role in the defeat of anarchist and pro-communist movements that had been associated with Greek anti-fascist resistance, from 1946;
- backing for the institution of martial law under President Ferdinand Marcos in the Philippines in 1972, which brought an end to a quarter century of democracy in the Philippines, inaugurated in the year of its independence from the USA in 1946;
- the overthrow of Salvador Allende in Chile (replaced by the military government of General Augusto Pinochet, 1973);
- the removal of Isabel Perón (legitimate successor to elected president Juan Perón, following his death in 1974), overthrown by the military junta led by Admiral Emilio Eduardo Massera, 1976;
- backing for the military coup in Thailand in 1976 which brought an end to the democratic period of revolution that had been initiated in 1973, and led to the installment of prime minister Thanin Kraivichien by the military;
- backing for the military coup in Turkey in 1980 which removed Prime Minister Bulent Ecevit and transferred power to Chief of the General Staff General Kenan Evren;
- the removal from power of Jean-Bertrand Aristide, President of Haiti, in 1990, his reinstatement in 1994, and his removal (in his second period of presidential office) and forced extradition in 2004;
- an attempted coup d'état against President Hugo Chávez of Venezuela in 2002;
- covert support for the coup d'état against Manuel Zelaya, President of Honduras in 2009.

Many of these episodes figure in William Blum's (2004) chronicle of US interventions.

Less dramatic forms of intervention included financial and other support for parties that the USA considered would be successful in fending off the electoral or revolutionary chances of Communist or left-wing parties, especially but not only if these were perceived to have been supported by the Soviet Union. Such was the case in post-war Australia, Britain, France and Italy (where the US role mainly took the form of channeling financial support to the Christian Democratic Party to ensure its triumph over the otherwise stronger Italian Communist Party) from the 1940s through to the 1960s and beyond.

Some major western governments, including those of Britain and France, were often complicit with US foreign policy objectives. The French traded extensively on their experience of counter-insurgency in Algeria, particularly their strategies of mass detention and torture throughout the 1957 Battle of Algiers – lessons that were later applied by the USA in Vietnam and by the Argentine junta during the Argentine "Dirty War" (1976–1983). Likewise, the British offered the lessons of their experiences from the Malay Peninsula and Kenya as a model for "pacification" in Vietnam (Mattelart, 2010). US intervention has often taken the form of secret CIA payments. In commenting on substantial CIA payments to the President of Afghanistan, Hamid Karzai, from 2002 onwards, Giraldi (2013) an ex-CIA agent who has had direct experience in such transactions, records the following:

> There is a long history of CIA buying foreign heads of state. In the Middle East, the late King Hussein of Jordan received $7 million yearly from the Agency and a succession of Christian presidents of Lebanon and their parties benefited similarly. Nearly all the Generals who headed military style governments in Latin America in the 1970s and 1980s were on the CIA payroll. In Europe, the process was more subtle, with the money generally going to a political party or even a faction within a party rather than to a politician.

COMMUNICATIONS RESISTANCE TO EMPIRE

Creation of the Movement of Non-Aligned Nations (NAM) in 1960 inaugurated an influential voice on behalf of former colonies, a voice that aspired to economic liberation from western interests so that members might realize the full potential of national self-determination. The movement was the outcome, in part, of the political philosophy of President Tito of Yugoslavia, who navigated his country, with some success, through the rivalries of the Soviet Union, China and the West, although the country would disintegrate violently not long after his death. The news agency of Yugoslavia, Tanjug, became an important media channel for the movement's vision (Vukasovich and Boyd-Barrett, 2012). At conferences sponsored through the 1970s by the United Nations Educational, Scientific and Cultural Organization (UNESCO), representatives of newly independent nations, with support from countries of the Soviet bloc, issued calls for a New World Economic Order (NWEO) and soon insisted, 1976–78, on a New World Information Order (NWIO, later renamed, on US insistence, the New World Information and Communication Order or NWICO). Achievement of economic reform, it was argued, required the prior reform of global media.

The UNESCO debates largely endorsed the perception that regardless of the achievements of movements for national self-determination the leading western powers and their corporations continued to enjoy disproportionate control over the global economy, in part through such institutions as the International Monetary Fund and World Bank that the allied powers under US leadership had founded at the Bretton Woods Conference in 1944. Western governments and corporations were also the principal players behind the construction of a global communications infrastructure and a global media system in which a relatively small number of large corporations exercised disproportionate influence. They framed stories of events around the world through the prism of the values of western capitalist democracy.

A revolution in information and information flows, the UNESCO's McBride Report (1980) indicated, was a necessary precondition for the achievement of an economic revolution. But NAM's influence reached its zenith in the 1970s, a period coinciding with the rise of OPEC (Organization of the Oil Exporting Countries) and its ability in 1973 to undermine western economies through applying upwards pressure on fuel prices. This had added to the growing clamor for attention from emerging nations in the United Nations (UN) at a time when US power had already been challenged by the defeat in Vietnam, recurring crises of terrorism and State terrorism in the Middle East and South America, and the perceived threat of the economic resurgence of Japan. These dynamics changed course radically, in part due to the inability of many emergent new nations to successfully implement autochthonous strategies for economic self-sufficiency. Emerging economies had insufficient technological means, know-how, infrastructure or market size to achieve economic independence. OPEC's influence on prices waned with the discovery of new sources of oil and overproduction of old ones. Under the Reagan presidency, the USA turned away from the UN as an appropriate global forum for international policy-making and entered an era of bilateral or multilateral agreements, increasingly conditional on the implementation of Chicago School monetarist economics and deregulation, prioritizing market considerations over social welfare. This development was intrinsic to an unfolding new phase of globalization, one that involved the opening up of world markets, intensification of the policing of international trade through GATT (established 1948) and, from 1995, the World Trade Organization, and a relative decline in the driving force of principles of national sovereignty in the economic and, therefore, political spheres.

COLD WAR INTERVENTIONS OF THE USA

US administrations, speaking through and generally with the enthusiastic or at least unquestioning support of mainstream media, typically presented their interventions during the Cold War as defensive measures serving to protect both local populations and western interests from predatory Communist expansionism by Russia or China. That these fears were sometimes greatly exaggerated, maliciously, at the service of domestic political objectives, corporate interests, and the military-industrial complex, is not in doubt (Noble, 2012).

Russia had considered itself pressured into an arms race by constant incursions of its sovereign air space by US spy flights after World War Two. On the other hand, western fears were not completely unfounded. This was never more evident than during the Cuban missile crisis of 1962. But Castro's acceptance of the Soviet offer to position nuclear missiles on Cuba was an understandable precaution following the covert US invasion of Cuba at the Bay of Pigs in 1961, which had attempted but failed to overthrow the revolutionary government under Castro that had taken power in 1959.

These Cold War interventions were not "imperialistic" in the classic sense that they involved the acquisition of territory and the substitution of local authority by that of the superpower. The USA was no stranger to the territorial model. Successful US machinations had acquired all of Florida from Spain in 1845, and California and New Mexico (along with parts of Arizona, Colorado, Oregon, Nevada, Utah and Wyoming) from Mexico in 1848 and, in effect, Texas, which the USA annexed in 1845. There was also the matter of its acquisition of island territories such as Guam and Puerto Rico, and its effective control over Cuba from the time of US victory in the Spanish-American war of 1898 (and later, through its support for Batista, up to the Castro revolution in 1959). Resulting from the 1898 war, the USA also acquired the Philippines, which it governed from 1898 up until 1946, excepting for the period of Japanese occupation from 1941 to 1945. The USA has continued to exercise significant influence in the Philippines subsequently, in part in order to safeguard substantial US military bases, as it has also done over much of Central America, Haiti and the Dominican Republic.

Anti-Communist interventions have more frequently resembled the USA's influence over Cuba (prior to 1959) than over the Philippines, since nominal sovereignty in Cuba was preserved between 1901 and 1959. US military bases proliferated in the territories of its allies, as did ties between US military and local security forces. Local interests that worked with the Americans could expect rewards; those that resisted were marginalized or punished. US "protection" was bought or imposed, often at the price of progress towards self-sufficient nationalism (that might have reduced the dependency on US imports or undermined the perceived necessity to host US military bases), communism, socialism or even social democracy, and the redistributive justice and human rights often associated with such systems.

Both information and entertainment media played a critical role in propping up Cold War pretexts for intervention. They represented the world beyond US borders through a simplistic Manichean lens: "us" versus "them." They demonized Communist systems and their leaders. They maintained consistently negative coverage of almost anything that happened in the communist world. Interpretation or framing of events quickly fell into line behind Washington definitions of the situation. The media paid most attention to developments that could be presented as contributing either to the failure or success of the West over communism (Herman and Chomsky, 2002) and ignored much else.

NEW RATIONALES FOR INTERVENTION

Interventions since the collapse of Soviet communism and of much of the communist world from 1989 (outside of China) could no longer be justified on the pretext of mounting a defense against Communist expansion. In the ensuing quarter century, interventions have been justified instead on the basis of the following four main pretexts: the "war" on drugs, "humanitarian" intervention, the "war" on terror (which also incorporates pretexts relating to "weapons of mass destruction"), and the promotion of "democracy." Sometimes more than one of these pretexts is employed simultaneously. Mainstream media almost universally and uncritically adapt the values that underwrite these rationales. I do not deny the painful realities that these labels sometimes invoke. The production, distribution and consumption of certain kinds of drug, for example, can be seriously detrimental to the health of individuals and communities. Horrific, sometimes genocidal offenses occur and understandably ignite popular outrage in developed countries, with demands that a stop should be put to such terrible abuses. There had been no such intervention in one of the worst genocidal atrocities since the Nazi holocaust of the Jews in the 1940s or the nineteenth-century white massacres of indigenous peoples of North America: the slaughter of Tutsis and moderate Hutus in Rwanda in 1994. Terroristic acts are, by definition, deplorable and deserve spirited condemnation; never mind that most terrorism is State terrorism and that the worst culprits include some of the largest and most powerful states. Critics of US foreign policy deny that interventions on the basis of the values that these pretexts represent (i.e. the harmfulness of drugs, virtue of humanitarian aid, and the evil of terrorism and the benefits of democracy) are altruistic or even effective on their own terms. They charge that the real motivations are invariably imperialistic, designed to enhance the global power of the USA on behalf of US corporate, military and other interests, so as to achieve greater leverage over particular territories and populations.

The role of the use of pretexts for going to imperial war – the official citing of reasons for aggression that are deliberately false or misleading – is beyond dispute (even if controversy surrounds the particular pretexts cited), in the case of the USA as well as other imperial nations. Reasonable certainty as to what are the "real" reasons at play is sometimes lacking. There are likely to be multiple interests at work behind particular interventions. The 2003 US-led invasion and occupation of Iraq is one example. Even some of the perpetrators, as we shall see, admit that the principal pretext cited (Iraq's alleged possession of weapons of mass destruction) was a bureaucratic or consensual device or, we may say, a lie of convenience. An imperial war may serve diverse interests, and each of these interests may have its distinctive rationales. In the case of Iraq these included the interests of the military-industrial complex in making substantial profits – through arms sales, supplies and post-war "reconstruction"; the interests of the energy establishment in securing more direct access to Iraqi oil fields for development and extraction, in order to make more money; the interests of politicians and ideologues in strengthening US hegemony in the Middle East and in advancing US-friendly "democracy"; and the interests of regional allies of the USA, in particular Israel and Saudi Arabia, in the eradication of a local rival or threat. Identification of "real interests" is inherently problematic. The main participants are generally loath to publicly articulate what these are. To do so would likely incur public wrath and could also lead to litigation and charges of war crimes, although a tolerance for US "exceptionalism," backed by the sheer clout of superpower status, will generally protect the culpable from actual punishment. None the less, evidence of "real" interests does emerge through the eventual publication of official archives, scholarship, and the memoirs and even the inadvertent remarks of members of the power elite.

Pretexts proffered to the media for intervention in particular cases are frequently wrong, provoked, and even fabricated. Authorities rely heavily on supposedly "independent" (but colluding) mainstream media for the widespread dissemination of their inaccuracies and deceptions. But more than that, they depend on the media to whip up patriotic fervor, boost support for the authorities, and marginalize and/or ridicule dissent and dissenters when these are not actively criminalized by the State (see Boyd-Barrett, 2003 for an analysis of such media management in the period surrounding 9/11 and in the run-up to the invasion and occupation of Afghanistan in 2001). This media practice has been evident throughout nearly every intervention in the period since World War Two (as well as before it). A few of the many possible sources – all of them relating pretexts of war, in various ways, to mainstream media complicity, whether enforced or voluntary – include Bamford (2005); Blum (2004); Chomsky (1998); Curtis (2002); Hallin (1989); McCoy (2003); Parenti (1995); Pilger (2010); Sanders (2002); Thrall (2000); and Zinn (2010). The prevalence of this phenomenon significantly calls into question orthodox academic interpretations of the role of the press in so-called "democratic" societies, and associated discourses about media and the "public sphere." These appear, unreasonably, to disregard the substantial subversion of the role of the press by "corporate democracy States" in matters of war or, in the case of a media mogul such as Rupert Murdoch and his manipulation of politicians in Britain, media's management of the State for corporate gain and plutocratic interest.

THE POLITICS OF PRETEXT

Morgenthau (1965) argues that it is the responsibility of elites to shape the public opinion that they need to support their already existing policies. Gibbs (2004) distinguishes between "orchestrated pretexts" that are actually manufactured as excuses for aggression, and "pretexts of convenience," or what McGeorge Bundy once described as "passing streetcars" (quoted by Kahin, 1986: 277, and Gibbs, 2004: 3) – that is to say, "opportunities" that policy-makers expected would arrive eventually in one form or another and which, when they do, are jumped upon in order to manage public opinion and push ahead with already prepared policies that hitherto had been too unpopular to contemplate.

The phenomenon of fabricated pretext has long been a feature of US war-making and of imperial power. It frequently comes with the motive of unseating foreign leaders, often former "assets" who have been helped into power by the USA, or of maneuvering such assets into positions of power. The former category includes Manuel Noriega, one-time "strong man" of Panama, and Saddam Hussein, one-time "strong man" of Iraq. These gentlemen failed to show that they would be eternally or sufficiently pliable on behalf of US interests. People of this kind apparently deserve not simply to be removed – at the cost of up to 4,000 Panamanian lives in the case of Noriega and up to a million Iraqi lives in the case of Hussein – but often to be brutally humiliated and crushed as well. Saddam Hussein's bungled execution was a fraction gentler than that of Libya's Colonel Gaddafi in 2011 who, if not a CIA asset (as Hussein once had been), had offered Libya to the USA as a suitable location for the interrogation and torture of victims of US rendition.

Assets who have been maneuvered into positions of power with the help of the CIA include Willy Brandt, Chancellor of the Federal Republic of

Germany 1969–1974; Hamid Karzai, President of Afghanistan since 2002, and his brother Ahmed Karzai; Ngo Dinh Diem, President of Vietnam 1955–1963, and his brother and chief adviser, Ngo Dinh Nhu; Moraji Desai, Premier of India 1977–1979; Eduardo Frei, President of Chile 1964–1970; King Hussein of Jordan 1952–1999; Thubten Jigme Norbu (eldest brother of the fourteenth Dalai Lama, Tenzin Gyatso; Gyatso has funneled CIA money to Tibetan paramilitary groups)(Ghosh, 2009); Mohammad Rezā Pahlavı, Shah of Iran (1941–1979); and many others, including some to whom I have already made reference.

By definition, pretexts emerge in the build-up towards hostilities, and therefore they frame the language of policy-makers and, in turn, of the news media which invariably privilege those same policy-makers as sources of information (see Shoemaker and Reese, 1995; Herman and Chomsky, 2002; Entman, 2003; and Bennett et al., 2008, for a detailed analysis of how events are "framed," "indexed," ignored or in other ways misrepresented by the mainstream US media). At many times throughout this volume I shall return to the politics of pretext and to the role of mainstream media in promoting them with the seriousness with which their progenitors hope they will be received.

CONCLUSION

In this chapter I have sought to dethrone the concept of imperialism as fundamentally about territorial acquisition – which it often but does not necessarily involve – and propose instead that imperialism must be seen as the manifestation of power of one tribe, community or nation over another, power that is exercised through different combinations of a wide array of available techniques and strategies. In its development of imperial power over North, Central and South America, through the course of two centuries, the USA has provided examples of many of these. The media have proven central to the imperial enterprise as agents whose function, knowingly or through confusion, is to obscure the unethical, treacherous, one-sided and generally brutal character of this enterprise both from the domestic population of the imperial center – only some members of whom could be said to actually benefit from its practice – and from its victims.

I have offered the example of Mexico that for many decades and still today has proven a plaything of US corporate and political power, extending to the promotion and removal of presidents (e.g. US support of Victoriano Huerta against Francisco Huerta and of Venustiano Carranza against Huerta). Indeed, it may be said that the USA – although it has had and continues to acquire plenty of experience in the exercise of the territorial variety – is principally a master of non-territorial forms of imperialism, none more effective than the empire of military bases which impacts the destinies of over 150 nations.

Communications resistance to the inequalities of empire has emerged at various times, both in the imperial center and in the colonies, and I have introduced the history of the New World Information and Communication Order as a laudable but stillborn effort. Yet the overwhelming force of mainstream communications – at all its levels from infrastructure and hardware through to software and content – is supportive of empire. This is particularly apparent and perhaps most important in relation to the pretexts that the empire provides for its interventions in the sovereign affairs of other countries and their peoples. For many decades following World War Two such pretexts were couched in discourses of anti-communism. These have now been supplanted by four principal, alternative, but overlapping discourses: the "war" on drugs, humanitarian intervention, the "war" on terror, and the promotion of "democracy." I argue that discourses of pretext are central to modern empires, and that the media are central to the formulation and dissemination of these discourses of pretext.

3 Classic Approaches to Media Imperialism: Three Models

Media Imperialism may best be thought of not as a theory, but as a field of study that still has only emergent form. Contributing to this field are studies that have their origins in many different disciplines, including media and communication, history, sociology, linguistics, and international relations. Common to most of these is an interest in the relationships between, on the one hand, the growth, maintenance and decline of empires and, on the other, the means of communication. Within this field, different scholars look at a wide range of different phenomena from different eras and different parts of the world. They posit different research questions, hypotheses and theories about these relationships between empires and communications.

It is important to acknowledge the diversity of scholarship for this is far too broad even to deal with each of its most important approaches. I shall be extremely selective. In this chapter I examine just a few of many possible influential approaches, while in a succeeding chapter I try to reach beyond the range of texts that are commonly invoked in this context, more with a view to prizing open the idea of media imperialism as an exceptionally complex and dialectical field of study than as an attempt to chronicle its history. One of the principal problems of a body of existing critiques of "media imperialism theory" is its simplistic presumption that there is indeed a single theory, rather than a multiple set of theories within a very broad field.

Existing scholarship shares an overriding interest in the level of determination between the two phenomena of media and imperialism, and in discovering whether different empires have sponsored different communications systems, or whether communications systems have given a distinctive shape to different empires. Scholarly formation of the topic from the mid-twentieth century onwards is an inevitable response to the development of so many radically new media forms inherited from the mid-nineteenth century onwards, the dazzling scale of their operations, reach, societal and corporate significance, in parallel with an intensification in the scale, ferocity and complexity in phenomena of imperialism, neo-imperialism or even post-imperialism.

I shall focus on three scholars whose influence has been fundamentally important in the development of theorizing about communication and empire and whose focus on this relationship tends to look outwards from imperial centers. They are certainly not the only scholars who could be cited, but their ideas are of particular importance for the direction of this book. In the next chapter I shall examine the work of theorists whose focus tends to be from the periphery looking back into the center. Their names may be less familiar, but they inspire ways of rethinking and extending study of the field.

HAROLD INNIS

The Canadian scholar Harold Innis is often considered one of the earliest representatives of this mid-twentieth century development. Innis's classic, *Empire and Communication*, was originally published in 1950. It is a relatively brief work of some 200 pages, but is also a difficult work. Except in its introduction, it offers little by way of clear articulation of a grand theory in the manner that is implied by many who cite him; its sourcing is inconsistent, and any assessment of the quality of those sources, more than 60 years after first publication, is virtually impossible without the aid of an army of historians each specialized in one of the many different civilizations to which Innis makes reference.

Inspired by his interest in the role of communications in helping unify his contemporary Canada, he observes somewhat casually in his introduction that "the subject of communication offers possibilities in that it occupies a crucial position in the organization and administration of government and in turn of empires and of Western civilization" (Innis, 2007 [1950]: 23). A foundational source is a work by James Byrce (1901) who had talked of the intensifying process of centralization from ancient times to the apogee of Roman empire, followed by slow disintegration and yielding to centrifugal forces over 700 years, prior to a reversal over another 600 years towards aggregation, nation and democracy. This prompted Innis to note how in the organization of effective government over large areas, efficiency of communication occupies a vital place. Byrce's three periods, Innis suggested, corresponded with a communications evolution from a phase in which clay and papyrus dominated, to a second characterized by parchment, and then a third dominated by paper.

The positing of a relationship between a prevailing method of communication and the degree of centralization of an empire represents a striking hypothesis, open to various forms of refinement, yet is one that relatively few media historians have returned to for more methodical testing. Innis illustrated complex relationships between the materials on which communication was inscribed, the instruments used for inscription, and the systems of writing which resulted. Complex systems of writing required more investment in training and application and were more likely to be monopolized by certain caste, priestly or professional groups. Equally powerful is Innis's second major hypothesis of a relationship between media, time and space. Media that favor space (i.e. geographical extension of reach) are more likely to be light in nature, less durable and (indicatively, although Innis does not spell it out), fostering decentralization and less hierarchical institutions. Media that emphasize durability over time are more permanent, more likely to use heavy materials and, Innis says explicitly, favor centralization and hierarchical types of institutions. Empires that persist, he claims, overcome the bias of any one type of medium so that the bias of one medium towards decentralization is offset by the bias of another towards centralization. He observes that the significance of a given medium to a civilization is "difficult to appraise, since the means of appraisal are influenced by the media," and adds, in an apparent reference to the inter-reflexivity between media and forms of intellectual activity and knowledge, "and indeed the fact of appraisal." It is easier to establish the contribution of monuments to a civilization that was dependent mainly on clay and stone for communication, and whose edifices still remain if only in ruin, than it is to establish the contribution of papyrus to a civilization that depended on it, since most of the products of papyrus and their contents have perished.

By the standards of conventional social science, Innis's language is lacking in precision or the "operationalization" of his key variables. Historical vindication of his hypotheses may be problematic because the evidence presented is selective and the quality of sources varying or unknown. Yet it is in the genius of his propositions that Innis opened up an endless vista of research questions on the relationship between media and empire.

Scholars who have examined the social and other impacts of the printing press and the mass circulation of information and ideas which this presaged vary as to whether they consider these impacts determining of social change or merely influences upon social change. There is indeed a tendency, especially but not only in popular writing about the media, towards "technological determinism" when talking about the impact on society of this or that medium of communication. With respect to the printing press, some have argued a wide range of momentous consequences: e.g. that it accelerated the decline of Latin and the proliferation of vernacular works of a much broader diversity of genres and topics; fostered the development of standardization of vernacular languages and of widespread literacy, newspapers and an educated citizenry; undermined the authority of the Catholic Church; fostered the growth of democracy, economy and the nation state. Further, it might have boosted the development of scientific thought and technology, preparing the way for the industrial age. The printing press contributed to the volume and speed of the storage and retrieval of massive amounts of information and equally to its codification. Simultaneously it reduced the amount of information that individual scientists needed to recall unaided and facilitated standardization of the reporting of scientific results (Eisenstein, 1979).

Critics on the other hand are skeptical of the grander claims, judging such outcomes as matters of degree only, not of radical change, and arguing that handwritten manuscripts had functioned in much the same way as printed manuscripts, that many other factors were at work contributing to outcomes attributed to the printing press and that some outcomes did not endure. Some social anthropologists point to evidence of the existence of scientific thought in pre-literate societies (Jensen, 2001).

Whatever the particular position one may take, it is facile to dispute the likelihood of some kinds of relationship between printing, thinking and expression and this in turn is likely to inform scientific discussion about the relationships between literacy, communication and empire. Empires such as those of the Portuguese, Spanish, Russian and French have typically advanced rationales for their generally coercive acquisition of alien territory, labor and resources that are closely intertwined with ideas of "civilization," a "true religion" and "modernization." Behind and central to all of such ideas are media and communication. These include sacred or revered texts such as the Bible, the US Constitution or the Communist Manifesto. They embrace works that the imperialists hold in high regard as symbolic of their elevated ethical, creative and intellectual genius, including the treatises of "great" scientists, philosophers and political thinkers. They extend to forms of communication which seem to the imperialists to resonate with their most noble, refined and public spirited virtues, such as the BBC, British Council, Voice of America, *The Guardian*, *The New York Times*. They also include creations which, while not elevated intellectually, may still, in their very popularity, speak to the humor, diversity, creativity, fun-loving colorfulness, essential innocence and harmlessness of the imperialists' purity of spirit, such as rock and roll, reality game shows or the morning news show. In their very physical manifestation the media, in the form of cinemas, newspapers, telephones, radio and television sets, computers, iPods and iPads, or mobile phones have all emanated from imperial powers and are iconic of their presumed scientific and technological superiority, versatility and generally carefree, magnanimous and fun-loving goodness.

This may be an appropriate moment therefore to invoke the classic works of Edward Said (1979, 1994) on the relationships between western literature and imperialism. These are devastating in their adumbration of what may now seem to many a repugnant, unmerited and uncritical sense of superiority, complacency and lack of reflexivity as to issues of colonialism that suffuse the greatest intellectual works of the nineteenth- and twentieth-century western worlds – and a reminder that these unfortunate characteristics still lie shallow beneath the veneer of post-modern sophistication.

HERBERT SCHILLER

Schiller's 1969 *Mass Communication and Media Empire* entitles the first chapter "Electronics and Economics Serving an American Century," the introduction of two terms that were not particularly common in the communications literature up to that point, and linked specifically to the concept of empire, a new form of empire in which the marriage of economics and electronics substitutes in part for the coercion exercised in former empires and whose aim was to promote, as articulated by two British economic historians in the nineteenth century, "free trade imperialism." Schiller regards communications as serving to overcome, by diversion, the lack of popular domestic enthusiasm for the "global role of imperial stewardship" (1992 [1969]: 2). US-originated and locally distributed information serves to deflect or confuse overseas opposition to a form of post-colonial servitude in favor of an "open-armed allegiance in the penetrated areas" (1992 [1969]: 3). Highly concentrated, advertising-driven, mass media entertainment "inform and instruct" audiences on the social patterns of consumerism necessary for a market-oriented economy. It places a high premium on impulse and immediacy. These social patterns are described as evidence of "freedom."

Schiller may be faulted for his unsophisticated presumption that what he regarded – and many today would still agree – as the low quality pabulum of broadcast content, was not healthy for listeners, viewers, or for society as a whole. But he coupled his critique with an attention to industrial structure, business models and regulatory systems that was unusual for his period. This unequivocally exposed the limited capacity of the system to deliver diversity and the corresponding opportunities foregone. Schiller was among the very

first media scholars to draw attention to the relationship between the rise of the media, the military-industrial complex to which a concerned Republican President Eisenhower had drawn the public's attention in 1961, and imperial interest. He argued that the media made an important contribution to the "structural transformation of society itself as it accommodates its routine functioning to a prolonged state of emergency" (1992 [1969]: 33). Here Schiller was indicating what was to become the half-century emergency of the "Cold War," in many ways a social construction or fabrication that served the cause of profit-making in the defense industries and helped consolidate domestic support for capitalism at home. This in turn has been followed by the "war on terror" that has morphed into a neo-liberal war in support of unregulated or extreme capitalism and whose principal enemies are nations or forces that do not subscribe to its doctrine.

Schiller turned his critical attention to the history of broadcast regulation. Regulators prioritized the needs of major investors, the manufacturers of radio and television sets, and their preferred business model – the sale of audiences to advertisers: "Corporate complexes struggled for monopolistic control of the broadcasting medium while the public was considered first only as a consumer of equipment and later as a saleable audience" (1992 [1969]: 22). In particular, he notes that patent rights for the manufacture of radio equipment and the transmission of signals were held by two groups – General Electric and Westinghouse and their joint creation RCA on the one hand, and on the other AT&T – both of them fired by the desire to sell radio sets as quickly as they could by providing mass programming. Educational uses of broadcasting were sidelined while UHF television frequencies were reserved for educational stations. Manufacturers were not compelled to provide television sets with both VHF and UHF until 1964. Exploiting the free gift bestowed on them by Congress, the people's airwaves, broadcasters separated entertainment from education, and sidelined the educational in favor of mass-oriented content that functioned to persuade audiences of the desirability of the status quo. From consideration of the corporate conglomerates who controlled the hardware and programming of broadcasting, Schiller turned his attention to the distribution of spectrum, finding that this was dominated by the militarization of communications capacity.

It is scarcely a surprise that Schiller in 1969 focused his attention on satellite rather than computing technology or the approaching marriage of computing, satellite and other telecommunications and electronics industries. This is a significant limitation of his 1969 work (his later books do indeed embrace the digital), but if satellite is taken merely as an example Schiller successfully demonstrated the significance of communications technology as lying at the very core of US global policing by means of a marriage between

military R&D and private enterprise in the construction of a private, US-dominated global network in which all the nations of the world would be invited to participate. COMSAT was established as a private US-led corporation in 1963. Four large US telecommunications carriers owned 90% of the industry segment of shares and 45% of the total issue. Foreign purchasers were expressly limited. The USA had already persuaded other countries to agree the reservation of radio spectrum for satellite communication at the 1963 Extraordinary Radio Administrative Conference. American interest also dominated the formation in 1964 of the international satellite consortium INTELSAT, of which the US share was 54% – a share that the agreement specifically acknowledged could never be allowed to fall below 50.6%. Given their technological advance, American companies could expect privileged access to the satellite market. Above all, the USA's lead in satellite technology ensured that as in broadcasting the need for profit would be paramount over educational or social objectives.

In the field of terrestrial broadcasting Schiller chronicled how utilization of the US spectrum had been divided between the private and the governmental sectors, but that the military accounted for up to 70% of the whole. While the private sector was regulated by the FCC, the governmental was regulated by the Interdepartment Radio Advisory Committee (IRAC), established in 1922. By the time of the Korean War, the IRAC had been coopted into the military. The FCC's membership of IRAC was terminated in 1953. The IRAC became the channel through which the Department of Defense's communications programs became national policies. In 1962 President Kennedy, citing the vital importance of telecommunications to national security, established the position of the Director of Telecommunications Management in the Office of Emergency Planning. This reflected growing government concern, in the wake of the fiasco of the Bay of Pigs, to maintain immediate communications with distant "trouble spots." This move was followed in 1963 by the establishment of the National Communications System with responsibility for all government communications, answerable to the Secretary of Defense, and whose first director, the Director of Telecommunications, was a former general.

Thus did Schiller trace a communications regulatory system that privileged and in large measure was governed by the military. He proceeded to demonstrate the close interconnections between this military apparatus and the private sector that was a beneficiary not just of more than half of all NASA and Defense Department R&D concentrated in aerospace, electrical machinery and communication, but also of the "enormous guaranteed market made available to these same concerns by the continuing military purchases of hardware and systems" (1992 [1969]: 51), within a context of growing corporate

concentration within the electronics industry. This included mergers of defense and broadcasting companies, such as that between RCA and NBC that at the very least invited reasonable doubt as to the capacity of these broadcasting operations to report objectively on matters that affected either defense or business interests. The nation's electronics industry sold well over 60% of its output in 1967 to the national government, mainly the armed forces.

As an illustration of the ways in which these interlocking interests panned out at the personal level, Schiller looked at the multiple roles performed by celebrated CBS president Frank Stanton who had also served as the Chairman of the United States Advisory Commission on Information, responsible for overseeing the operations of the United States Information Agency (USIA); Chairman of the Board of the Rand Corporation (funded almost entirely by the Air Force); and as Chairman of the Executive Committee of Radio Free Europe. Institutionally, Schiller cited the Armed Forces Communications and Electronics Association as indicative of the close interrelationships between government, defense and electronics industries, its officers and members representing the "highest corporate and military echelons" and occupying as well "the most important governmental posts in these areas" (p.58).

Whereas Schiller seems to have viewed the government and military as the strongest partners in this three-way relationship, later critics were to presume the dependence of government on the private sector. The principal driving force of the three-way partnership, he noted, was a US strategy of counter-insurgency aimed at pacifying the have-not nations and dissuading them from transferring to the communist camp. This was the primary interest in satellite communications that promised unparalleled opportunities for instantaneous intervention: "The nation's electronic sophistication, a product of massive research and development supported by huge federal expenditures, has been commissioned to oversee and sometimes to overpower primitive economies steeped in social misery if they give any sign of rebellion" (1992 [1969]: 65).

Schiller's critical appraisal of the global influence of both US military and private dissemination of propaganda and entertainment programming, that was very important and useful at the time of publication, may appear to many in the 2000s an out-of-date preoccupation. Yet this period in the history of international broadcasting primed the rest of the world as to the capabilities, purposes and business models of the medium, namely relatively low-cost, uncritical and consumerist fodder sufficient to capture eyeball attention and sell it to advertisers, whether multinational or local. Schiller understood that it was not so much the content but the business model that determined the content that counted. He said it plainly and simply, though perhaps not loud enough, when he wrote in 1969 "The United States communications presence overseas extends far beyond the facilities owned, the exports, and the licensing agreements secured by major American broadcasting companies and electronics equipment manufacturers, considerable as these are. Equally, if not more important, is *the spread of the American system, the commercial model of communications*, to the international arena" (1992 [1969]: 93; emphasis added).

This system was so compelling that it caused alternative models of publicly owned and non-commercial television to teeter, and for what reason? "Nothing less than the viability of the American industrial economy itself is involved in the movement toward international commercialization of broadcasting" (1992 [1969]: 95). As American corporations sustained their rate of growth by invading overseas markets, and as US advertising agencies travelled alongside them, so did US corporate expenditure on advertising on overseas television – often to the accompaniment of US-originated content. Schiller tells us who the advertisers were (US-based global brands) and how much they spent on television, in the USA and in other countries, a singularly important if fairly simple arithmetical demonstration that is still relatively rare in media studies. The overall product of this coordinated machinery is not the television program – wretched in quality but profitable because it has been written exclusively to persuade advertisers to spend (even then, Schiller notes, advertising agencies sometimes sat in at each stage of a script's development) – but *homo consumens*, cynosure of the entire machinery of modern US-led capitalism.

The pressure on non-commercial European TV networks to incorporate private programming and commercials was unrelenting. In Great Britain, it took the form of pirate radio stations on ships anchored off-shore or in the Thames Estuary and funded by overseas advertisers. Satellite communication, just like transnational transmission spills before it, was welcomed as a means that would further propagate the commercialization and privatization of television. This in turn provided conduits not just for western programming to reach the rest of the world but also western ideas and concepts even if, as Schiller described it, the television products with the least value would receive the widest circulation. Ultimately, few countries could resist the attraction of financing television systems with advertising. Schiller was writing at a time when US content still dominated the air-time of many nations. More significant in the longer term has been the US media community's understanding of the potential of the medium, and – because of US superpower status and influence – how that understanding has come to be adopted by or pushed on governments everywhere in response to noisy corporate lobbyists.

EDWARD HERMAN AND NOAM CHOMSKY

Manufacturing Consent, the oeuvre by Edward Herman (a Professor of Finance) and Noam Chomsky (a Professor of Linguistics), appeared in 1988 and a second edition in 2002. They borrowed the term for their title from Walter Lippmann who talked about the manufacture of consent in his influential 1922 book *Public Opinion*. Both Hermann and Chomsky are extremely well published, but I propose that *Manufacturing Consent* deserves a special place in the field of media imperialism studies. They provide a compelling framework for understanding how it is that the mainstream media of the USA, in theory constituting a "free press," often appear to march more or less in uniform behind an administration's foreign policy, behaving not unlike the media for an authoritarian society. This was evident, for example, in the immediate aftermath of 9/11, the run-up to the invasions and occupations of Afghanistan and Iraq in 2001 and 2003, the campaign against Iran's (non-existent) nuclear weapons program, the demonization and annihilation of the Gaddafi regime in Libya, and the attempted annihilation of the Assad regime in Syria. Later research has demonstrated that the longer a war endures the greater the divergence between administration and media narratives, although media very rarely question the underlying premises of war (King, 2014).

While celebrated by many, Herman and Chomsky's formal "propaganda model" is often ignored by those who should know better, including many scholars and journalists who write about international communication and propaganda. Many media students are familiar with the five "filters" that Herman and Chomsky proposed as the principal factors that determine whether news stories will get to be published. Stories must not threaten the business or political interests of the media behemoths that control most of the US mass media. They must not be seen to undermine the advertising revenue stream on which many news media depend or, more generally, the news and information climate that is favorable to the interests of advertisers and consumerism in a capitalist society. Stories must observe the basic procedures of journalistic routine, among them an overweening dependence on and prioritization of official or "authoritative" (usually established institutional) sources. They must preempt the 'flak" of irate, powerful sources who could interfere with the prosperity or survival of a news medium or an otherwise promising reporting career. Journalists need a continuing flow of invitations to official press conferences and cozy encounters with sources for "off-the-record" briefings if they are to continue to be of value to their employers. In their original work, Herman and Chomsky wrote that stories had to conform to the overwhelming presumption of US foreign policy that communism (and anything that administrations could smear with the label, which they often applied to socialism or nationalism) was evil. Since the fall of the Berlin Wall in 1989, the hegemony of anti-Communist ideology has been replaced by an ideology of various but integrated stripes that include support for the "war on terror," and the wholesale adoption of neoliberal principles favoring deregulated, "free" trade, capitalism. The propaganda model also works in application to media genres other than news (Alford, 2011, applies it convincingly to movies).

Much of the debate about Herman and Chomsky's book has focused on their propaganda model. In some ways this is a pity because the comparative evidence they present throughout the greater part of their book is a good deal more interesting, complex and nuanced than the model itself, although, as the authors argue, the model enables them to predict which news actors will be favored and which will be smeared or marginalized. Whereas the model may be criticized for its systemic bias (cf. Boyd-Barrett, 2010a) the case studies actually provide substantial evidence of agency and of how particular news media and journalists sometimes go out of their way, not infrequently through the relay of lies, omissions and misrepresentations, to serve as handmaidens of US foreign policy. Because the book focuses on major international news stories it focuses on the very stories that are most sensitive to the interests of empire.

In their analysis of specific cases the authors start by examining how mainstream news media represent the victims of war and oppression. Media bestow sympathetic attention on some victims, to whom they give the benefit of the doubt for any culpability those victims might bear. Others, by contrast, receive little if any attention, and less sympathy. Media imply that these victims have brought their misfortunes upon their own heads. Herman and Chomsky examined coverage of the killing of Polish priest Jerzy Popieluszko, and contrasted this with coverage of the treatment of a hundred religious victims in Latin America in the 1980s. Popieluszko was an activist Catholic priest and a strong supporter of Solidarity, the trade union movement so favored by the West because it helped embarrass and eventually bring down Communist rule in Poland. Popieluszko was killed by Polish secret police in 1984. The US mainstream media provided copious details of the murder and the violence inflicted, repeating these details across many stories. They also stressed the indignation and shock felt by the priest's sympathizers, and joined in the clamor for justice, seeking accountability from the very top of the political establishment and, when the culprits were punished, congratulated themselves on their success.

Herman and Chomsky contrast this to the media treatment of multiple killings of religious (many of them also Roman Catholic) in Central America. There were several simultaneous US interventions in support of authoritarian governments against progressive movements of the 1980s. A particularly notorious incident involved the assassination of the most prestigious critic of the US-supported military government of El Salvador, Archbishop Oscar Romero (killed by an agent of the junta in 1980), and the massacre of 40 persons who had attended Romero's funeral. The *New York Times* privileged the protestations of the Salvadoran government that it was caught as a neutral party in a civil war between right-wing and leftist forces. The *Times* prioritized the government's claim that the massacre was an unavoidable security reaction to a panic that had been instigated by leftist forces. More credible sources, on the other hand, indicated that the panic was caused by a bomb thrown from the National Palace. The paramilitary forces and death squads of El Salvador were known to have extensive interlocking relationships with the official military and security forces and their US counterparts. Romero was killed by an agent close to the Deputy Defense Minister. The *Times* even misrepresented Romero's own views, suggesting that he had blamed both right and left forces whereas the Archbishop had been critical only of the Salvadoran oligarchy – a position confirmed to the press, in private, by the US embassy. In contrast to their coverage of Popieluszko, US media showed little interest in hunting down those responsible for ordering Romero's killing at the uppermost levels of Salvadoran authority. Even when the culprit who ordered the assassination (D'Aubuisson) was identified and linked to official forces the media paid scant attention and any possible US involvement was buried.

Next, Herman and Chomsky consider the different treatment US media accord to "legitimizing" versus "meaningless" Third World elections. They cite coverage of El Salvador, Guatemala and Nicaragua. Whenever western governments favor a particular Third World regime, then its elections, however flawed or farcical (think Libya in 2012: author), are promising evidence of democratization, albeit stumbling. But whenever western governments are opposed to a particular Third World regime, then the elections in such a country, even when quite robust and administered amidst external aggression and destabilization (think Iran, 2009: author), are declared to be fake and meaningless.

During the 1980s Nicaragua's revolutionary Sandanistas overthrew the long, brutal dictatorship of General Samoza and held elections in 1984. These contrasted with what Noam and Chomsky deride as "demonstration" elections whose purpose is to placate US public and world opinion, as in elections introduced under the military-controlled regimes of El Salvador in 1982 and 1984, and Guatemala in 1984–1985. Whereas Nicaragua rated reasonably well on the criteria for "free elections" (i.e. a free press and assembly; freedom of organization of intermediate groups; the freedom to organize parties, field candidates and campaign for office; the absence of state terror and of a climate of fear; and freedom from the coercion to vote), El Salvador and Guatemala did not. Yet the US mainstream media were highly critical of the elections in Nicaragua, while excusing profound abuses in El Salvador and Guatemala. Covering Guatemala, the *New York Times* depended heavily on uncontested State Department sources, US officials and official observers, prominent Guatemalan politicians and generals. Spokespersons for the "insurgents" (essentially, the majority) were ignored. Available to the media but unused were statements dismissive of any possibility of fair elections issued by the Guatemala Bishops' Conference in 1984, and again in 1985 when the bishops queried whether an election could be meaningful in a situation "close to slavery and desperation" 1988: 103).

By contrast, the US media cast the Nicaraguan elections in a poor light, in a tone of negativism and apathy, overlooking the many ways in which the Nicaraguan elections were superior to those of the US client states, El Salvador and Guatemala. Attempts by rebels to disrupt the elections in these client states went unreported whereas in Nicaragua, when US-backed contras called for abstention, and threatened or attacked polling stations, they were lauded. In the client states, US media forgot to mention that voting was a military-backed requirement, whereas in Nicaragua they did not report that voting was voluntary.

Herman and Chomsky next dissect the strange and unlikely case of the alleged KGB-Bulgarian plot to kill the pope. On May 31, 1981, Mehmet Ali Agca shot and seriously wounded Pope John Paul II in St Peter's Square. Agca "was a Turkish rightist and assassin long associated with the Gray Wolves, an affiliate of the extreme right-wing Nationalist Action Party" (1988: 144), whose friends were violently anti-communist. The US mass media lent credibility to the unlikely claim that Agca had acted as hit-man in a KGB-Bulgarian plot. The story helped foster an image of the Soviet Bloc as terrorist, a trope in line with its elevation by President Reagan to the status of evil empire. It was fed by repetition and a disregard for alternative frames. It first surfaced in a document sourced to the Italian secret service, SISMI, and later found to have been fabricated. From there the allegation surfaced in a book that led to other citations. There were two major players responsible for disseminating the falsehood in the USA. One was ex-CIA officer and propaganda specialist Paul Henze, who had once headed the CIA bureau in Ankara and had even been accused by an ex-premier of Turkey as having destabilized the country. The other was Claire Sterling. Both were contracted by the *Reader's Digest* to write a story about "The Plot to Kill the Pope." This was followed up by an NBC program narrated by Marvin Kalb, and helped account for why Sterling became both a columnist and reporter on the affair for the *New York Times*. Herman and Chomsky argue that the Sterling and Henze accounts "suffered from a complete absence of credible evidence, a reliance on ideological premises, and internal inconsistencies. As problems arose, the grounds were shifted, sometimes with a complete reversal of argument" (1988: 147).

Herman and Chomsky devote two chapters to what they describe as the Indochina wars in Vietnam, Laos and Cambodia. They debunk the argument – often associated with *Washington Post* correspondent Peter Braestrup, who authored a two-volume analysis, *Big Story*, of media coverage of the 1968 Tet offensive – that the media (not the politicians, not the State Department, not the Department of Defense, not the military) had somehow "lost" the war in Vietnam. Yet throughout the war, Herman and Chomsky argue, the media not only supported Washington's war policy, they also performed their cheer-leading role with a degree of enthusiasm often exceeding any such sentiment in Washington. The scope for disagreement and debate permitted to surface in the mainstream media was narrow. It rarely extended to (1) a consideration of the legitimacy (or rather, the complete illegitimacy) of the US presence in Vietnam in the first place; or (2) an acknowledgement that the most serious opposition to the USA came from the South Vietnamese, with some support from North Vietnam, who were battling for repossession of their country from an aggressive invader and occupier, namely the USA; and never (3) regarded the USA as anything other than a warrior angel battling selflessly to protect a poor Third World country from the perils of communism while (4) restricting any disagreement to issues of strategy and tactics and (5) swallowing, as required, the lies and disinformation of presidents and politicians – as when Washington chose to totally misinterpret the terms of the Paris peace accords that the USA had already signed with North Vietnam, in a manner that encouraged the puppet government in Saigon, with US help, to continue its aggressions against what it claimed to be communist sympathizers, and in this way provoking the final North Vietnamese invasion and the ignominious expulsion of the USA from Vietnam in 1975.

Opposing viewpoints in US media were "limited to the domain of tactics – that is, limited to the question of 'whether the policy enunciated worked,' viewed entirely from the standpoint of US interests, and with official premises taken as given" (1988: 178). The USA had subverted the 1954 Geneva agreements struck after the departure of the French (whose restored imperial reign following World War Two was almost completely paid for by the USA). The accords were intended to prepare the way for national unification by means of elections that the USA knew would be won by Ho Chi Minh. By the official start of the war in 1965 the USA had not yet established a sufficiently reliable puppet government in Saigon that could do its bidding and "invite" in the USA; instead, the USA "simply moved in without even the formalities of request or acquiescence by a supposedly sovereign government" (1988: 178). Herman and Chomsky suggest that "these intriguing facts reflect the overwhelming dominance of the state propaganda system and its ability to set the terms of thought and discussion, even for those who believe themselves to be taking an 'adversarial stance.' Media departures from these doctrinal principles were negligible; indeed, they may well have been literally zero in the vast coverage and commentary on the war, while it was in progress or since."

Answering the charge that the media "lost" the war in Vietnam, Herman and Chomsky cite evidence that for the first five years the public did support the war, and that many did so because of the television coverage. Most television news anchors supported the war to the end. They were optimistic about US successes, reinforcing the impression given by government propaganda that the USA was in control, or at least up until Tet in 1968. Network news editors were instructed to delete excessively grisly or detailed shots. Few viewers appear to have considered that television reduced their satisfaction with the conduct of the war. Coverage focused mainly on the US effort, not on the GVN or the civilian leaders. The post-Tet "accelerated pacification program" – a program of mass, murderous slaughter inflicted on the South Vietnamese – received little attention. There was little or no coverage of US racism, the hatred felt by American servicemen towards the Vietnamese. The political opposition was treated with considerable hostility. Utterly fraudulent elections in South Vietnam were presented as triumphs of democracy. Civilian casualties (overwhelmingly the result of US firepower) were downplayed. The war was presented as a struggle for democracy against aggression.

The deceptions surrounding the Gulf of Tonkin incidents are well known. At the time the media swallowed the administration's stories of North Vietnamese aggression even though the first attacks, in which the *Maddox* was hit by a single bullet and the attacking craft were crippled or destroyed, are now known to have been a response to deliberate US provocation, and at a time when the National Liberation Front would have likely sought a political solution to the conflict. The second incident probably never happened. Daniel Hallin concluded that on "virtually every point, the reporting was either misleading or simply false" (1988: 208). Yet these incidents became the pretext for war. Herman and Chomsky conclude that "the nationalist media, overcome by jingoist passion, failed to provide even minimally adequate coverage of this crucial event" (1988: 209).

In *Big Story*, the *Washington Post* reporter Peter Braestrup argued that US media had misreported the Tet offensive of 1968 as a failure when really, he claimed, it was a US success. He ascribed the media coverage to incompetence and its "adversarial stance." Herman and Chomsky contest this, noting that if US media were held to account to the same standards as, in the 1980s, those media judged Soviet media reporting of the Soviet invasion of Afghanistan, then their coverage of Tet "provides another striking illustration of the subservience of the media to the state propaganda system" (1988: 213). They say that Braestrup adopted uncritically the same presumptions as US media: that the USA had a right to conduct operations in South Vietnam; that its goals were democracy and self-determination; that its forces brought security to the South Vietnamese peasantry; and that the South Vietnamese had been invaded not by the USA but by the North Vietnamese. Because Braestrup was unconscious of the presumptions that framed his own thought processes he could not recognize them in the media that he studied.

There can be no doubt that the Tet offensive had a strongly deleterious impact on the military situation for the USA, leaving two thirds of the country in the hands of the NLF. Internal US assessments cited by Herman and Chomsky were considerably more pessimistic than were US media. Even before the offensive, Secretary of State Robert McNamara privately concluded that the war was not winnable. Contrary to Braestrup's claims that the media had little dampening effect on public opinion, immediately after Tet public opinion was more strongly supportive of the war although it declined later to pre-Tet levels. Nor were the media particularly critical or despondent over Tet. At CBS Walter Cronkite even insisted that the Vietcong had suffered a military defeat.

Turning to the tragedy of Laos, the USA had struggled to prevent a political settlement following the 1954 Geneva Accords. Nonetheless, a coalition government was formed following the elections of 1958 which had favored the Left. US clandestine operations against Laos began in 1961 and regular bombing in 1964. Aid was cut off so as to make things much more difficult for the 1958 government, something that the US press chose not to mention. As conditions worsened through three distinct wars (the bombing of the Ho Chi Minh trail in the South; the bombing of peasants in northern Laos; and the clandestine CIA war against the Pathet Lao) press coverage declined and the terrible destruction of northern Laos was ignored or suppressed: when this did finally surface the media lied in their attempts to provide justifying explanations for the carnage alleging, for example, that it was targeted against North Vietnamese infiltration routes to South Vietnam, or that US planes were providing tactical support to government forces fighting North Vietnamese aggressors. In fact the bombing went well beyond such areas.

In the case of Cambodia, Herman and Chomsky argue that while the atrocities of the regime of Pol Pot were well covered by the media (and actually exaggerated), the previous reign of terror, almost as bad and caused by US bombing (which created the conditions that made it possible for Pol Pot to succeed), received barely any media attention. The authors conclude that "the dramatic differences in the information available for the two phases ... are readily explicable in terms of a propaganda model" (1988: 265). They refer back to the horrors, disregarded by western media, perpetrated by French imperialists when "government forces led by Lon Nol, who was to head the US-backed client government in the early 1970s, carried out wholesale massacres in villages as the French withdrew, including such 'individual tests of strength' as 'grasping infants by the legs and pulling them apart,'" actions that "had probably not been forgotten by the men of that area who survived to become the Khmer Rouge troops whose later atrocities in this 'gentle land' aroused such outrage in the West" (1988: 267). Despite concerns about the Khmer Rouge and the later regime of Pol Pot (media outrage peaked before the numbers of deaths had reached those of the previous era of US bombing and western incursions) the USA took the attitude that there was nothing to be done. Herman and Chomsky compare this to media coverage of the US-backed Indonesian atrocities in Timor where western media coverage declined sharply as the massacres increased. Later, when Vietnam invaded Cambodia to push out the Khmer Rouge, the USA in effect sided with Pol Pot.

CONCLUSION

In this chapter I have introduced the ideas of four theorists of media imperialism. Each of these is a mainstream media scholar, in the sense that each is widely cited in the scholarly literature. This is one reason why I call their theories "classic." Although they would not necessarily apply the term "media imperialism" to their writings, their central preoccupation has to do with the relationships between phenomena of imperialism and phenomena of media and communication. All may be considered strong exemplars of the political economy approach to media study, and three would identify themselves as such. Herman and Chomsky sub-titled their work a "political economy" of mass communication. Schiller is very aware that his object of study is the media and communication system of a country that exercises inordinate power around the world, and considers that communications have become an essential ingredient to nurturing and sustaining that power. Innis was a political economist in as much as he was interested in the relationships between communication systems, the economic factors that contributed to the choice of one system over another, and their relationships to major centers of power in the ancient societies he studied.

At the conclusion of Chapter 4 I will consider these scholars in relationship to a different range of researchers. Here it suffices to note that despite the shared preoccupations that these scholars have with the relationship of empires to media, they each have different ideas about the nature of this relationship – I made a similar point in Chapter 1 when I briefly compared the works of Tunstall, Innis, Schiller and Boyd-Barrett. Innis suggests that there is a direct relationship between the form of an empire and its prevalent means of communication. While the choice of the means of communications is a factor of physical environment and the state of knowledge, that choice is seen to have significant causal consequences for the nature of power and its exercise. Schiller is also inclined to attribute considerable influence to technology – in 1969 he was principally interested in the satellite – but his main contribution lies in his identification not only of the multi-layered connections between political and military power and technology, but also the dialectical relationships between these and the economics of the media business and their overall implications for the maintenance and expansion of advantageous trading relationships abroad. Herman and Chomsky are also interested in these things, but their primary focus and passion led them to examine primarily journalistic practice and the contrasting representations by leading US media of official US allies and enemies. Theirs is a close-up examination – in other words, of the construction and expression of an imperialist ideology through the media – and it demonstrates the extent to which "media imperialism" is a process that is every bit as toxic within the imperial center as it is in the peripheries, and maybe more so.

4   Colonial Communication Reframed

We need pause only briefly to digest the extraordinary vista of issues that opens up once it is accepted that media imperialism is about the study of the relationship between these two complex but essentially inter-related things: media and imperialism. Regretfully, the kind of sophistication that Innis hints at has been generally lost sight of in the literature. This is not to say that the works of scholars such as Herbert Schiller and Herman and Chomsky (or others I have not so far mentioned, including Armand Mattelart) who have done much to advance our understanding of media imperialism are anything other than sophisticated. But they, and some of their critics, were following one particular trajectory within the broader realm of media imperialism, one that had to do with the political economy of US power in the world and the role of US media in it. This is a worthwhile and important concern, one with which I have a great deal of sympathy and will be considering in some detail, but nonetheless within the broad span of the field as a whole, it is a relatively modest component. In this chapter I will examine the works of two additional authors who have made very different contributions to the field, starting with distinctive ideas as to what the terms "communication" or "information" or "media" might mean, and pointing in new directions for future research. These are C.A. Bayly (about the British in India) and Alfred McCoy (about the USA in the Philippines). The chapter concludes by identifying the common themes that emerged in the writings of all the authors discussed in both this and the previous chapter.

C.A. BAYLY

C.A. Bayly's monumental (1999) work, *Empire and Information in India 1780–1870*, is relevant here for several reasons. It helpfully reminds us of the "pre-modern history" of media imperialism from a time when, of the media of information and debate" (1999: 372). Diffuse pieces of information once collected and organized by newswriters, runners, diwan and munhi were now "ordered into files, and processed through official publication and the Anglo-Indian press, giving news a formality and fixity previously unknown" (1999: 372). The British could further access and mold the ways in which Indians "knew" what they knew, and what they reported, through colonialist systems of public instruction and schoolbook committees.

ALFRED MCCOY

Alfred McCoy's (2009) work, *Policing America's Empire*, explores similar themes in the context of American empire, with particular reference to the Philippines which the USA acquired among the spoils of victory after its defeat of the Spanish in the Spanish-American war of 1898. A stunning feature of this transition to a US takeover of the Philippines is that there was already a well-established national resistance movement against Spain in the Philippines. The nationalists at first expected that the US victory would mean their liberation, as the USA itself had promised, but this hope was almost immediately eradicated when the Americans turned their army against both Spanish and Filipinos.

McCoy pays close attention to the establishment of a constabulary to operate both as a political and a paramilitary force (the Philippines Constabulary, later the Philippine National Police) which had the consequence of embedding within the Philippine executive a powerful security apparatus that has been used by all succeeding Filipino presidents. The "covert doctrines" of surveillance, infiltration, disinformation and assassination that were developed under US rule have persisted through independence. In the bigger picture, the USA used empire as a crucible for experimentation in social control, an experiment that was not possible at home but one that yielded lessons which US administrators would later incorporate into domestic policy and practice. "Back home," McCoy writes (2009: 39–40), "these colonial veterans imbued the new U.S. domestic Intelligence apparatus with an imperious dominion over those deemed other, and thus lesser, whether ethnic communities, political dissidents, or ordinary workers," yielding a "repressive capability manifest during periodic political crises throughout much of the twentieth century."

McCoy here discerns a pattern that distinguishes the US empire from the 70 other empires that preceded it. Whereas European empires "operated under a costly command-style bureaucracy, American colonialism employed a decentralized market model" depending on the mobilization of a cadre of contractors, consultants on short-term secondment, and rotating military officers: "a transitory A–Z army of technical consultants in administration,

that we commonly recognize as such today, only the book, pamphlet and newspaper existed. It explores with rare precision the fundamental contribution of intelligence-gathering to statehood and imperial control generally, reminding us of the continuing interconnections between the worlds of the media and the worlds of the intelligence services. This has never been more resonant than in the second decade of the twenty-first century when the extent of the "surveillance" state, now characteristic of all developed economies, operating with the voluntary or involuntary assistance of major telephony, Internet and computing companies, was publicly exposed by celebrated whistleblowers such as Julian Assange and Edward Snowden. These interconnections have mainly to do with (1) the use by intelligence services of the products available to them through "open source" media; (2) manipulation of the media by intelligence agencies in the pursuit of particular tactical and strategic goals, through such means as suborning, cajoling (by money or threat) or threatening publishers, editors or journalists; (3) use of the media as convenient perches for intelligence agents who have either already penetrated the media or have been suborned by intelligence services for the purpose of gaining covert access – in the guise of journalistic credentials – to certain locations or sources. These remind us that the information acquired through or from such networks is always partial, is the product of many diverse motivations, and that its value may often reside not in the information itself, but in how that information can be used to undermine or support particular people, institutions, movements and causes.

The history of the media in India, as in many of the colonial territories of Britain and France, is a reminder of what Christian Vukasovich (2012) has called the "weaponization" of media both to impose imperial power and resist or undermine it via "home rulers" (representatives of the imperial classes who clamor for independence from the motherland, usually in an alliance with wealthy and influential sectors of the indigenous people) and indigenous nationalists or revolutionaries seeking to remove all traces of imperial power. The period chronicled by Bayly starts from around the time of the East India Company Act (1784) whose purpose was to subordinate the company to the British Crown in political affairs. A succeeding Act of 1813 asserted the Crown's sovereignty over all territories acquired by the company (by that time encompassing most of India). The East India Company finally lost all its possessions to the Crown under the Government of India Act of 1858 following the Indian Mutiny of the preceding year. Central to Britain's ability to control India for as long as it did was a combination of military force, trading advantage and intelligence. The term "intelligence" is used by Bayly very broadly to signify not just the covert collection of information but the development and distribution of different forms of knowledge.

Bayly argues that the British "took over and manipulated the sophisticated systems of internal espionage and political reporting which had long been deployed by the kingdoms of the Indian subcontinent ... The British had learnt the art of listening in, as it were, to the internal communications of Indian polity and society" (1999: 365). This "empire of information" however was undermined by prejudice or ignorance. By the 1860s officials sought to boost their intelligence system by establishing closer links to "natural leaders of the people," men of power at estate and village level, even though British prejudice against indigenous religious and cultural institutions often continued to exclude these as significant sources of information. Officials made some effort to use the patronage of the Education Department to reward and punish editors: "The loss of a hundred guaranteed sales to the Department could make the difference between success and failure for a struggling broadsheet" (1999: 342). Some newspapers were sponsored by the British, but this sponsorship did not necessarily make publications popular with their readerships. Future founder of the Indian National Congress, A.O. Hume, established *The People's Friend* in an effort to establish "loyal, sensible and moral vernacular newspapers" (1999: 342), articulating a form of popular imperialism that would attack the sort of calumnies that Hume believed had contributed to the rebellion of 1857, and that could counteract the influence of the editors of "Native papers" who might aspire to rich patronage from wealthy Indians. By the 1860s larger towns had one or two printing presses and most printed works were now original publications.

Bayly notes elsewhere that "the book, the pamphlet, the newspaper and the British post office had been pressed into use by critics of colonial rule and by those who questioned the West's cultural domination nearly sixty years before the formal date of birth of Indian nationalism" (1999: 366). While on the one hand these can be regarded as potential and actual sites of resistance to British control, their influence and/or popularity, or both, also made them indispensable sources of intelligence for the rulers, which helps to explain the uneasy and frequently interrupted tolerance for local publications exhibited by the British in most of their colonies. Bayly notes that Indian editors could tap into networks that were largely inaccessible both to the government and to Anglo-Indian editors. Many of their reports were picked up through marriage connections or the custom of charitable subscriptions for the easement of famine, or from the reports of pilgrims arriving into Banaras and Allahabad. The vigor of an Indian press contributed to a national consciousness of India, of its points of unity and its divisions of language, caste, religion and culture.

Bayly's work is sensitive to the many grey areas between "media," as the term is generally understood today, and the much broader and deeper phenomena of knowledge and information from which media draw and into which they feed. This includes formal intelligence networks, as we have seen, and extends to the concept of "archival depth" which would include such phenomena as public libraries, collections of sacred and other historical texts, journals, literary and educational societies and the like, and which flourished with the additional input of departments of state, and the legal profession, with its demand for written precedent and documentation. To these sources of formal knowledge may be added what Bayly calls affective knowledge through membership of religious sects and other "communities of emotion" (1999: 350) and "patrimonial knowledge" related to old court centers and landed magnates.

The British desire to remedy the mistakes made before the Mutiny led them to take a much closer interest in the diversity and multiplicity of Indian communities, including domestic and female spaces, and to develop a knowledge base of this richness, an approach that some have described as "a discursive strategy to bury change within tradition." In other words, local knowledge and the systems of knowledge-collection favored by the imperialists had implications for what knowledge would be available and prized by either imperialists or the indigenous and whether that knowledge would support or contest local knowledge. Bayly talks of the "life, death and transfiguration" of "different knowledges," and describes how the penetration of global capitalism into the hinterland rendered many skills of production and medicine for example redundant, and which both British officials and Indian nationalists struggled to record before they vanished. He also notes that the survival of indigenous knowledges was determined by their relevance to the emergence and mobility of influential new groups.

Bayly concludes that the "most common epistemological strategy of colonial rule was, in fact, a form of syncretism in which European knowledge and technique were vaunted as superior, but were required to be grafted onto the indigenous stock when planted in the great extra-European civilizations ... Since the British were dependent on Indian administrators, soldiers and merchants, and since Indians controlled the bulk of the means of production, commerce and capital throughout the colonial period, such syncretism was the only possible course" (1999: 370–1). Even as the British developed their knowledge of India, Indians developed their knowledge both of India and of Britain, albeit increasingly through epistemologies derived from the new rulers. What emerged, says Bayly, "was a dual economy of knowledge: an advanced sector which used western forms of representation and communication within an attenuated but still massive hinterland employing older styles

agronomy, entomology, ethnography, economics, meteorology, plant biology, public health, urban planning and zoology" (2009: 43). In effect this is an empire of information coupled with covert intelligence-related activities, including disinformation and the fomenting of scandal to embarrass or potentially embarrass opponents, tied to a nominally prohibited and convenient "vice economy of criminal syndicates, police corruption, political collusion, and periodic crisis." Philippine policing, initiated in order to combat insurrection, swept up scandalous knowledge about both Filipinos and Americans that could be selectively released as an instrument of colonial control in a political regime that was free from the legal constraints on the invasion of privacy that pertained on the US mainland. Ambitious Filipino politicians often contributed as informants, spies or political operatives, leaving behind trails of the evidence of their treachery that could be used against them and which circumscribed their capacity for resistance. Governor William Taft and his interior secretary Dean Worcester established a "total information regime" – one that reminded visiting Americans of a police state based on fear and honeycombed by the secret service – with every means at their disposal, including punitive libel and sedition laws, prosecuting editors for criminal libel, forbidding any political activity deemed "subversive," exiling radicals, jailing dissidents, and compiling files on gambling, corruption and "caciquism."

The Information Division of the Philippines Constabulary in the early 1900s built a network of some 200 paid Filipino agents, their identities concealed by numeric codes, who penetrated nationalist groups. In this way the Constabulary elevated spies to the most senior levels of leadership. Sometimes the purpose was to maneuver favored nationalist leaders into positions where they could be most helpful to the Americans: for example, the Constabulary worked hard to advance the cause of future President Manuel Quezon. McCoy remarks that it is possible that many of the agitators at any Manila meeting "were spies maneuvering for both popular leadership and PC rewards" (2009: 129).

In field operations spies proved useful during dragnet operations for the identification of their former colleagues as subversives. While the spy network was extensive and controls on the press were severe, the administration could not close down or control the press completely. In the Philippines, as elsewhere, there is significant evidence of the media acting as a vehicle of resistance to empire. It was a form of resistance that the authorities felt compelled to allow some leeway, given the wisdom in any complex society to allow some circulation of expression and ideas. This is especially true wherever it is deemed advantageous to secure the willing consent of the local aristocracy to imperial control, a class who, if properly corralled, will become important sources of intelligence. A local or indigenous press is also a key source of intelligence for the authorities.

Imperial condescension has its limits however. In the wake of the extremely brutal methods of repression exercised by the Constabulary on the island of Cavite (among other locations), the nationalist newspaper *El Renacimiento* printed damaging exposés that provoked outrage among educated Filipinos in Manila. Constabulary leaders considered such reportage "bitter and reckless" (2009: 139), and filed charges of criminal libel (which under the law of the day placed the burden of proof on the accused), arresting the editor, publisher and writer. The court case supplied major drama, eagerly reported by all the press. The outcome was vindication for the newspaper and punishment for those Constabulary leaders most responsible, leading to a Washington-instigated purge of the force in favor of men who could work more harmoniously with Filipinos, eventually culminating in a relationship of mutual dependency between rulers and local elites that worked to the advantage of both.

The case of *El Renacimiento* might also be seen as a relatively loose leash being applied by the imperial power to those media and leaders who were prepared to comply with it or who could be persuaded or coerced into taking a moderate path that urged collaboration between Americans and Filipinos on the long road to national independence, in preference to a more radical or revolutionary route. The latter included a measure that was favored by some revolutionary leaders, and its threat much exaggerated by the Constabulary: an alliance with Japan. *El Renacimiento* did not survive being later sued for libel by Dean Worcester, one of the colony's most powerful and vindictive rulers.

Most histories of the media – even when dealing with such complex issues as imperial pacification and revolution – stop at the media, or at media and political figures, rather than regarding the media as just one element in a complex intelligence network. McCoy notes how "radical or non-cooperating leaders who operated outside the bounds of electoral politics through union organizing or street rallies were subjected to surveillance, infiltration, and ultimately arrest and prison"(2009: 176). Secret agents were sent to all secret meetings or street rallies. They arrived armed with facts and information which they deployed, spontaneously it seemed, to combat calls either for revolution or an alliance with Japan. The Information Division of the PC infiltrated Filipino nationalist circles "so deeply that they were able to provide the Constabulary with both accurate Intelligence and considerable control over the movement. Gradually, the Constabulary moved beyond mere surveillance to covert penetration ... damaging the radical movement and embroiling the division in political intrigues" (2009: 186). This had the ultimate effect of creating fear and recrimination throughout the nationalist network in the period 1907–1912.

The Constabulary "turned" several celebrated nationalist leaders. These included Aurelio Tolentino, a famous radical dramatist, and Manuel Quezon, the future president. These became spokespersons for US-Filipino collaboration and provided key intelligence to the Constabulary that assisted it in neutralizing the more revolutionary arm of the movement: "By discrediting the leaders and disbanding their militant organizations, the constabulary in effect cleared the colony's narrow democratic space for political moderates willing to collaborate with colonial rule" (2009: 186). Quezon played it both ways, winning "nationalist credentials by defending radical leaders and colonial patronage by spying on them" (2009: 187) and helping preempt uprisings that "might have complicated his negotiations with the U.S. Congress over independence" (2009: 187). In the period 1907 to 1908 Constabulary pressure on Tolentino diminished him from his notoriety as an author of incendiary drama to the status of hack, producing theatrical metaphors for US-Filipino marriage and praising US rule "as a model of colonial governments, the worthy production of a people who had freed slaves" (2009: 190). His scripts were submitted in advance to the Manila police for censorship.

To combat a radical movement that the Constabulary did not like – the Dimas Alang society – the Constabulary set up a much more radical rival, the Makabuhay, with a view to luring out the most dangerous militants from the moderate group. By such techniques did Filipino policing and intelligence marginalize the militant nationalist movement: "By advancing the moderates and checking the radicals, the imperial information regime subtly, almost invisibly, kept Filipino political development within colonial bounds" (2009: 204).

The media played other important functions for the imperialists that help to explain the (limited) degree of tolerance shown them. Imperialists did not constitute a monolithic block, but were made up of many different political and other inclinations. The most significant divisions mirrored varying allegiances to (1) Republican or Democratic parties back in the USA – these parties had distinctively different policies with respect to the future of American control of the Philippines and to support or oppose promotion of Filipinization of government and administration; (2) support for or opposition to tough Constabulary actions against indigenous rebellions and labor protests; and (3) outrage against, or complicity with, scandals relating to gambling, prostitution, police and political bribery, and corruption. These scandals included the egregious abuse of power by American colonialists for the purposes of amassing land, business opportunity and wealth, often at the expense of indigenous populations. Colonialists could also sometimes be victims in need of press protection. In 1911, the *Free Press* undertook an exposé of police corruption in support of Captain John Green and his "heroic efforts" to stamp out corruption.

The different divisions among imperialists required corresponding media mouthpieces to promote particular policies or viewpoints and denigrate others; sometimes, as in the case of the *Free Press*, this denigration was based on well-substantiated investigative reporting. Press freedom leveraged the bitter disputes that broke out between different personalities and levels of the hierarchical institutions of imperial control. In these disputes officials could choose which media they wished to favor with news scoops or disinformation designed to discredit others, sometimes in the certain knowledge that local publications would catch the attention of politicians in Washington. When Police Commissioner Percy McDonnell was subjected to investigation and muck-spreading by Governor-General Taft, he bought sufficient shares in the *Cablenews-American* to become its chief editor, using this position to fight back – requiring, for example, that all mention of Constabulary Chief Bandholtz must be "detrimental." McDonnell was further enabled to conceal his espionage in the form of genuine press inquiries.

Following the Democratic presidential win of 1912 and the consequent push for Filipinization under new Governor Francis Harrison, Republicans fought back, sending stories of Filipino incompetence to US newspapers. This misinformation was traced by the Constabulary's secret service to a single cell inside the business office of former Constabulary Chief Harding. In the crisis of the "Conley Case" of 1923, Detective Ray Conley, apparently an effective scourge of the Manila underworld and who enjoyed the support of Governor Wood, was brought to criminal trial. The press were divided in their reactions: catering to American readers the *Manila Times* hailed Conley as the "terror of gamblers," while Filipino and Spanish dailies such as *La Vanguardia* were more suspicious. *El Debate* led the Filipino press in exploiting the scandal as a means of attacking the governor, Wood, and undertook apparent investigative journalism against Conley which actually had more to do with the relationship between *El Debate*'s owner – ex-mayor Fernandez, a close ally – to the nationalist leader and later president Quezon. McCoy notes that reporters "pounded out detailed accounts for front-page stories that appealed to the biases of their separate American and Filipino audiences" (2009: 276). In addition to the imperialists, of course, there were Christian and Muslim Filipinos augmenting the already rich diversity of belief systems among the indigenous. There were English, Spanish and Tagalog speakers as well as other language groups. There were conservatives, revolutionaries and bourgeois nationalists. All of these groups and their allied interests sought some kind of media representation.

The strategies and techniques of information management, control and manipulation that are invented by imperial powers in their colonies, McCoy argues, are imported back to their motherlands. In the USA the experience and lessons of empire in the Philippines have had a strong influence in shaping domestic US information control in both World Wars, and in combating left-wing, labor, civil rights and antiwar movements, and this influence persists even today in the aftermath of 9/11 and the war on terrorism:

> The pacification of the Philippines served as both blueprint and bellweather for Washington's nascent national security state. In its search for security in the midst of revolution, the U.S. colonial regime at Manila drew untested technologies from the United States, perfected their practice, and then transmitted these refined repressive mechanisms back to the metropole, contributing to the formation of a federal internal security apparatus ... More broadly, colonial rule had a profound influence on metropolitan society, introducing an imperial mentality of coercive governance into U.S. domestic politics. (2009: 346)

Early evidence of this became apparent in World War One. "President Wilson's wartime America circa 1918" writes McCoy (2009: 294), "came to bear a marked resemblance to Governor Taft's colonial Philppines circa 1901" – in the shape of legislation limiting civil liberties, secret services that engaged in arbitrary arrests, rigid censorship, mass surveillance, covert penetration, and black operations:

> World War 1 transformed the U.S. state through the mobilization of a four-million-man army, massive industrial procurements, and the creation of an Argus-eyed internal security apparatus. (2009: 296)

The commander of the Philippine's Division of Military Information, Van Deman, later drew up the design for the first US internal security agency. His appointed secretary, Captain Alexander B. Coxe, was also a veteran of the Philippine DMI.

McCoy identifies the following similarities between Van Deman's Philippine campaign and US internal security during World War One: the reduction of voluminous information to a single card for every subject; covert surveillance and infiltration; an ethnic or racial template for the perception of threat (in the Philippines as in the USA, Van Deman relied on native agents); the mass relocation of subject populations; the systematic use of scandal for political disinformation, social ostracism or blacklisting; and omnipotence over people deemed to be alien and inferior. Reminiscent of the use by the Philippine Constabulary of hundreds of Filipino operatives were used in the USA by the Military Intelligence Division of the 300,000 citizen spies of the American Protective League (APL). This alliance between state security and civilian institutions persisted, under different names, for the next 50 years, "as a sub rosa matrix that honeycombed American society with active informers, secretive civilian organizations, and government security agencies, federal and local." Van Deman presided over the APL's transformation into an almost exclusive WASP civilian counter-intelligence auxiliary, with 350,000 volunteer agents in 1,400 local units, their leaders mostly recruited through elite networks, who concentrated their attention on German Americans and conducted a total of three million wartime investigations for the government. The accused were never allowed to confront their accusers; the cloak of secrecy allowed members to harass commercial rivals. The MID itself concentrated on covert counter-intelligence against radical unions and socialist parties, often aligning itself to the security forces of individual factories and even joining violent vigilante groups to crush unions. Arbitrary arrests, infiltration and provocation were common. McCoy traces similar tactics through World War Two, post-war labor unrest and the subsequent Red Scare, including the Hollywood blacklists. Even then, Van Deman and his relationship with Richard Combs, chief counsel to the California Committee on Un-American Activities, served as a conduit that "allowed the US Intelligence community to leak damning but unconfirmed information about suspected subversives from classified files into the committee's public hearings" (2009: 334).

CONCLUSION

This short review indicates scope for the integration of scholars whose works in Chapter 3 I termed "classics" of media imperialism, for whom the media are central to their inquiries into imperialism, and a newer generation of scholarship that is equally concerned with imperialism but for whom the media are not necessarily central. Inevitably, and mainly for reasons of space, I have not referred to the many other works that have also contributed substantially and with great originality to our understanding of the complex range of relationships of media and empire. Among these I would include, and recommend the reader to consult, Dwayne Winseck and Robert Pike's *Communication and Empire: Media, Markets and Globalization 1860–1930* (2007). Together these writings, old and new, span the course of more than 60 years, and they provide compelling proof that the connections between media and imperialism are important, complex, multiple, multi-layered, reciprocal and dialectical. Innis drew attention to the relationships in antiquity between prevailing media forms and forms of imperial control. This basic insight informed the work of Schiller who unraveled the relationships between electronic media (notably satellite communication) and imperial surveillance and ideological manipulation, tying together the military-industrial complex, communications hardware industries, mass entertainment and information, advertising, and the eternal need for the extension of markets in systems of consumer capitalism. In his way he prepared us for discourses of the role of media in the "surveillance society" (cf. Mattelart, 2010) and even more recently the disclosure of intimate ties, sometimes enforced by secret court (FISA), between the national security apparatus of the USA and of leading computer hardware, software, social media and telephony corporations.

McCoy identified the most distinctive feature of US empire as decentralized, market-driven control. Eminently suited to this context is the illusory appearance of press (and media) freedom and plurality. A devolved "freedom" from direct political control offers corporations, and the media that serve them, the flexibility that the market requires for a constant adjustment of image, tone and narrative to suit the varying and always evolving life conditions of specific market segments in different parts of the world. Herman and Chomsky disclosed how far such "freedom" is sustained through a close integration of the operations of both the press (as an institution) and of journalism (as a practice) with the requirements of political elites, themselves the servants of both the plutocracy in general and the large corporations, and rarely more evident than in the case of foreign reporting. This partnership is ever more evidently at work to denigrate the last hold-outs against the global expansion of US-generated neoliberalism (cf. Chapter 1) and deregulated oligopoly corporatization. While Herman and Chomsky are themselves concerned mainly with the operations of the press, this book shall examine comparable and parallel evidence of similar ideological work in the industries of the entertainment media. The connections go far beyond ideological hegemony and control.

Both Bayly and McCoy demonstrate an earthier level of interrelationship between media and the ruling apparatus through the mutual functioning of media and intelligence. This goes a long way towards explaining the US system of media imperialism, its decentralized character and the scope for discretion and difference that it tolerates (nearly always narrower than at first seems to be the case), just as it also explains not dissimilar levels of tolerance demonstrated by the British in their relationships to colonial media. Herman and Chomsky expose how media tolerance varies as between subjects who enjoy the support of imperial authority and those that do not.

Media that appear to be and even are indigenous, even when supposedly "free," function as covert instruments of surveillance for the imperial state, even when they present themselves to readers as centers of intellectual energy for resistance, in the forms of nationalist, radical and other movements. They also provide credible channels for covertly-implanted elite frames and perspectives. Such media serve multiple uses in support of the efforts of intelligence agencies to exercise control by such means as punishment by actual or threatened disclosure or the withholding of disclosure, in addition to more conventional tactics of manipulation and disinformation.

The information at stake here is far broader than the merely political, as Bayly shows, but has to do with the promotion of ways of knowing about the world that are consonant with the ways of knowing that serve the imperial interest. What "counts" in an examination of the control of information on behalf of empire does not belong only to the realm of the colonial world. Empire is sustained as much at home as abroad. This happens through the supply to domestic audiences of frames for the understanding and interpretation of world events and of the world itself in ways that anchor their intellectual and emotional support to imperial maneuvers and flatter them with an elevated perspective on their own goodness and intelligence. This would be one juncture among many at which I could reasonably move from media to cultural imperialism, although it is my intention to remain focused on the role of media in this nexus.

5 Selling Pretexts for Imperial War

FALSE PRETEXTS FOR IMPERIAL WAR 1846–1983

In the concluding section of Chapter 2 I introduced the concept of pretexts for war and what I have called the "politics of pretext." I shall show in this chapter that frequently US imperial expansion (and, for that matter, the expansion of many other empires) has been initiated through the construction of false or at best questionable pretexts for war. Far from declining in importance, the tactics of false pretext have become more frequent and sophisticated. Mainstream media play an indispensable role in routinely accepting these pretexts with little or no critical investigation. Mainstream media function to maintain US and world public opinion in a state of suspended innocence if not gullibility. In this chapter I shall have space for only a few selected and significant examples. As is the case with almost any other historical events there is room for controversy and dispute. The persistence of such controversies, often supported with strong evidence, should counsel extreme press caution against uncritical acceptance of the reasons given by officialdom for going to war.

It is a history that could be picked up from 1846 when President Polk ordered US forces south of the Nueces River, knowing this to be territory claimed by Mexico. The encounter of this patrol by the Mexican army, as anticipated by Polk, resulted in the killing of 16 US soldiers, an event that he then construed as a case for a war that within two years would substantially increase the size of the USA (the territories then acquired today represent 15% of the USA). US newspapers almost uniformly supported Polk's war plans (Moreno, 2007). The bombing and sinking of the USS *Maine* in the harbor of Havana in 1898 triggered US contingency plans drawn up in 1894 for a war against Spain. The bombing was almost certainly not the work of the Spanish, as the Americans had claimed, but the result of either an accidental explosion on board the ship or a "false flag" operation by the USA. The war demolished a rival to US power and netted

the USA some 50 years' control over Cuba and the Philippines, the colonization of Puerto Rico and even the annexation of Hawaii when, at the
behest of American sugar planters, the USA deposed Queen Liliuokilani
(Sanders, 2002; US Department of State, 2013). Of critical importance to
the mobilization of public support for the Spanish-American war were the
leading newspapers of the day and their publishers William Randolph
Hearst (*New York Journal*) and Joseph Pulitzer (*New York World*).
Unrestrained by the absence of evidence, they decided that the Spanish were
to blame for the sinking of the *Maine* and ordered sensationalistic stories of
so-called "atrocities" that had been committed by the Spanish in Cuba.

US entry into World War One was a reaction in part to the sinking of the
British liner, the *Lusitania*, on May 7, 1915, by a German submarine that
killed 1,198 people including 128 Americans. In addition to passengers the
ship was carrying six million rounds of US ammunition bound for Britain.
Before its departure from New York, the German Embassy had published
prominent warnings in 50 US newspapers of the danger to passengers if
they sailed into waters that Germany had already described as a war zone.
In his listing of such pretexts, Sanders (2002) cites sources showing that
British First Lord of the Admiralty Winston Churchill had previously commissioned "a study to determine the political impact if an ocean liner were
sunk with Americans on board," and that a week before the incident he had
written to the Board of Trade's president saying it was "most important to
attract neutral shipping to our shores, in the hopes especially of embroiling
the U.S. with Germany."

The Japanese invasion of Pearl Harbor in 1941 was a response to measures taken by the Roosevelt administration that amounted to an act of war,
a war that Roosevelt had promised the public he would avoid but which his
administration wanted. With apparent recklessness, a substantial portion of
the American fleet was concentrated in Pearl Harbor as an irresistible target
for the Japanese (see Stinnett [2001] for what is probably the best of several
book-length analyses). This was one component of an eight-stage plan to
provoke war, drawn up in October 1940 by a close advisor to Roosevelt,
namely Lieutenant Arthur McCollum, head of the Far East desk for US
Navy intelligence. To this day mainstream media coverage of Pearl Harbor,
as in the press commentary during anniversaries or in movie representations
such as Michael Bay's 2001 *Pearl Harbor* (released a few weeks' prior to
September 11, 2001), ignores or marginalizes such evidence in favor of
simplistic "day of infamy" rhetoric.

The US invasion of Korea in 1952 was presented by the USA to the world
as a response to the invasion by "North" Korea (then under Soviet army
occupation following the liberation of Korea from Japan) of "South" Korea

(under American army occupation) across a totally arbitrary border that had been imposed by the occupiers at the 38th parallel – against widespread Korean opposition. The North Korean invasion had been anticipated by the USA (Gibbs [2004], drawing on Halliday and Cumings [1988] and declassified documents). Although the USA had not previously considered Korea to be of vital strategic importance, news of the invasion in the USA was greeted by an official hysteria whose purpose was to convince the public to accept the "need," otherwise unpopular, for a substantial rearmament program and what ultimately was to become the remilitarization of the USA. Thus was accomplished the threefold increase in military spending that had been proposed by the National Security Council in NSC-68 as necessary to allay inter-service resource rivalries while at the same time enabling direct economic support to Europe. NSC-68 was drafted early in 1950 and approved by President Truman two months prior to the invasion of Korea in June that year. The USA, Gibbs argues, lured North Korea into attacking the South. Secretary of State Dean Acheson had publicly expressed doubt in January 1950 as to whether South Korea fell within the "defense perimeter" that the USA had established, possibly giving an apparent green light to North Korea to attack ROK. President Syngman Rhee, and triggered the war "with behind the scene support of John Foster Dulles." Dulles was a former-US Secretary of State, and met Rhee (June 18, 1950) just days before the outbreak of war. Dulles told Rhee that "if he was ready to attack the communist North, the U.S. would lend help, through the UN ... He advised Rhee ... to persuade the world that the ROK was attacked first, and to plan his actions accordingly" (Sanders, 2012).

As discussed in Chapter 3, the pretext for the formal US engagement of troops in Vietnam was the pair of so-called Gulf of Tonkin incidents of August 4 and 6, 1964, of which the first resulted from provocation and the second never even occurred. The Tonkin pretext extended and formalized the war in Vietnam at the eventual expense of an estimated four million Vietnamese dead and the lives of 60,000 US servicemen and women. In the USA the White House and Pentagon blamed the press for losing the war, although Herman and Chomsky (1988) have shown that if anything the press maintained a stronger faith in the war than the administration itself.

The invasion of the island of Grenada in 1983 was the first significant US aggression since its humiliating defeat at the hands of the Vietnamese in 1975, signifying the new right-wing unilateralism of President Ronald Reagan. The invasion followed a decade's impassioned western defense of an extreme right-wing leader, Eric Gairy, ex-premier and first prime minister of an independent Grenada, whose leadership of the island was so unpleasant that when Britain offered independence Grenadians themselves preferred to "shut down the country ... prior to Independence Day, February 7, 1974" (Sanders, 2002) to forestall the continuation of Gairy's power. When the opposition New Jewel Movement (NJM) overthrew Gairy in a bloodless coup, the USA sought to remove the NJM whose leader, Martin Bishop, was assassinated by Deputy Prime Minister Bernard Coard, serving as the pretext for the US invasion.

The operation was also a laboratory for the US administration to apply a new or at least rediscovered methodology of press control. It excluded the press from the main action – and, therefore, from the main scenes of atrocity – until it was too late. Access was restricted to selected members of a press "pool." The military carefully monitored and controlled where these pool journalists went and to whom they talked. The "pool" model of management of the press by military and political authorities was further perfected through the Panama invasion in 1989 and the first Gulf War of 1990–1991, and by the second Gulf War in 2003 which was supplemented by "embedding" the press with troops.

OPERATION DESERT STORM 1990–1991

The green-lighting of North Korea by Dean Acheson in 1950 was reprised in the lead-up to the Iraqi invasion of Kuwait in 1990. US Ambassador April Glaspie on July 25, only one week before Iraq launched its invasion (its plans already known to the USA), told Iraq that the US administration did "not have an opinion" on the disagreement between Kuwait and Iraq and that the USA did not intend to "start an economic war against Iraq." This was wildly at variance, of course, with the aggressive enthusiasm with which the USA led an international UN-supported operation (the first of two) against the regime of Saddam Hussein. Various interests and motives have been alleged here, with the usual suspects including the defense industry and oil interests (Chomsky, 1998).

The USA indirectly contributed to Hussein's long path to power by colluding in his overthrow of President Qasim in 1963, and supported both Iraq (primarily) and Iran in their eight year war (1980–1988). Hussein started the war only a year after he became president and one year after the anti-US Iranian revolution. The conflict took one and a half million lives (Karsh, 2002). The USA did not merely assist Saddam Hussein's use of gas and chemical weapons against Iranian troops and Kurds by identifying targets for him (Porter, 2014), while Iran refused on religious principle to engage in chemical warfare, but even allowed the export of dual-use products that contributed to the manufacture of WMD.

In Hussein's eyes Kuwait was merely an artificial creation – contrived by the British in the aftermath of the dissolution of the Ottoman empire following World War One, and serving to block Iraq from having access to the Gulf – as well as an upstart whose oil companies were now allegedly ramping up their production by slant drilling from Kuwait into Iraq's Rumaila oil field (Hayes, 1990). At a time when Iraq desperately needed to raise revenue to help repair the damage it had suffered from the war with Iran, furthermore, Kuwait chose to ignore OPEC policy and lowered the price of its oil on international markets, thus pulling global prices downwards.

Wars provide opportunities for the testing of new weapons and the invasion of Iraq saw the first major application of a new generation of computerized, so-called *"precision bombing"* (a term that successfully deceived western mainstream media who were encouraged to present the war as one in which only military targets would be attacked). Most of the bombing, however, was conventionally indiscriminate and even so-called precision bombing (advertised in footage released by the military and gleefully broadcast throughout the world) was anything but precise. The USA claimed that the intervention was urgent because Iraq intended to invade Saudi Arabia. Satellite evidence did not support this claim, which might have been a pretext to pressure the Saudis into allowing the USA to establish military bases (a measure considered greatly offensive to Islam by Osama Bin Laden) (Ungerman and Brohy, 2001).

To help ensure domestic US support for a war to protect the oil-rich sheiks of Kuwait, a country that few Americans knew or cared about, a major public relations outfit, Hill and Knowlton, was pressed into service on behalf of both the Kuwaiti royal family and the White House. Using as dramatic "evidence" the pre-coached story of an "anonymous" 15-year old Kuwaiti girl who later turned out to be the daughter of the Kuwaiti ambassador to the USA, Hill and Knowlton fabricated a tale that Iraqi soldiers in Kuwait city had grabbed babies out of hospital incubators and left them on floors to die (Fifth Estate, 1992; Grigg, 2011). This story was referenced endlessly by the president and his executive team for their pre-war propaganda campaign, and consumed uncritically by the mass media.

THE SOVIET INVASION AND OCCUPATION OF AFGHANISTAN 1979

Before the Soviet invasion Afghanistan was not seen by the USA to be as vital a security interest as neighboring Iran (Gibbs, 2004). The invasion was a pretext for the USA to swing public opinion behind a massive increase in military expenditure, which otherwise would have been deeply unpopular among a citizenry still smarting from the humiliation of defeat in Vietnam. Gibbs (2004) argues that the Soviet Union was lured into the invasion. President Carter approved funding for Mujahidin forces six months before the Soviet invasion. Such aid constituted a serious provocation on the southern frontier of the Soviet Union. Carter's national security advisor, Zbigniew Brzezinski (who has written on this many times; see Brzezinski, 1997), advised the president that aid would induce a Soviet military invasion which could then entrap the Soviets into an equivalent of the USA's own Vietnam "quagmire." Parenti (2009) adds that the Taraki government of the People's Democratic Party (PDP), which had been returned to power with military support in 1978, had promoted egalitarian and collectivist economic policies while opposing opium production. The PDP incurred the enmity of the CIA which was in alliance with Saudi and Pakistani militaries, lending their weight to what Parenti describes as "ousted feudal lords, reactionary tribal chieftains, mullahs, and opium traffickers." Taraki was executed in a *coup d'état* staged by Hafizulla Amin, possibly a CIA asset, in September 1979. The PDP government sought Soviet assistance against CIA-funded mujahidin and foreign mercenaries.

9/11 AND THE "WAR ON TERROR"

This kind of contextualization was predictably absent from mainstream US media coverage of 9/11 (Boyd-Barrett, 2003; Kellner, 2003), which has very rarely questioned either the official narrative of 9/11 or the official explanation for the invasion and occupation of Afghanistan (King, 2014). It is one of history's strangest ironies that within two decades of the Soviet invasion it would be the USA's turn to invade and occupy Afghanistan, on an even less robust pretext than that employed by the Soviets. The Soviets, at least, could argue that they had been invited in to help the Kabul regime maintain order.

Gibbs (2004) considers that the attacks of 9/11 were again used by the US administration as a pretext (under the pseudonym of global "war on terror") for massive increases in military and defense expenditure following several years when defense budgets had languished in the wake of the fall of the Soviet Union and the consequent "peace dividend."

The "war on terror" appears to have been eagerly anticipated by senior members of the neoconservative movement, many of whom had ascended to leading positions in the government of George W. Bush when he came to power following a deeply disputed election in 2000 (whose final result was determined not by voters – Al Gore won the majority of votes nationwide – but by thuggish GOP shenanigans in Florida and by the Supreme Court). The movement's manifesto was published in September 2000 by the Project for the New American Century, a so-called think-tank (1997–2006). Entitled *Rebuilding America's Defenses: Strategies, Forces and Resources for a New Century*, it called for additional annual defense spending of $15–$20 billion. It also advocated a reformulation of power in the Middle East, "if America is to retain its militarily dominant status for the coming decades." The sought-for transformation was expected to be a long one, "absent some catastrophic and catalyzing event – like a new Pearl Harbor."

Neoconservatives who held positions of power in the administration of George W. Bush indisputably made use of 9/11 to press their PNAC agenda. Among the most powerful were Vice-President Dick Cheney, Secretary of Defense Donald Rumsfeld (both of whom had spearheaded the campaign to exaggerate the Soviet threat in the 1980s) and Deputy Secretary of Defense Paul Wolfowitz.

First application of the opportunity presented by the 9/11 pretext was the (principally) US invasion and occupation of Afghanistan, launching a war that continued for the ensuing 13 years up to the time of writing in 2014, is likely to involve some form of continuing US presence for the indefinite future, and which has in recent years significantly destabilized Pakistan, a nuclear power. The original pretext for this war, namely to punish the supposed perpetrators of 9/11, never made compelling (if any) sense. The supposed instigators of the 9/11 attacks were mainly Saudis, yet as Bob Graham (a former chair of the Senate Intelligence Committee and chair of the 2002 joint congressional investigation into 9/11) has noted the US administration took unusual precautions to protect Saudi Arabia from suspicion or investigation (Real News Network, 2013). The Saudis in question were said to be members of an organization later known to the world as Al Qaeda, as to whose institutional existence at the time of 9/11 there is reasonable doubt (Curtis, 2006) and whose name owes its origin to the US/CIA recruitment of the Mujahidin resistance during the Soviet occupation in the 1980s. Even assuming that Osama Bin Laden, widely considered to have been a CIA asset in the 1980s, had been a meaningful "head" of this organization would not explain a 13 year (and counting) US war against a different target, namely the Taliban, closely associated with the ethnic Pashtuns of Afghanistan.

THE US INVASION AND OCCUPATION OF IRAQ

Even more egregiously evident as orchestrated pretext, building on the manipulation of public opinion that had been achieved in the wake of 9/11, were the invasion and occupation of Iraq in 2003. These were heralded by the 2002 articulation of the "Bush Doctrine." This doctrine encompassed a policy of preventive war and expounded the right of the USA to depose foreign regimes that the administration perceived to pose a threat, even if that threat was not immediate (a violation, many would argue, of international law). The 2003 invasion was based on the manifestly false pretext that the regime of Saddam Hussein possessed "weapons of mass destruction." Paul Wolfowitz has admitted that the pretext was merely one of bureaucratic convenience, one that the instigators of the conspiracy could most easily agree upon (competing pretexts considered were "terrorism" and the "abuse of Iraqis by their own government," [Associated Press, 2005]).

Mainstream media almost universally hailed the fine reasoning and "evidence" of Iraqi weapons of mass destruction that Secretary of State Colin Powell presented to the United Nations on February 6, 2003, evidence that was quickly pulled apart by knowledgeable critics outside of the mainstream at the time, and was soon to be demonstrated as tragically wrong and treacherous in the immediate wake of the invasion. Powell later disavowed his 2003 speech, describing it as a "blot" on his record (Associated Press, 2005). Yet well before the invasion many knowledgeable sources, generally disregarded by the mainstream press, were extremely skeptical.

The concept of "weapons of mass destruction" was not precisely defined by the administration. None the less, with the help of the media the public were encouraged to think that Saddam had massive nuclear and biological capability, which he clearly had not. The British government produced two briefing documents in September 2002 and February 2003 that together suggested Iraq could deploy biological weapons in 45 minutes of an order from Hussein to that effect and that the country had reconstituted its nuclear program. At least one of the two British reports had plagiarized considerably from, and exaggerated, a published source (by a graduate student). A story in May 2003 by BBC journalist Andrew Gilligan to the effect that the previous September's "45 minutes" report had exaggerated the likelihood of Iraqi WMD and that intelligence had "sexed up" the evidence – hardly a preposterous claim – was manufactured into a subject of bitter dispute between the Blair government and the BBC. It was one focus among others of the Hutton inquiry into the death of Gilligan's main source, Dr David Kelly, an employee of the Ministry of Defense. Notwithstanding Hutton's conclusions, Kelly's death remains deeply controversial – mooted causes other than suicide include his covert assassination by British intelligence or, much less likely, by the Iraqi government (Marsden, 2014).

By early 2004 the scandal had brought about the resignations from the BBC of Gilligan himself, the BBC Chairman Gavyn Davies, and the BBC

Director-General Greg Dyke. Gilligan's comments had represented a single paltry attempt within the prestigious mainstream media to warn the public that the evidence that was being touted to justify an upcoming brutal war of invasion and occupation, a war crime of hideous proportions, was at best dubious. Even this humble attempt was successfully derailed by the British government and used instead to distract media and public attention away from illegal war mongering towards fabricated issues about journalistic quality.

In its Duelfer Report (US GPO, 2005), the Iraq Survey Group – a 1,400 member force put together by the Pentagon and CIA after the invasion to find the weapons of mass destruction – reported that it had found no such weapons. That there were elements of chemical weaponry, some of which were found by US troops in the years following the invasion, cannot be a huge surprise. Ex-UNSCOM inspector Scott Ritter (Ritter and Pitt, 2002) wrote that nuclear facilities had been 100% eliminated and that other mass destruction capability had been 90–95% eliminated by 1998, and noted that any remnants still to be found on any sites that had previously been sealed by the UN would have long since lost their potency.

There was considerable evidence prior to 2003 that any weapons of mass destruction in Iraq had long before been destroyed. Furthermore it is barely conceivable that Iraq, a country under constant surveillance in practically every way, could have reinstated such programs in the period 1998–2003. In the John Pilger 2010 documentary *The War You Don't See*, FAIR's Steven Rendell related how stories by AP special investigative reporter Charles Hanley in 2003 recounted that he had personally accompanied the UN weapons inspectors who were visiting all the sites that had been identified as suspicious, and told how they had found that these remained as sealed as they had been when examined by the UN in 1991. Few news media chose to use these stories.

The build-up to the invasion was aided and abetted by the *New York Times*, which ran several front page stories by reporter Judith Miller, and some in partnership with Michael Gordon, that were heavily dependent on anonymous and, as it turned out, highly dubious sources, such as Ahmed Chalabi, chairman of the US-supported Iraqi National Council, and Rafid Ahmed Alwan al-Janabi, or "Curveball," who later admitted that his "evidence" was fabricated (Boyd-Barrett, 2004, 2010a; Chulov and Pidd, 2011).

Mainstream media frequently replayed the Bush lie that Saddam Hussein had kicked out UN inspectors in December 1998 whereas in fact the head of UNSCOM, Richard Butler, had withdrawn them from Iraq for fear that they might be caught up in the four-day bombing campaign against Iraq launched that month by the USA and the UK (to "degrade" rather than eliminate Iraq's ability to manufacture and use weapons of mass destruction) (Ritter and Pitt, 2002). *MediaLens* (2002) cited a FAIR finding (2002) that the media who in 1998 had reported that the inspectors had left on their own volition were reporting in 2002 that they had been "thrown out." *MediaLens* also found similar evidence of duplicity in the UK press – only six of 497 *Guardian/Observer* stories, for example, even mentioned that the previous UNSCOM inspections team might have been penetrated by spies. Furthermore, a modified inspections team, UNMOVIC, was created in 1991 and was allowed back in by Saddam Hussein in November 2002, accompanied by AP's Charles Hanley (see above). Just like the Iraq Survey Group after the invasion, UNMOVIC had found nothing before it.

Many leading media and news professionals have expressed regret for their coverage during the lead-up to the war. In addition to celebrated published *mea culpas* from the *New York Times* and the *Washington Post*, these include the BBC's Jeremy Paxman who considers that the media were "hoodwinked," CBS's Dan Rather who has talked about how journalists succumbed to a climate of fear of not seeming to be sufficiently patriotic, and the *Observer's* David Rose who now feels nauseated by his own and others' coverage and admits that journalists allowed themselves, wittingly or otherwise, to become accomplices to a war fought on a false pretext (all three have been interviewed or recorded by John Pilger [2010]).

THE WAR ON DRUGS AS A PRETEXT

Armed or violent interventions instigated by the USA and its allies on the basis of one or more of the most common contemporary pretexts for war – the "war on terror", the "war on drugs," "humanitarian intervention," or to achieve "democracy" – can often appear grossly disproportionate and possibly counter-productive, even if taken seriously on their own terms.

In its first significant intervention as the world's *sole* superpower, in December 1989, the USA killed up to 4,000 Panamanians, destroyed the homes of 20,000 people, and unleashed a period of lawlessness and looting. The pretexts cited by President George H.W. Bush Senior, swallowed in their entirety and uniformly by US mainstream media, were the need to protect US lives, apprehend the Panamanian leader Manuel Noriega – the "drug lord" – and protect the "neutrality" of the Panama canal. Noriega had been a CIA asset precisely because of the usefulness of his knowledge of drug trafficking and his help to the USA in its fight against the Sandinista revolutionaries of Nicaragua in the 1980s, and he was also involved on behalf of the USA in the Iran-Contra scandal. His CIA salary had been increased substantially by George H.W. Bush when Bush headed the CIA in 1976, but

Noriega had also intervened in a process of democratic election against the candidate that was backed and funded by the USA.

Noriega was heir to control of Panama after the death, in an air crash in 1981, of the *de facto*, progressive military leader of Panama, General Omar Torrijos, who had achieved power by a *coup détat*. Torrijos negotiated the treaty with President Carter to hand US sovereignty over the Panama Canal zone back to Panama by the end of 1999. This hand-over would allow a continuation of US military bases and the USA's right to ensure the neutrality of the canal. When relations with the USA began to deteriorate from the mid-1980s, many in the Reagan administration who were opposed to the treaty in principle worried that Noriega might incline more towards Cuba and the Soviets, although the Soviet bloc was already in the process of transformation under Gorbachev at that time, so was unlikely to have had an interest in Panama.

The 1989 attack on Panama may be construed in part, therefore, as a war of false pretext launched with a hideous absence of proportionality under the banner of the "war on drugs." If this "war" was to be taken seriously, on its own terms, it would be judged as one of the most manifestly stupid, ineffective, and needlessly expensive policies ever pursued by any government.

Although first use of the term has been attributed to President Richard Nixon in 1971 (Payan, 2006: 23), in response to a scare about heroin addiction among returning Vietnam war veterans, its antecedents reach back, at federal level, to the Harrison Narcotics Tax Act of 1914 and to 1860 at state level. It was George H.W. Bush who, as Director of the CIA, pushed for CIA and military involvement in the war on drugs. Such involvement has often contradicted the policies and actions of the Drug Enforcement Administration (DEA), which was established in 1973.

The CIA and its predecessors already had a track record of participation in drug trafficking as a means of financing covert and sometimes illegal activity from long before George H.W. Bush's stint at the agency (Scott and Marshall, 1998; Cockburn and St. Clair, 1999; McCoy, 2003). Complicity began at least as early as World War Two, when US forces turned a blind eye to US and Sicilian mafia operations in return for mafia assistance in fighting labor mobilization that the US administration feared would hinder the war effort.

After the War, the CIA was instrumental in drug trafficking through French and Italian ports in an effort to support and fund anti-communist forces in the labor movement and elsewhere. This trade (the "French Connection") was networked with CIA support to KMT activity in harvesting and smuggling opium throughout the "Burmese triangle," a key area of opium production and trade that persists to the present day. In this way the

CIA had tried, vainly, to bolster the fortunes of Chiang Kai-Shek against the rise of Maoist communism.

The CIA was involved in the US counter-insurgency program in support of the "Contras" against the ultimately successful Sandinista revolution in Nicaragua, where the agency was responsible for overseeing the illegal (because outlawed by Congress) channeling of weapons to the Contras that had been paid for from the equally illegal sale of arms to Iran, using empty planes returning from Central America to the USA for drug smuggling, much of which ended in the sale of crack cocaine in African American neighborhoods of Los Angeles (Webb, 1996).

There is widespread consensus that the war against drugs is a failed policy (see for example the 2011 Global Commission on Drug Policy report signed by a panel of highly esteemed international figures). At the Summit of the Americas in 2012 the presidents of Guatemala, Mexico and Colombia pronounced the failure of the war (Clark and Jimenez, 2012). But "failure" is hardly a recent discovery. A RAND study in 1988 had determined that use of the military for drug interdiction was pointless (Reuter, 1988), and a 1994 RAND study recommended a wholesale switch from enforcement to treatment (Rydell, 1994). In 2008 a Harvard economist calculated that legalization of drugs would inject $77 billion into the US economy (Rodricks, 2008). Bunker (2011: 5) estimated that since the Nixon presidency, one trillion dollars had been spent on the war on drugs.

Artificial suppression of the supply of a commodity that is in demand simply pushes up prices and profits. The lesson should have been learned, permanently, from the history of the Prohibition (1920–1933) which failed to eliminate alcohol production or consumption yet handed control of the business to criminal gangs. Prohibition was supported by interests whose motivations had little to do with morality (see Dighe, nd., for a nuanced discussion). These included oil titans such as Standard Oil who would have had little to gain from the adaptation of alcohol as a fuel for the likes of Henry Ford's Model T.

The cost of Plan Colombia in the period 2000–2006 was $4.7 billion. Yet the flow of cocaine from Colombia to the USA went up during this period (US GAO, 2005). The Merida Initiative channeled $1.4 billion to the Mexican government in the period 2008–2012. In January 2012, the Mexican government reported that 47,515 people had been killed in drug-related violence since President Felipe Calderón initiated a military assault on criminal cartels soon after taking office in late 2006 (*New York Times*, 2012). The USA expended $15 billion overall in the war against drugs in 2010 (ONDCP), while the DEA employed 5,000 agents on a budget of approximately $2 billion. Enormous expenditures are dedicated to the tracking, arrest, trial and imprisonment of civilians for drug offences, the vast majority of them relatively minor. Villar and Cottle (2012) argue that the war on drugs institutionalized state terrorism and promoted the war on FARC.

What, then, is "really" going on? As often happens in the face of such apparent absurdities, the supposed mission turns out not to be the "real" mission at all, and many special interests have been and continue to be at work. Before listing some of these specifically, the compelling argument of Paley (2012) that the war on drugs has become a component of an aggressive policy of neoliberalism deserves mention. It connects with transnational corporate control over markets, labor and natural resources. In particular it has been used successfully to expand foreign direct investment (FDI) in Colombia, Mexico and Central America. FDI in Colombia rocketed from $2.4 billion in 2000 to $14.4 billion in 2011, much of it from the oil, gas and mining sectors. Even though Plan Colombia failed to reduce the flow of drugs into the USA, it has allowed for an effective new model of US intervention, at the expense of indigenous and local peoples, and was quickly followed by Plan Merida for Mexico. The emphasis is less on drugs than on enabling foreign competition against local monopolies in telecommunications, banking and energy, and especially targeting the State oil monopoly, Pemex. In December 2013 the Mexican Congress approved a bill that would bring an end to this monopoly.

This policy has survived alongside an intensification of demands for privatization, deregulation and increased FDI. It relies heavily on what Paley calls "paramilitarization" in the service of capital. This takes the form of death squads, displacement of communities (especially indigenous communities with collective title to lands of interest to speculators), the "discouragement" of union organization and the pushing out of small businesses (160,000 closed in Mexico in 2011 alone because of "insecurity") which are then replaced by branches of transnational corporations. Paley discusses the evidence of collusion and financial links between paramilitary organizations and US or transnational corporations (as shown in legal proceedings against Chiquita Brand), a phenomenon that extends to the use of so-called gangs like the Zetas for the criminal importation of oil to Texas, and intimidation of opponents.

Opposition to both cannabis and hemp production in the 1930s and passage of the Marijuana Transfer Tax Act of 1937 was related to the concerns of industrialists who feared that hemp production would be a threat to timber and nylon interests and their spokesmen (including the publisher, Randolph Hearst, and Andrew Mellon, Secretary of the Treasury). Industrial interests that are threatened by legalization today include the US law enforcement and prison industries, increasingly privatized. In 2008, one and a half million Americans were arrested for drug offenses and 500,000 were imprisoned (Will, 2009). A disproportionate number of those held on drugs charges and who are sent to prison are African American, so racist agendas are also served.

The US defense, helicopter and pharmaceutical industries (notably Monsanto) earn considerable profits through counter insurgency and fumigation programs in Colombia (see Goff, 2003; Ungerman and Brohy, 2003). Aerial fumigation negatively impacts the health and crops of many farmers who do not produce cocaine and who are often forced off their lands, while the actual cocaine growers move their operations into more remote locations and even neighboring countries (Peru became the number one producer, ahead of Colombia, in 2012). Legitimate coca production and consumption, widespread throughout the Andes, are needlessly criminalized.

Anti-drug money has been linked also to the suppression of unions, support for the brutalities of right-wing paramilitaries (often connected with figures in the mainstream military), and assassinations of political, union and community leaders. Total cocaine production was not impacted by the War on Drugs in the period 2000 to 2006. Oil and business interests are served where anti-drug money provided by the USA is used directly by US agencies or through foreign beneficiary militaries and paramilitaries for the purposes of counter-insurgency, and for driving peasants off land that is considered of potential value for oil. Perhaps the most important interests that are served by the War on Drugs, therefore, are those that lie behind US or US supported counter-insurgency operations, as in Colombia, Mexico and Peru where anti-drug war money is spent on armed operations against rebel organizations such as FARC. These also participate in the drug trade, as do the paramilitary organizations that seek their elimination.

HUMANITARIAN INTERVENTION AS A PRETEXT

US /NATO bombing in Kosovo was a 78-day concerted action conducted from March 1999 by the air forces of 13 of NATO's 19 member nations. Fought allegedly for "humanitarian" reasons, it was the second major NATO air intervention in the Yugoslav wars. The other episode (1994–1995) primarily targeted the Bosnian Serbs in the Bosnian war of secession. In 1999 US Secretary of State Madeleine Albright declared that the Serbs were guilty of genocide in Kosovo. This was from the same US administration that in 1994 had indulged in extraordinary linguistic contortions to avoid using the word "genocide" in application to the massacre of 800,000 Tutsis in Rwanda (Frontline, 2004). President Clinton publicly compared Serbian actions to the Holocaust. Tensions in the Serbian province of Kosovo were long-standing. The Kosovo Liberation Army (KLA) had appeared in 1996, and was described by Serbia, Yugoslavia and the USA as a terrorist organization until after 1998 when it entered into talks with the USA. By 1999 it was absorbed by the Kosovo Protection Corps (KPC). The KLA and its later manifestations have been associated with criminal activity, a turn that was fed in part by the chaos that ensued after the fall of Communism in Albania, 1992. This accelerated ties between Albania and Albanian Kosovars. Criminal actions have included trade in human organs (extracted, among others, from Serb prisoners captured in 1999), drugs and extortion, implicating, among others, Hashim Thaci, who became independent Kosovo's first prime minister in 2008 (Seper, 1999; del Ponte, 2008).

DEMOCRACY (AMONG OTHER) PRETEXTS IN IRAQ

The claim to be promoting democracy often accompanies other pretexts, as in Panama in 1989. US mainstream media routinely treat this pretext as serious even in the face of the most obvious indications that democracy as it is understood in western industrialized countries is a barely sustainable if not farcical ambition (Ricks, 2006). The "democracy" pretext was foregrounded by the George W. Bush administration in Iraq in 2004 only after the manifest failure of the main original pretext to materialize – Hussein's (non-existent) weapons of mass destruction. Democracy was not uppermost in the mind of Lieutenant General Jay Garner, appointed Director of the Office for Reconstruction and Humanitarian Assistance after the 2003 invasion, nor was it a top priority for his successor, Paul Bremer, the top civil administrator of the former Coalition Provisional Authority (reporting to the US Department of Defense and the US president) who was permitted to rule by decree. When democracy did come, if it can be said to have come at all, it came via the barrel of an American gun, on terms largely dictated by the occupying forces. Bremer appointed the members of the Iraqi Interim Governing Council from among groups and people who had supported the invasion. These included Al-Jaafari, Nuri Al-Maliki, and Ayad Allawi – each of whom was to become a future prime minister. These choices presided over Bremer's policy of the de-Baathization of Iraq and the privatization of much of the country's infrastructure and mineral wealth. In 2004 the CPA transferred limited sovereignty to the Iraqi Interim Government. Allawi was voted by the Governing Council to the position of interim Prime Minister of Iraq in 2004 with the grudging support, under American pressure, of UN special envoy Lakhdar Brahimi. Allawi participated in the setting up of the Iraqi National Intelligence Service, with the advice of the CIA, and also supported the brutal military incursions of Najaf and Falluja. Al-Jaafari was first prime minister of post-invasion, occupied Iraq from 2005 to 2006. He was succeed by Al-Maliki in 2006, following close US involvement in his selection as candidate since the USA was particularly anxious to veto anyone who was too close to Iran.

DEMOCRACY (AMONG OTHER) PRETEXTS IN AFGHANISTAN

Much the same could be said of the introduction of "democracy" to Afghanistan after the invasion of 2001. Hamid Karzai, who had worked as a contractor for the CIA in the 1980s, and had several siblings in the USA, was also affiliated with US allies in the Northern Alliance, led by Ahmad Shah Massoud. A UN-sponsored conference of an unrepresentative and small body of Afghan leaders was convened after the US invasion and appointed an Afghan interim administration, with Karzai as its chairman. Under US auspices, an emergency "Loya Jirga" or grand assembly of Afghan chiefs met in 2002 to elect US-backed Karzai as president of the transitional administration of Afghanistan, after the leading alternative contender, the former King of Afghanistan, Zahir Shah, was pressured by the USA and UN to withdraw. The second most likely contender, former President Burhanuddibn Rabbani, followed suit.

Karzai's ensuing cabinet was dominated by Northern Alliance commanders and Tajik warlords. Several press reports implicated Karzai's half-brother, Ahmed Wali Karzai – sometimes described as the "political boss of Southern Afghanistan" or the "ruler of Kandahar" – as a CIA informer who also had ties to narcotics and the Taliban. He was assassinated in 2011. Woodward (2010) claimed that Wali Karzai was recruited by the CIA before 9/11 and that he later also received CIA funds through his brother the president. A *New York Times* report (Filkins, 2010) cited sources claiming that Afghan and US officials had decided that the president's brother should be allowed to stay in place despite the allegations against him. Among these were that he helped the CIA to operate a paramilitary group called the Kandahar Strike Force, that he rented out a compound to the CIA in the region of Kandahar, oversaw several armed gangs in Kandahar, and had helped organize a large-scale campaign for the forging of ballots on his brother's behalf in the 2009 elections.

The CIA paid the entire budget for Afghanistan's spy service, the National Directorate of Security, from 2001 onwards, and around one third of the budget of Pakistan's equivalent agency, the ISI, which had long-established ties to Afghani Taliban. Sources referenced by Filkins indicated that the CIA was making secret payments to multiple members of the Karzai administration. One was Juma Khan, a drug lord, supplier to the Taliban and long-time informer to the CIA. After a brief detention by the Americans in 2001, he developed a narcotics empire and even worked with Wali Karzai to take control of the drug network that had been left behind when the Americans arrested one of Khan's rivals, Mr. Noorzai. Khan subsequently met with top CIA and DEA officials in Washington in 2006. Filkins' sources estimated that he received over $2m from the CIA and US military before his arrest in 2008.

The entire Karzai administration benefited for many years from monthly cash payments from the CIA. The money did not go to the president directly, but to the Afghan National Security Council (Giraldi, 2013; Rosenburg, 2013) and amounted to tens of millions of dollars. In the estimation of the *New York Times* editorial board (*New York Times*, 2013), their purpose was to "buy agency influence at the presidential palace and to cover such off-the-books costs as buying the loyalty of warlords and politicians, many of whom have ties to the drug trade – and even, in some cases, to the Taliban." Giraldi (2013) also speculated as to whether such money might have helped the CIA plan the running of counter-insurgency operations using its own militias post-2014.

The governments that such "democratic" interventions induce into existence may justly be termed "puppet" regimes. Yet US mainstream media persist in reporting on these just as they might the activities of long-established, independent governments. Press use of the term "democracy" in this context is generally vague, incurious as to the species of democracy that is at play, its inclusiveness or effectiveness, and uncritical of the supposed "democratic," generally two-party-in-one elite or plutocratic regimes of the countries that are claiming to act on behalf of democracy by invasion and occupation.

DEMOCRACY AS A PRETEXT IN THE "COLOR REVOLUTIONS"

Intervention in the name of "democracy" was a feature of many of the so-called "color" revolutions in Central and Eastern Europe and Central Asia following the collapse of the Soviet Union. Typically, such interventions were activated or manifested during times of street protest and disruption against autocratic regimes, or regimes that the United States deemed to be autocratic. These included Georgia's "rose" revolution of 2003 and the "orange revolution" in the Ukraine in 2004 as well as the failed "green" revolution in Iran in 2009.

The agencies of intervention in these cases are supposedly non-government organizations but include bodies or front organizations whose sources of funding include the US State Department, USAID, the National Democratic Institute for International Affairs, the International Republican Institute, the NGO Freedom House and George Soros's Open Society Institute. The National Endowment for Democracy, a foundation backed by the US government, for example, supported non-governmental democracy-building efforts in the Ukraine from 1988 (Diuk, 2004). It also helped fund Otpor in the case of Serbia, 2000. The Otpor model (Cartalucci, 2011) was adopted by CANVAS (the Center for Applied Non-Violent Action and Strategies). The Egyptian April 16 Youth Movement, instrumental in the street protests of 2011, had attended a US State Department Conference in New York City in 2008 and met with CANVAS in 2009. CANVAS partners include the Albert Einstein Institution and Freedom House and they have been involved in the Rose Revolution of Georgia, the Orange Revolution of the Ukraine and similar partnerships with at least 50 other countries. Meyssan (2012) cites social scientist Gene Sharpe (author of *Making Europe Unconquerable*) and Israeli Army psychologist Reuven Gal as being implicated, singly or together, in the stirring up of youth activists for the objective, not always successful, of organizing coups in China (1989), Russia and the Baltics (in the 1990s), and in Serbia (1998). Cover organizations have included the Albert Einstein Institute, CANVAS and the Academy of Change. The purpose is usually regime change without social transformation (as had occurred in the "lotus" revolution in Egypt in 2011). The "orange revolution" in the Ukraine is one of the best known from the 1990s, and may be deemed an eventual failure. It was provoked by popular unrest following what were considered the fraudulent election results in the 2004 contest between incumbent Viktor Yanukovych and Viktor Yushchenko. Following a court-ordered re-election, Viktor Yushchenko was declared president. But unseemly conflict between Yushchenko and his prime minister Yulia Tymoshenko brought discredit to the Ukrainian political establishment, leading to the return to power of Yanukovych in the 2010 elections. If this experience might have seemed to irretrievably besmirch the "color" brand of intervention, in which protest movements are funded and trained by western pollsters and professional consultants, funded by a range of western government and non-government agencies, then the Western-backed and supported coup against Yanukovych early in 2014 would suggest otherwise.

CONCLUSION

In this book I argue that imperialism is not, nor ever has been, only a matter of territorial acquisition. Equally important, if not more so, has been the will to control resources and peoples to whom the empire can establish access, and as many of these as possible. The essential economics of capitalist imperialism have to do with corporate competition, domestic market consolidation and oligopolization, and the declining rates of profit that result. The process of expansion of control, and the means by which it is achieved, are typically a matter of potential shame and embarrassment for imperial governments and the elites they serve because they are often in deep contradiction with the basic value systems, religious and secular, to which these elites allegedly adhere and on which they depend in order to legitimate their control over their own domestic populations and over the members of their own fighting forces (whose motivation to fight must be pumped high for as long as possible). But the elites also understand that not only are their strategies and tactics deeply questionable in terms of domestic value systems but also that domestic populations will benefit relatively little, if at all, from the riches of imperial plunder, which are monopolized by corporations and the plutocratic classes. As compelling as imperial expansion must seem for the maintenance of capitalism and capitalistic growth it must also proceed with maximum caution, in such a way that it appears to be moral. Hence the need for pretexts and for compliant mainstream media to avoid undermining the pretexts that ruling elites provide for imperial expansion.

6 Media and the Hybrid Pretexts for Wars in Libya and Syria

DEMOCRACY, HUMANITARIAN INTERVENTION AND THE "WAR ON TERROR" AS PRETEXTS FOR THE INVASION OF LIBYA

In this chapter I consider western interventions in Libya (2011) and Syria (2011–2014). Previous episodes of "Arab Spring" uprisings – of which only one, in Tunisia, appeared to have achieved a demonstrably improved, sustained emancipation of the suppressed by the time of writing in 2014 – had accustomed international audiences to the positive media framing of fresh-faced, young "rebels" protesting against autocratic regimes, including the variety of autocratic regimes such as Mubarak's Egypt that the West had enthusiastically supported over many decades. Had these protests manifested in western countries, along the lines of the uprisings of Muslim youth in the towns of France from 2005, the mainstream media might more likely have appropriated the language of French President Sarkozy and dubbed them hooligans. In the Middle East, then, was their youth sufficient reason for western countries to contribute to and intensify the bloodshed in defiance of international law?

Recent experience in Iraq had amply demonstrated how the violent removal of a demonized dictator such as Saddam Hussein could quickly unleash possibly worse bloodshed, instability and social breakdown, and for longer than had ever been experienced under the said dictator. More measured reflection might have suggested that dictators sometimes endure precisely because they have learned how to contain explosive conditions created in part by western imperialists of the nineteenth and twentieth centuries and far more effectively than those western powers could ever dream. For a short period prior to destabilizing both, western powers had appeared to be reconciling with the regimes of Muommar Gaddafi (Libya) and Bashir Assad (Syria). Upon the emergence of seemingly popular (if sporadic and localized) rebellions in the wake of the so-called "Arab Spring," and taking advantage of sympathetic coverage by western mainstream media (and by Al Jazeera English, reflecting the interests of its principal financier, the emir of Qatar, which had moved into closer alignment with those of the West), the USA, NATO and even some autocratic Arab regimes such as Saudi Arabia channeled support to the rebellions, in extremely bloody efforts at "regime change." Among the rebel groups were Sunni and other Islamist fundamentalists, with connections to or, as western media sometimes claimed, "inspired" by, Al Qaeda, and who, in other contexts, western powers had attempted to eradicate, continuing to refer to them (e.g. in Afghanistan, Iraq, and Pakistan) as "terrorist."

Reversing a long record of anti-western policies, Gaddafi had moved closer to the West following the collapse of the Soviet Union. To do so he had to negotiate around western presumptions of Libyan guilt for the 1988 Lockerbie bombing of Pan Am flight 103. Up until 1990, coinciding with Syria's support of the USA during the first Gulf War, western intelligence agencies had blamed not Libya but Iran and Syria. In line with his shifting stance towards the West, Gaddafi accepted responsibility. In 1999 he handed over for trial two men whom western powers had claimed were responsible, and he eventually committed over $2 billion in reparations. One of the accused, Ali Al-Megrahi, found guilty by a Scottish court in 2001, was released on compassionate grounds in 2009. Gaddafi's acceptance of responsibility was likely motivated by a desire to put an end to the UN sanctions imposed on Libya in 1996. These were lifted in 2001. There is widespread disquiet concerning the veracity of the judgment bought against Al-Megrahi. Although all this was known at the time of the NATO invasion of Libya, the mainstream western media continued to assert, as fact, Al-Megrahi's responsibility (Parry, 2012). A later *New York Times* obituary of Al-Megrahi in 2012 conceded that his guilt was in serious doubt.

In 2003 Gaddafi agreed to dismantle his weapons of mass destruction program and permit entry to UN inspectors. His was not a particularly impressive armory – there was virtually nothing to dismantle. Curtis (2012) argues that Gaddafi was playing a game of seeming more dangerous than he really was, to the gratification of UK Prime Minister Tony Blair and other western leaders in need of indirect vindication for their Iraqi pantomime. The Bush administration rewarded Libya by removing it from the always politicized US list of nations who supported terror in 2006. Because his own country suffered attacks from Islamic fundamentalists from the late 1990s onwards, Gaddafi was opposed to Al Qaeda. Indeed it was Gaddafi who issued the first arrest warrant for Osama Bin Laden, in 1998, and after 2001 he cooperated with the CIA and MI6, even offering assistance to the

CIA's rendition and torture program in return for intelligence on Libyan dissidents. He met with former British Prime Minister Tony Blair in 2004. Blair commended Gaddafi's role in the "war on terror," and went on to agree a deal with Gaddafi favoring Shell oil interests in Libya. Gaddafi also met with US Secretary of State Condoleezza Rice in 2008, and with President Obama in 2009.

Western back-peddling from their rapprochement with Gaddafi possibly set in with his 2008 threat to reduce oil production and/or expel US oil and gas companies. Senator Frank R. Lautenberg's legislative efforts to make it easier for families of the victims of the Lockerbie bombing to seek compensation from Libya's hidden commercial assets irritated Gaddafi. Additionally, he smarted from the loss of 98% of the value of the Libyan Investment Authority's deposits in a scheme that had been originated and managed by Goldman Sachs. The loss followed on from the collapse of Lehman Brothers in September, 2008. Subsequent discussions between Goldman Sachs and the Libyan Investment Authority did not come to fruition (Wachtel, 2011).

Explorations of the full range of motivations behind NATO intervention in March 2011 – occurring a mere month after the outbreak of civil war in Libya, and having, as its official objective, the protection of civilians while unofficially siding with the rebels – were difficult to locate in mainstream media accounts. NATO acted under the mandate of a UN Security Council resolution that authorized "all necessary measures" to protect civilians in Libya. Van Auken (2011) argues that this clearly did not give NATO the right to take sides in a civil war (still less, encourage its development in the first place), with a view to regime change. The *New York Times*, he notes, even editorialized in favor of NATO use of AC-130 and A-10 flying gunships, whose "killing areas" of more than three quarters of a mile had already ensured their notoriety for the slaughter of civilians in high density population areas – precisely where the *New York Times* saw fit to encourage their use. NATO's apparent enthusiasm for the spirit of the "Arab Spring" had a surface aura of credibility, but of greater significance was the fact that Libya had the largest proven oil reserves in Africa and the third largest proven natural gas reserves.

The role of oil was rendered more transparent than usual following the release of *Wikileaks* documents (*MediaLens*, 2011), including diplomatic cables, that disclosed how much the USA and US oil companies resented Gaddafi for insisting on billion-dollar sweetness deals before green-lighting joint ventures in Libya, and indicating that Libya had grown more protective of its natural resources. The UK mainstream media were even more silent about the oil connection than US counterparts: *MediaLens* reported in June 2011, that "we found nothing in any article in any national UK newspaper" that made the connections between *WikiLeaks*' revelations, oil and Libya. US companies such as ConocoPhillips and Marathon had each invested some $700 million in the previous six years and were growing concerned. Considerations of interest to European participants in the anti-Gaddafi campaign included the hope that they might push Russia's Gazprom out of Libya in favor of French and Italian oil companies. As it turned out, France's Total and Italy's ENI were obliged by the new Libyan Oil Company – formed by the NATO-supported Transitional National Council – to wait in the queue behind more "deserving" oil companies such as ExxonMobil, Chevron, BP and Shell, for a chance to grab new contracts for exploration and production. Robert Neate in the *Guardian* (Neate, 2011) quoted Nuri Berruien, head of the Libyan Oil Company, to the effect that the government would "favor our friends" in the development of Libyan reserves.

Mainstream media approvingly amplified the call by Paul Wolfowitz (a principal architect of the invasion and occupation of Iraq in 2003) for the implementation of a no-fly zone over Libya, which would give NATO unhampered freedom to bomb (Grigg, 2011). Media sympathetically supported demands for the seizure of Libyan overseas funds, although no such calls were heard throughout the Egyptian, Tunisian, Bahraini or Yemeni uprisings. Of the five, only Libya had significant oil deposits. Media barely seemed concerned that President Obama might be acting illegally by going to war without Congressional approval, in contravention of the War Powers Act; nor was there any outrage when NATO commander General Sir David Richards, in defiance of international law, called for everything to be bombed in Libya, including its infrastructure (Bowles, 2011). On its website, the BBC offered no content that questioned the legality or morality of Operation Odyssey Dawn.

Media swallowed suspicious atrocity propaganda such as the claim that Gaddafi was ordering mass rapes and providing Viagra to his troops to support their efforts (FAIR, 2011a). Even public service media were reluctant to give voice to those who were anti-war, US foreign policy critics or critical legal experts (FAIR, 2011b). They overlooked the significance of Gaddafi's plan to drop the oil trade in US dollars in favor of a gold-backed Dinar. They were largely silent about the CIA connections to Khalifa Hafter, and hence to control over the insurgency, when Hafter was appointed the top military commander for Libyan rebel forces. Media avoided mention of his name even after this had been publicly announced by the Transitional National Council in Benghazi (Martin, 2011). They tip-toed around evidence of the involvement of extreme Islamic and even Al-Qaeda connected forces in support of the rebels – an apparently unholy alliance (not simply between Islamic and non-Islamic rebel forces, but between western intelligence and Islamic forces) that became even more problematic for Western countries in their support of the rebels in Syria through 2011–2013.

The call by Libya's new leader Mustafa Abdul Jalil for the application of sharia law provoked the barest ripple of embarrassment among these media warriors for western "civilization." *Time* magazine did report the presence of Salafis who were said to be applying a rigid form of Islam in many communities, especially close to the border with Tunisia (Sotloff, 2011). Scant attention was paid to the history of Libyan rebel commander Abdel-Hakim Belhadj who had once headed an anti-Gaddafi Islamic military group backed by the CIA (McDonnell and Dilanian, 2011). It was Belhadj who established the former anti-Gaddafi Libyan National Army in 1988, with backing from the CIA (Martin, 2011). In the *Guardian*, Simon Jenkins (2012), citing a BBC *Panorama* investigation, recalled that Belhadj and his wife had been kidnapped from Thailand by M16 and rendered for torture to Gaddafi by MI6's Mark Allen (head of the counter-terrorism unit) in a *quid pro quo* for a favorable oil deal for BP which was finalized when Tony Blair visited Gaddafi in his tent in 2004.

As in Iraq, the outcome permitted an unconvincing species of "democracy." This was heralded by elections in thoroughly inauspicious circumstances – what Herman and Bodhead (1984) have called "demonstration elections," whose main function is to sway public opinion in the imperial powers, providing assurance that their governments' interventions are working out. In practice, the elections in both Iraq and Libya were achieved at enormous cost to human life and suffering. As in Iraq and Afghanistan it was understood that the only acceptable candidates would be those enjoying the approval of the occupying powers. In Libya candidacies were restricted by the NATO-installed National Transitional Council to a relatively small group approved by the Elections Commission.

Voting conditions were execrable. Cromwell (2012) argues that western media made no serious attempt to judge the integrity of the elections against rational criteria. The elections were held only a year after Amnesty International produced its 2011 report *The Battle for Libya: Killings, Disappearances and Torture*, and only a month or so after conducting research for its 2012 report *Libya: Rule of Law or Rule of Militias?* These confirmed that Libya was increasingly lawless, subject to arbitrary and often abusive behaviors, including detention and torture, by militias who enjoyed impunity for their misdeeds and whose actions stoked a widespread civil reluctance to speak out for fear of brutal reprisals. Additionally, entire communities had been displaced. An AP report of February 2012 further noted that Libya was splintering into largely autonomous city states. The oil rich region around Barca (Cyrenaica) was even seeking autonomy within the federal state.

One function of war propaganda is to suppress compassion, noted *MediaLens,* which might help explain the media's apparent callousness in the face of appalling war crimes – so long as these were committed by their favored "rebels". Rebel attrocities included the bombing of Libyan State Television; the weeks-long siege of Sirte; the brutal, racist persecution of black Sub-Saharan Africans; and the criminal execution of Gaddafi himself and of dozens if not hundreds of those who were with or close to him at the time. Instead, *MediaLens* recalled how broadcast media rushed to vindicate these western-backed "warrior-leaders." Western media overlooked or downplayed the significance of peace initiatives when these came from Gaddafi, but supported the rejection of such overtures by the Transitional National Council. For the media it seemed hardly important that the UN Security Council's 1973 resolution emphatically called for a "ceasefire" and not for regime change, and that ceasefire offers from Gaddafi were routinely rejected by the Transitional National Council. The media seemed unfazed by the relative lack of evidence for the contention that Gaddafi seriously planned a massacre of rebels in Benghazi, or by the overall cost of the war in terms of lives lost.

Western media typically neglected evidence of the extent of previous popular support for these regimes, or exaggerated evidence of popular discontent. Gowans (2012) has noted of Syria, for example, that like most targets of western campaigns for regime change, the country demonstrated a "predilection for independent, self-directed, economic development … state-ownership of important industries, subsidies to domestic firms, controls on foreign investment and subsidization of basic commodities," all measures that are less conducive to western corporate profit than western governments would prefer. Despite his support for some notoriously brutish leaders in Africa, among them Idi Amin of Uganda and Charles Taylor of Sierra Leone, Gaddafi also enjoyed widespread popularity. He had opposed apartheid and was a close friend of Nelson Mandela. Western mainstream media were incurious with respect to Libyan policies of wealth redistribution – Gaddafi proposed in 2009 to share out Libya's oil wealth directly to its people – and full employment (with equal rights for women and minorities), education (achieving a literacy rate of 90%), free social security and health care (yielding a life expectancy of 77), housing aid, and the highest per capita wealth in Africa (although poverty persisted in the Eastern provinces). This constituted prosperity to a degree never previously experienced in Libya, and was unlikely to be quickly restored, if ever, under western-imposed neoliberal "free" market conditions. Under Gaddafi,

Libya experienced some extraordinary if not always effective experiments in direct democracy, for prolonged periods, through the institutions of Peoples Congresses and the Revolutionary Committees.

DEMOCRACY, HUMANITARIAN INTERVENTION, THE "WAR ON TERROR" AND WEAPONS OF MASS DESTRUCTION AS PRETEXTS IN SYRIA

Far from being spontaneous popular uprisings – the script that western media had spun for previous chapters of the "Arab Spring" – the roots of Middle Eastern destabilizations went back at least to 2001, when a future US presidential candidate, General Wesley Clark, was informed by Pentagon insiders of a plan to take down seven countries including Iraq, Iran, Lebanon, Libya, Somalia, Sudan, and Syria (Clark, 2007). This extended the strategizing of the neoconservative think-tank, Project for a New American Century, and its 2000 report, *Rebuilding America's Defenses: Strategy, Forces and Resources for a New Century*. Of stunning significance, Clark's record of these conversations, which indicated the existence of a long-term plan for regional transformation, and even of a US battle for global supremacy, received little attention in western mainstream media. One year later, US Secretary of State John Bolton added Syria, along with Libya and Cuba, to the Bush regime's designated "axis of evil" countries, a prelude to what by the following year (alongside the invasion and occupation of Iraq) had morphed into what Stephen Gowans (2012) described as a program of economic warfare against Syria.

This had intensified by 2005 when the USA started to "funnel money to opposition elements to mobilize energy for regime change," as revealed in a US embassy cable published by *WikiLeaks* and cited by Blum (2012). Recipients of State Department aid included opposition groups in Syria, and the London-based oppositional satellite TV channel Barada TV, run by Syrian exiles. Davies (2012) cited former CIA officer Philip Giraldi for his claim that as early as December 2011 unmarked NATO planes were delivering weapons and militiamen from Libya to Turkish air-bases near the headquarters of the rebel Free Syrian Army (FSA) in Iskanderum. The FSA received training, equipment and intelligence from British, French and US intelligence. Gowans noted that for western powers listed terrorist organizations had become a "central pillar in their planning and execution" of regime change operations. Blum (2012) quotes an email in December 2011 from Reva Bhalla, Stratfor's Director of Analysis, alleging Pentagon sources for the information that Special Operation Forces teams "were already on the ground focused on reconnaissance missions and training opposition forces." The initial event that sparked the uprising on March 17, 2011 – when unknown snipers opened fire in the Southern Syrian town of Deraa, killing several policemen and innocent protestors – appeared, in the judgment of Canadian economist Michel Chossudovsky (*MediaLens*, 2012), to have "all the appearances of a staged event involving, in all likelihood, covert support to Islamic terrorists by Mossad and/or Western intelligence." Even with evidence of sophisticated weaponry that included pump action shotguns, machine guns, Kalashnikovs, and RPG launchers western media avoided the term "armed insurrection" and persisted on seeing only a "protest movement" that, as Chossudovsky predicted, would divide the country and justify western intervention.

Mainstream media were slow to acknowledge that the Syrian resistance, whom they overwhelmingly favored, seemed increasingly to be populated if not dominated by Islamist radicals, including some who were allied to Al Qaeda. The USA had even helped gather and train activists from Tunisia, Egypt, Syria and the Lebanon (Cartalucci, 2012), their numbers soon to be augmented by Libya's Islamic Fighting Group whose leader Abdul Belhaz pledged NATO-supplied weapons and money to the cause of the Free Syrian Army (FSA).

Media-favored battlefield narratives invariably originated with the FSA who also helpfully supplied estimates of casualties – not just to the media but also to the UN (ibid.) whose November 2011 human rights report for Syria, compiled in Geneva, was based solely on the accounts of the FSA and its allies in the Washington-based Middle East Policy Council. *MediaLens* (2012) noted that a key source for the BBC (and, we can note, much other media reporting) had long been the British-based "Syrian Observatory of Human Rights," and quoted Aisling Byrne (2012) of the *Asian Times*:

> Of the three main sources for all data on numbers of protesters killed and numbers of people attending demonstrations – the pillars of the narrative – all are part of the "regime change" alliance. The Syrian Observatory of Human Rights, in particular, is reportedly funded through a Dubai-based fund with pooled (and therefore deniable) Western-Gulf money … What appears to be a nondescript British-based organization, the Observatory has been pivotal in sustaining the narrative of the mass killing of thousands of peaceful protesters using inflated figures, "facts", and often exaggerated claims of "massacres" and even recently "genocide".

In the *Guardian*, Charlie Skelton traced the imposingly-named Syrian Observatory for Human Rights to Rami Abdul-Rahman and his wife, in Coventry (UK), owners of a clothes shop. Skelton admonished his profession that it had been too passive when it came to Syrian opposition sources, not scrutinizing their backgrounds and their political connections. Skelton looked into the backgrounds of figures that the media routinely dubbed "spokespersons" for the Syrian National Council (the exiled body preferred by western governments and media over the internal, pacifist and left-leaning National Coordinating Body for Democratic Change – which also happened to be nonsectarian and opposed to foreign intervention) and found them to be high-ranking members of what Skelton describes as the "Anglo-American democracy-promotion industry." Bassma Kodmani, SNC's most senior spokesperson, had previously worked for the Ford Foundation in Cairo, where she had directed its governance and international co-operation program. In 2005 she was appointed executive director of the "Arab Reform Initiative," initiated by US lobby group, the Council on Foreign Relations, just as Washington was diverting aid away from the Damascus regime and beginning to funnel money to opposition groups. Kodmani also held the position of research director at the Academie Diplomatique Internationale, headed by a former chief of the French foreign intelligence service. Ausama Monajed, another member of the SNC and adviser to its president, was also founder and director of the pro-opposition and London-based Barada Television, and was previously director of public relations for the Movement for Justice and Development (MJD) which from 2006 received $6 million from the US State Department for opposition activities in Syria, including Barada Television. Monajed's "Strategic Research and Communication Center" was located at a virtual office, shared by many other organizations in Holborn, London.

THE CASE OF CHEMICAL WEAPONS

In a reprise of the attempt by the USA to justify its invasion of Iraq in 2003 with false claims of Iraqi possession of weapons of mass destruction, US media were quick in December 2012 to highlight anonymous US claims that the Syrian military was poised to use chemical weapons against its own people. Thus did they prepare world opinion for what they were soon to claim were actual chemical weapons attacks in 2013. Two of these attracted significant international and media attention: an attack in Aleppo in March; and in East Ghouta, near Damascus, in August.

Aleppo

Reacting to western allegations in 2012 of the Assad regime's intent to use chemical weapons, Edwards (2012) quoted US media watchdog *FAIR*, which asked:

So where did all of this new information come from? The familiar, ominous answer: Anonymous government officials talking to outlets like the *New York Times* ...

NYT reports included some by Michael Gordon. Gordon had co-authored some of the *Times*' stories about Iraqi weapons of mass destruction with Judith Miller in 2002–2003, and had spearheaded his paper's subsequent beating of the drums for war against Iran on the equally false pretext that the country was building nuclear weapons. Edwards took *Guardian* reporters Matt Williams and Martin Chulov to task for their sensationalist reporting of claims that the Syrian regime was "considering unleashing chemical weapons on opposition forces," while citing in support of this only a CNN story which in turn had cited an "unnamed US official as the source of its report."

By April 2013, the USA and other western states had been warning for over a year that as the government of Bashar al-Assad had begun to "topple" (still a long way distant at the time of writing in 2014) the danger had increased that, in a desperate action, it would resort to chemical weapons. Fisk (2013) reported four potential chemical attacks of uncertain provenance that had occurred by the end of April 2013: in Aleppo, Homs, Damascus and the northern Lebanese city of Tripoli.

Allegations that the Assad regime had used chemical weapons in April were based on a supposed intercept by the Intelligence Unit of the Israeli Defense Forces in March 2013 (the same source as for the later attack in August) regarding the attack at Khan al-Assal near Aleppo that killed some 30 people. The allegations received ambivalent support from the White House and the Pentagon. By May, US lawmakers were calling for a full-scale assault on the grounds that the Syrian army already had used chemical weapons. An apparently more informed source, Carla del Ponte, on behalf of the UN Independent Commission of Inquiry on Syria (separate from the team of inspectors assembled by the UN Secretary General to investigate the April attack in Aleppo), told the press that there were strong, concrete suspicions, but not yet incontrovertible proof, that it was western-backed opposition forces and not the Syrian Army that had used chemical weapons.

The Syrian government invited a UN inspection team to examine the evidence at Aleppo. Their eventual arrival in August coincided with the more severe attack at East Ghouta, close to where the inspectors were lodged. The investigation was stalled for four months because some Western countries insisted on a more thorough inquiry. This would have encompassed the alleged chemical weapons used in Homs in December. The investigators also wanted access to Syrian military installations, which the UN said Damascus had prohibited (not unreasonably, as this could have compromised Syrian security – author). In addition, the UN had excluded Russian and Chinese experts despite the presence of inspectors from NATO countries. Moscow opposed the delay and warned its UNSC partners to draw no conclusions before the findings were complete, even though the USA and UK claimed "with varying degrees of confidence" (i.e. anything from full confidence to no confidence whatsoever – author) that Assad's forces were behind the use of chemical weapons. In August, Russia disclosed that it had handed the UN a 100-page report in July that blamed Syrian rebels for the Aleppo sarin attack. The UN Commission of Inquiry on Syria which investigated the Aleppo attacks released its report on September 9. It found that it was "not possible to reach a finding about the chemical agents used, their delivery systems or the perpetrators." The majority of the casualties were the result of conventional weapons. It noted that atrocities had been committed both by forces loyal to President Bashar al-Assad and by anti-government groups.

The rebels had received training from US contractors in handling chemical weapons, according to a CNN report in December 2012. Opposition fighters had posted a video of themselves on YouTube showing them testing chemical weapons and materials. On May 30, local Turkish media and *RT News* also reported that Turkish security forces had found a 2kg cylinder with sarin gas after searching the homes of Syrian militants from the Al-Qaeda linked Al-Nusra Front. The gas was reportedly going to be used in a bomb (Edwards, 2013). Van Auken (2013b) noted that this discovery was "virtually blacked out by the corporate media in the US." In Turkey, media covered the story even in face of attempts by Prime Minister Erdogan's government to censor the extensive evidence that attacks that had occurred two weeks previously in the border city of Reyhanli were the work of Syrian opposition groups (Van Auken, 2013a). On September 14, 2013, the Turkish Republican Prosecutor in Adana issued a 132-page indictment, alleging that six members of the Al-Qaeda-aligned Al-Nusra Front and Ahrar ash-Sham – one Syrian and five Turks – had tried to acquire chemicals with the intent to produce the chemical weapon sarin (Bisturek, 2013)

In May, the *New York Times* reported that the USA, Britain and France were "secretly" discussing coordinated air strikes for the purpose of imposing a no-fly zone over Syria (an option supported by a *Wall Street Journal* editorial of May 7) and disclosed that the US military had been planning to attack Syria for months (Gaist, 2013). Narwani (2013) quotes Charles Blair in *Foreign Policy* to the effect that if Assad had used chemical weapons his "regime would risk losing Russian and Chinese support, legitimizing foreign military intervention, and, ultimately, hastening its own end. As one Syrian official said, 'We would not commit suicide.'"

Narwani also quotes a reference in *The Times* (London) to a video taken of a supposed victim of a sarin attack in Aleppo. The video was deemed suspicious by a senior researcher at the European Union Institute for Security Studies interviewed by *McClatchey News*. The *Times*' report also mentioned the strange arrival in the "immediate aftermath" of this alleged attack, that had occurred in the middle of the night, of an "American medical agency" to collect samples for testing in an "American laboratory," which placed further doubt as to the authenticity of the entire incident.

Sources interviewed by CNN indicated that Israel's Mossad had a widespread presence in Syria, were likely sources of information concerning the alleged chemical weapons' incident, and that UN officials had repeatedly stated that investigations inside Syria showed that opposition forces, and not the Assad regime, were responsible for previous chemical attacks. *FAIR* quoted *GlobalPost*'s Tracey Shelton and Peter Gelling's report that "the spent canister found in Younes' house and the symptoms displayed by the victims are inconsistent with a chemical weapon such as sarin gas, which is known to be in Syria's arsenal" (FAIR, 2013a), and cited a Reuters' report that the UN team of investigators had heard from victims and medical personnel who claimed that sarin had been used by anti-government rebels. Noticing continuing efforts by the *New York Times* to support the Israeli/White House claims, *FAIR* (2013b) concluded a week later that "It is clear that the *Times* has promoted a storyline that treats the chemical weapons claims as more definitive than they are, and has given scant attention to subsequent revelations about the evidence."

East Ghouta

The attack of August 21, 2013, involved two rocket missiles carrying poisonous gas said to have been launched from a government-controlled suburb of Damascus, Douma (or Duma) (this was later contested) against a rebel-controlled suburb called East Ghouta. Given the doubtful evidence of the Aleppo attack in April, considerable caution by both government and media sources in arriving at any certain judgment as to culpability should have been in evidence.

The USA did not wait for independent evidence of culpability for the resulting deaths (numbers varied between 300 and 1,300) but asserted from the start that Assad was guilty (as outlined in the three-page document *U.S. Government Assessment of the Syrian Government's Use of Chemical Weapons on August 21, 2013*). Evidence released by the USA was far from satisfactory. It certainly did not include the quality of proof that only soil, blood and environmental samples could have provided. And whatever samples it did have in advance of the UN investigation, according to Porter (2013), citing rebel sources, were provided through the rebels. No better could be said for the conclusions of British, German and French intelligence that Assad was responsible. The US evidence was based on videos, doctors' reports of victims, and the fact that the missiles were still largely intact (i.e. had not exploded). On the face of it, Syrian government responsibility was highly implausible. The attack took place on the very day that UN weapons inspectors began their work in Damascus at the invitation of the president. Assad hardly needed such an attack, since he was at that point of winning the war against the rebels. Most importantly, he understood perfectly well that any such attack would provide a pretext for formal US /NATO intervention.

Did use of chemical weapons deserve a special status in the hierarchy of evil in the conduct of war? The CIA had already coordinated massive flows of arms and Islamist foreign fighters into Syria, unleashing a sectarian civil war with the aim of achieving regime change. It had armed and trained anti-government forces in Jordan and sent them back into Syria under effective US command to carry out mayhem (Van Auken, 2013a).

The official US reaction to the possible use of chemical weapons dripped with hypocrisy, given its history of deployment of chemical weapons, including napalm and Agent Orange in Vietnam, and in Iraq where, at Fallujah, it dropped phosphorus bombs, and its complicity with Iraq under Saddam Hussein regarding Hussein's use of chemical weapons against Iran. The USA has also frequently accused others, falsely, of using chemical weapons. Under President Clinton in 1998, it had even bombed an alleged chemical weapons factory in Sudan that turned out to be making only pharmaceutical drugs.

Having at first demanded that Syria give the UN immediate access, the USA on August 24 then tried to stop a UN investigation once Assad had invited the UN to investigate. The USA now claimed the investigation would not be necessary since (a) there was already sufficient evidence, (b) Assad would have already cleared up the evidence against him, and (c) an investigation would take too long. Obama said the UN investigations were "pointless." Effectively, the administration's position was that the evidence did not matter because the USA would blame Assad anyway (Ditz, 2013b). The USA then beefed up its already significant military presence in the region even though any attack without the support of the UN Security Council (highly unlikely since both Russia and China would have voted against this) would be in violation of international law. US intelligence sources were reported by AP as saying proof of a link to Assad was "no slam dunk" (Dozier and Apuzzo, 2013). None the less, the USA, backed by

France, some other NATO nations and conservative Arab states, asserted that responsibility lay with the Assad government and sought, unsuccessfully, to secure UN Security Council agreement to a Chapter VII authorization to use military force against Syria.

The US unclassified evidence to the UNSC was weak. Draitser (2013) contested the US evidence on five principal grounds. Terminology such as "human intelligence" and "witness accounts" indicated dependence on rebel sources and "activists." US officials had cherry-picked their eyewitness accounts. The very notion that "social media reports" constituted credible evidence to be used in making a case for war has to be discounted, given that US and other intelligence agencies are able to manipulate Twitter, Facebook and other social media in whatever way they see fit. Video images are easily manipulated and even if they are left untouched videos of victims cannot determine culpability. Videos merely show what is visible, not the underlying motives, means and opportunity. Use of journalist reports in a "high confidence assessment" was suspect given that most western coverage of the conflict in Syria had come from journalists outside the country or those already sympathetic to the rebel cause.

An AP report, already cited, noted that even some US intelligence officials were unconvinced. Some considered that the rebels could have carried out the attack in a callous and calculated attempt to draw the West into the war. Russia's ambassador in the UN Security Council, Vitaly Churkin, presented evidence – based on documents and Russian satellite images – of two rockets carrying toxic chemicals, fired from an area controlled by the Syrian rebels (Cartalucci, 2013). Dale Gavlak and Yahya Ababneh, reporting for a local news agency, *Mint Press News*, interviewed numerous doctors, Ghouta residents, rebel fighters and their families who testified that certain rebels received chemical weapons via the Saudi intelligence chief, Prince Bandar bin Sultan, and were responsible for carrying out the gas attack. The rebels noted that the tragic use of chemical weapons was the result of an accident caused by rebel mishandling of the chemical weapons provided to them. More than a dozen rebels reported that their salaries came from the Saudi government. Both Saudi Arabia and Qatar were among authoritarian Arab states involved in supporting rebels in Syria. The Saudi Arabian Sunni regime was opposed to rival regional powers led by the Allawi-based Shia leadership of Syria and its Shia-dominated ally Iran. Some reports suggested that Saudi Arabia had tried to both bribe and threaten Russia to walk away from its support for Assad (Snyder, 2013). Qatar had invested in a natural gas pipeline out of the Persian Gulf that would run through Syria and into Europe.

The *Mint Press News* account was supported by a Belgian hostage held by rebels for five months who reported that his captors denied that

President Bashar al-Assad was responsible for the Ghouta massacre (Bacchi, 2013). In a report by Umberto Bacchi (2013), Pierre Piccinin said that he and fellow hostage Domenico Quirico, an Italian war reporter, heard their jailers talking about the chemical weapon attack and saying that Assad was not to blame. In September, likely Russian intelligence sources told *Interfax News Agency* (2013) that the August chemical weapons attack in the Syrian capital's suburbs was undertaken by a Saudi Arabian black operations team. In the *Independent*, Robert Fisk (2013) was skeptical that the Assad regime would have used gas when it had so much other lethal weaponry, in an area where its own soldiers and administrators were present, and in the knowledge that it would invite a western reaction. Fisk also reported doubts among UN and NGO communities that the missiles had been fired by Assad's army. There was particular skepticism that Assad would wait until UN inspectors were ensconced at a hotel in Damascus, four miles from East Ghouta, before using the weapons.

Adam Entous for *Democracy Now!* (2013) claimed that Saudi Arabia, Qatar and Turkey ("and, to a certain extent, the CIA in more of an observatory capacity") started arming the rebels out of Turkey from 2012, but that there were tensions among the arms suppliers as to whom the arms should go – "moderate" Islamists or others considered more extreme? The Saudis in particular were concerned by the supply of arms to the Muslim Brotherhood, and transferred their operations from Turkey to Jordan with considerable CIA support, flying in weapons bought in Eastern Europe and Libya and providing extensive training.

The British parliament voted down an attempt by the government to secure the authorization for war, doubtless heeding Prime Minister Cameron's own admission that there was not "100% certainty" that Assad was responsible, and ignoring the report of the Joint Intelligence Committee which was as lacking in conclusive evidence as the US unclassified release. In the US Congress, President Obama conceded that he would seek (but not necessarily be bound by) Congressional approval, which was unlikely to have been forthcoming. Embarrassment was camouflaged by agreement to a Russian plan for the dismantling of all Syrian chemical weapons (Russia would be punished a year later by western support for a pro-Western uprising in the Ukraine).

The USA had at first claimed (Porter, 2013) crucial evidence for its allegations from one of its own intercepts of Syrian army communications, although this was later exposed by an Israeli leak to have actually been an *Israeli* intercept by the Intelligence Unit of the Israeli Defense Forces, supposedly of communications among Syrian regime officials. But the US statement provided neither transcripts nor explanation as to how the intercepts were translated. Later reports, including a *Wall Street Journal* article, indicated that the transcripts had actually been supplied to the CIA by Mossad or, more specifically, as the German magazine *Focus* reported, by the 8200 intelligence unit of the Israeli Defence Forces. Two agencies were now implicated, Mossad and the CIA, that were highly compromised by their participation in preparing the ground for war in Syria. Bowles (2013) considers the Israeli source notoriously unreliable, the same that in the past had disseminated scare allegations of the Iranian intent to launch a nuclear weapons program. Pulitzer Prize-winning journalist Seymour Hersh in his 2007 *New Yorker* article, *The Redirection: Is the Administration's new policy benefiting our enemies in the war on terrorism?*, had long before claimed that the USA was planning to fund a terrorist overthrow of the government of Syria.

No audio recordings of the intercepts were made available. *FAIR*'s Jim Naureckas (2013) complained that the evidence was strikingly vague. The officials whose conversation was allegedly intercepted were not identified. It was also not clear what exactly it was that they said that had "confirmed" use of chemical weapons, nor what evidence there was for the assertion that Syrian chemical weapons personnel had been operating close by nor for how their alleged presence would constitute proof of the manufacture of sarin gas. The US evidence itself indicated that at the time the activities of such personnel were not regarded as out of the ordinary. For *Inter Press Service*, Gareth Porter's (2013) investigation was equally skeptical. The description of the phone calls, he argued, did not answer the most obvious and important question as to whether the purported chemical weapons officer had actually said that the regime had used chemical weapons. Instead, he suggested, the significance of the intercept was that an admission of chemicals weapons use was not made and could be interpreted as showing that Syrian officers wanted the UN inspectors to be able to ascertain that there was no use of chemical weapons by Syrian forces in eastern Ghouta.

The regime agreed within 24 hours of the first formal request on August 24 from UN envoy Angela Kane for unimpeded access to eastern Ghouta. Porter was struck by the fact that the US intelligence summary made no effort to explain why the Assad regime had promptly granted access to the investigators, and ignored the fact that UN investigators were already present in Damascus, having been initially requested by the Assad regime to look into the April gas attack in Aleppo. While intelligence suggested that the regime might have been preparing for a chemical weapons attack, such intelligence in itself does not show whether they were preparing an attack of their own, or for an attack that might be launched by the rebels. The language of the report seemed to suggest "high confidence" (not proof, therefore) there had been a chemical weapons attack, but no level of confidence that a nerve agent had been involved. Despite the large numbers of videos alluded to by the USA in support of its allegations, most of the alleged victims being shown in the videos posted online, noted Porter, did not show symptoms associated with exposure to a nerve agent.

RT (2013) reported the skepticism of a local Catholic nun. Noting that Reuters had made video files public at 6.05 in the morning of August 21, and that the chemical attack was said to have been launched between 3 and 5 o'clock in the morning, she asked how it was possible to collect a dozen different pieces of footage, get several hundred young people together, dead and survivors, in one place, dispense first aid, conduct interviews on camera, and to do so in less than three hours. Where were the parents? Where were the female bodies? Some bodies appeared in different videos in different locations.

A specialist on chemical, biological and radiological weapons and adviser to the White House, Dan Kaszeta (cited by Porter, 2013), considered that a nerve gas attack should have been accompanied by symptoms not shown in the videos posted online. For example, there would be more or less universal vomiting, but no vomiting or evidence of such vomiting on the clothing or on the floor was indicated in any of the videos that he saw. Personnel were shown handling the victims without any special protective clothing and did not exhibit symptoms themselves. Treated survivors far outnumbered the dead, contrary to what would be expected in a nerve gas attack. While the absence of symptoms might be explicable by a "low dose" attack, there was not sufficient leeway between incapacitating and lethal doses for this to be an adequate explanation in the case of sarin.

There was also curiosity about the US calculation of death – 1,429 – much higher than the 300–400 estimated by humanitarian organizations such as Doctors Without Borders (although these were not first-hand observations, as McClatchy correspondent Mark Seibel has pointed out). One chemical weapons expert, Jean Pascal, noted that the US figure coincided with the higher range cited by insurgent sources (Wise, 2013). Porter (2013) added that US intelligence had provided no indication of how the analysts arrived at such a precise estimate, although the normal practice would be to provide a range of figures reflecting different data sources as well as assumptions. Even a British report indicated that the highest casualty rate of Syrian chemical weapons attacks that it had counted was only 350 (Sanger and Schmitt, 2013). Since some of the intercepts had occurred in the days leading to the attack, there were questions as to what the USA had done with this evidence to stop the attack from happening, or why Israel had not alerted the world earlier.

House representative Alan Grayson complained that the US Congress was deprived of sufficient evidence and referred to reports that the

Israeli-supplied intercepts had been doctored. He demanded that the administration provide the transcripts, claiming that members of Congress were not being given any of the underlying elements of the intelligence report, and were unable to discuss among themselves classified intelligence unless they were inside an approved reading room beneath the US Capitol Visitor Center where questioning the official account of events, he said, was "actively discouraged" (Nelson, 2013).

Some commentators considered that the ultimate US goal of destabilization of Syria was to weaken Iran, Syria's ally. Not incompatible were Israeli interests as these had been outlined in 1996 in a policy document prepared for later Prime Minister Benjamin Netanyahu by a study group led by American neocons Richard Perle and Douglas Feith, among others. Recalling that Hilary Clinton had said that "Assad must go" two years previously, McGovern (2013) described how the Israeli policy was to force regime change on hostile states in the region, thus isolating Israel's close-in adversaries. The plan envisaged the containment of Syria, with the aid of Turkey and Jordan, by engaging in proxy warfare and using as a pretext alleged Syrian possession of weapons of mass destruction.

The UN inspectors' report on the attacks of August 21, released on September 19, found "clear and convincing evidence" that chemical weapons had been used. But it did not assign culpability. Nor could it even identify the number of victims. That the report appeared only after a deal had been reached between Washington and Moscow on ridding Syria of its stockpiles of chemical weapons indicated declining western confidence either in the evidence that it had previously asserted against Assad or in popular support for action against Assad. The UN's chief human rights investigator on Syria, Paulo Sergio Pinherio, reminded the UN Human Rights Council that "the vast majority of the conflict's casualties (100,000 dead since March 2011) result from unlawful attacks using conventional weapons such as guns and mortars," rather than chemical weapons.

The findings of the UN report were immediately interpreted by western governments as supporting their claims. A close examination of the report's own charts by Narwani and Mortada (2013) showed a massive discrepancy in lab results from east and west Ghouta. There was not a single environmental sample in Moadamiyah that tested positive for sarin, yet it was in Moadamiyah where alleged victims of a chemical weapons attack tested highest for sarin exposure, with a positive result of 93% and 100%. In Zamalka, the results were 85% and 91%. The authors concluded that it was scientifically improbable that survivors would test that highly for exposure to sarin without a single trace of environmental evidence testing positive for the chemical agent. This source noted that the UN investigation team had centered only on the rebels; almost all those interviewed were pre-selected by the opposition.

McClatchey reporter Mathew Schofield (2014) reported the conclusion of a meeting of security and arms experts that the range of the rocket that delivered sarin in the largest attack on the night of August 21, 2013, was too short for the device to have been fired from the Syrian government positions where the Obama administration had insisted they originated. Schofield cited a report entitled *Possible Implications of Faulty U.S. Technical Intelligence* authored by Richard Lloyd, a former United Nations weapons inspector, and Theodore Postol, a professor of science, technology and national security policy at the Massachusetts Institute of Technology, which argued that "the question about the rocket's range indicates a major weakness in the case for military action initially pressed by Obama administration officials."

CONCLUSION

Dimaggio (2009) suggests that at least in their editorials it is the media of weaker or marginal powers, and who are not complicit with the foreign policies of the majors, that are most inclined to challenge the Washington consensus. But Dimaggio gives insufficient weight to the inability of such media to invest anything remotely like the reporting resources committed by the media of the major powers. The media of weaker powers may have alternative opinions, but for the *facts* they are dependent on the classic global (dis)information apparatus that is still dominated by news organizations in New York, London and Paris. Examining the histories of coverage of Libya, Syria, and in the next chapter Iran, we can see that western media are far from above clinging to a simplistic, official narrative until it becomes untenable. Rather than jettison improbable or weak narratives they are too often dependent on the vagaries of their official foreign policy sources. Media executives who have grown up in a popular culture suffused for decades with images of espionage, spycraft and double-dealing would nonetheless have their audiences believe that in the "real world" everything that is of great sensitivity for authority is pretty much the way that authority tells it.

7 Western Media Propaganda and Iran's Non-Existent Nukes

A CAMPAIGN OF IMPERIAL WAR PROPAGANDA

Harassment of Iran by western powers on the bogus pretext that it has credible and demonstrable plans to build nuclear weapons that in turn would constitute a real threat to other countries has been explored in detail by many authors (see Dimaggio, 2009; Porter, 2014). Glaser (2012) correctly comments, "Despite the official position that Iran has no weapons program and has not demonstrated an intention to build one, the whole of the political, military, and media elite are constantly regurgitating lines about blocking 'Iran' from obtaining 'nuclear weapons.'" Their complicity with what Porter (2014) justifiably derides as a "manufactured crisis" in itself represents an outstanding exposé of western media's subordination to power.

Iran is a voluntary signatory to the Non Proliferation Treaty (NPT), which it signed in 1968. The NPT allowed five nations (the USA , the Soviet Union, Britain, France and China) to possess nuclear weapons but not to divert nuclear materials to other nations, and on the understanding that they would eventually get rid of their nukes, while all other signatories (190 by 2007) renounced nuclear weapons altogether. Countries that have not signed the NPT include Israel, India, Pakistan and South Sudan. Both India and Pakistan have staged nuclear weapons tests. India's first test was as early as 1974. Almost immediately after India's second test in 1998, Pakistan followed suit with its own nuclear weapons test. In response, the USA and Japan imposed sanctions on India that they later lifted. North Korea signed the NPT in 1985 as a non-nuclear state and entered into the regime of the NPT Safeguards Agreement in 1992, but withdrew from the IAEA in 1994 (while sustaining the Safeguards Agreement) and then from the NPT entirely in 2003, an eventuality that the NPT itself allows for (Kirgis, 2003).

Iran's nuclear program (for energy, not weapons) was launched in the 1950s with the help of the USA and West European governments up to 1979. The original Iranian program was resuscitated after the Ayatollah Ruhollah Khomeini's death, albeit, as the Iranians have consistently claimed, for peaceful purposes. Prather (2007) notes that the IAEA has consistently verified that there was no evidence that any amount of NPT-proscribed materials has been diverted from a peaceful to a military purpose. The IAEA and the US intelligence establishment have continued to confirm this conclusion. At best, there might have been times prior to 2003 when elements within Iran's nuclear science community engaged in studies relevant to nuclear weaponization, or were less than transparent about efforts taken towards the enrichment of uranium for peaceful purposes, even though this is perfectly legal under the terms of the NPT, in order to protect their suppliers from US sanctions. Porter's (2014) account allows for perceptions within some elements of the Iranian government that even the taking of legal steps towards the mere capability of producing nuclear weapons (such as the production of low enriched uranium), without any other action or intention towards actual production, can itself act as a form of deterrence and provide Iran with a bargaining chip in negotiations with the USA.

Iran's enriching of a small quantity of its uranium to 20% (90% is required for successful weaponization) is required for producing medical radioisotopes to treat nearly a million Iranian cancer patients. Production started in February 2010 only after the West had several times refused to negotiate Iran's being allowed to purchase the enriched uranium from other countries, and delayed negotiations that otherwise would have allowed Iran to send its own fuel to a third country like Russia or Brazil for enriching to 20% and then being sent to France for production of the fuel roads (Shirazi, 2013). From early 2012 Iran began enriching fuel to 20% at its Fardow facility under IAEA supervision, although in 2013 it planned to phase out enrichment to 20% altogether.

Persistent scare-mongering by western politicians, experts and media commentators has fomented the notion that Iranians could produce a bomb in a very short space of time (although Khomeini and his successors have been consistent in the view that nuclear weapons are non-Islamic). For the *Christian Science Monitor* Scott Peterson (2011) even provided a timeline of such predictions over 1979–1984. In 1992 Israeli parliamentarian Benjamin Netanyahu, Foreign Minister Shimon Peres and ex-Mossad official Joseph Alpher each predicted that within three to seven years Iran would have nuclear warheads.

Mainstream media make constant references to "talks" and "negotiations" between Iran and senior western nations, and frequently represent

Iran as a reluctant and bad-humored participant. Any balanced perspective would surely consider the aggressions committed against Iran by western countries both in the past (too long a history of imperial aggression to cover here) and in the present. Contemporary western aggressions would include involvement in instigating an eight-year war between Iran and Iraq and providing military support to both sides during that conflict. More recent would be responsibility for the deaths at the hands of western or, more specifically, Mossad agents of at least three Iranian nuclear scientists from 2010 onwards, perhaps with the involvement of America's CIA and Britain's MI6 (Broad et al., 2011) and the attempted assassination of a fourth. Of equivalent significance is the western attempt to cripple the country's nuclear program through a computer "worm," Stuxnet, which is widely believed to have been created by the USA and/or Israel. Throughout 2008, the USA repeatedly refused to rule out using nuclear weapons in an attack on Iran, and the 2002 US Nuclear Posture Review (NPR) envisioned use of nuclear weapons on a first strike basis even against non-nuclear armed states (in violation of UN Security Council Resolution 984), a possibility which is still extended to Iran in the otherwise more moderate 2010 NPR.

Iran has many times proposed workable solutions to the "problems" of Iran's development of nuclear energy – as these problems have been defined, principally, by the USA, other western members of the UN Security Council and Israel. Such proposals are routinely rejected by the USA, or by other western countries on behalf of the USA, which persists in requiring that Iran should desist from all uranium enrichment for whatever purposes. This insistence is an indefensible restriction on Iranian sovereignty; it is in apparent violation of the NPT. It is also discriminatory, since equivalent harassment has not been deployed against nations that might have flouted the terms of the NPT more egregiously (questions arise in the cases of Brazil and Japan, for example), or against nations that have never signed the NPT yet whose nuclear weapons development is of a much greater magnitude and threat than in the case of Iran (Israel, India and Pakistan are examples).

The USA, the only country ever to have used nuclear weapons in war (in Japan, where the USA killed at least 120,000 citizens when it dropped atomic bombs on Hiroshima and Nagasaki in 1945), may be argued to be or to have been in violation of the Non Proliferation Treaty, since it has failed to achieve nuclear disarmament and has recently modernized its nuclear armory. Article VI of the NPT treaty constitutes a specific obligation on nuclear-weapon states to disarm themselves of nuclear weapons. Instead, the USA adopted a policy of pre-emptive war in 2002 that did not exclude the use of nuclear weapons against non-nuclear states (Shah, 2004). It withdrew from the Anti-Ballistic Missile (ABM) Treaty which it had signed in

1972 and which prohibits the use of defensive systems that might give an advantage to one side in a nuclear confrontation, and under the Bush administration indicated that it would develop newer generations of nuclear arms such as the nuclear version of "bunker-buster" bombs (Van Auken, 2009).

There are several good reasons why Iran might want to (and since 2011 actually does) generate its own nuclear energy. While the country has large quantities of petroleum, it has a shortfall in refining capacity, lacking even sufficient refineries (see Webb, 2007) to meet its own domestic traffic needs. It cannot easily expand refinery capacity in line with increased demand because of international sanctions that impede or scare off overseas investors in Iran's oil and gas industry. The USA maintains that Iran's shortage of refining capacity gives the USA leverage in its attempts to control the country's nuclear industry. So Iran is heavily dependent on overseas refineries for the supply of oil. It knows that one day the oil will run out, so it is advisable that it prepares for that eventuality well in advance. The less petroleum Iran consumes domestically, the more it can make available to the international market to boost is export earnings.

PROPAGANDA STRATEGIES

In what follows, I have assembled a range of examples of prevalent forms of western media propaganda and critiques of such coverage from the period 2006–2012. The overarching purpose of this propaganda is to present Iran as an ever-present threat to the world on account of its falsely alleged ambition to build nuclear weapons. The manipulation of public opinion may in turn be used to support western attempts to destabilize Iran and open up its economy and resources for western exploitation.

Beefing up the propaganda machinery

In February 2006, Secretary of State Condoleeza Rice asked Congress for $75 million for anti-Iranian propaganda, including radio and television broadcasts into Iran and for the fomenting of internal opposition to Iranian religious leaders, and Iranian student exchanges. $50 million of the proposed funds would be used to significantly increase Farsi broadcasts into Iran by federal government stations and US-funded Radio Farda, and to build the capacity to broadcast 24/7. Other money would go to Iranian labor unions and human rights activists via nongovernmental organizations and "democracy" groups such as the National Endowment for Democracy, and to "independent" Farsi language Internet, radio and television activity.

Iran the authoritarian state

Mainstream media continuously represent Iran as an autocratic and/or theocratic state. Iran today (and since 1979) is a functioning democracy, even vibrant, yet also one in which the clerics have a constitutionally privileged and sometimes commanding place, perhaps comparable to that of the military-industrial complex, large corporations and plutocratic oligarchs in the USA (Ervand, 2008; Balaghi, 2013). Herman and Peterson (2009), for example, finger the role in the USA of an "unelected dictatorship of money" in vetting nominees of the Republican and Democratic parties (comparable to, if less transparent than, the influence in Iran exerted by the Islamic Council of Guardians), with the result that the options available to US citizens are two candidates, "neither of whom can change the foreign or domestic priorities of the imperial US regime." Al Jazeera (2009) has described Iran as a mixture of theocracy and democracy, a balance of appointed and directly elected institutions.

Misrepresenting the democratic process in Iran

The elections of 2009 resulted in the re-election of Mahmoud Ahmadinejad – demonized by western media on the false pretext, among other things, that he had called for Israel to be wiped off the map – amidst fierce street demonstrations that stoked western media to a fury of indignation. The general western presumption, on behalf of defeated candidates (that the outcome of the election was the result of fraud) is contested by the close analysis of Herman and Peterson (2009). They concluded that the street protests were not "home grown" but were directly linked to destabilization campaigns that had their provenance from outside of Iran, citing misleading statements by the *New York Times* which reported incorrectly, for example, that Iran's Guardian Council had said that the number of votes recorded in 50 cities exceeded the number of eligible voters there by three million. Parry (2009) comments that when the campaign of opponent Hossein Mousavi acquired the appearance of a "velvet revolution," with Mousavi claiming victory before any ballots had been counted and then organizing a mass demonstration when the vote went against him, "the U.S. press corps mocked any suggestion from Ahmadinejad's government that foreign operatives might have had a hand in the disruption."

Herman and Peterson note, first of all, that the "only relatively scientific, non-partisan poll of Iranian opinion conducted in the pre-election period between May 11 and 20, found a very strong lead for Ahmadinejad (33.8%) over Mousavi (13.6%), Karroubi (1.7%) and Rezai (0.9%)." Parry (2009) discusses the claim that the fact that Mousavi lost in his home Azeri district suggests the likelihood of fraud. But the New America Foundation pre-election poll had shown Ahmadinejad with a 2-to-1 lead in that area, undercutting the assumption that Azeris would surely support one of their own, in a region that had benefited from considerable resources invested in it by the Ahmadinejad regime.

Presuming that official sources tell the truth: (1) Iran in Iraq

In early 2007 official US administration sources spread the word that Iran was involved in attacks on the USA in Iraq, in support of Shiite militias. FAIR monitored copious media coverage accepting these claims (February 2, 2007). Such stories were not only too trusting of official and usually anonymous sources, but were also unaccompanied by sufficient third party expert scrutiny. They overlooked important contextual factors that might undermine the claims: for example, that Iran was actually encouraging Shiite participation in electoral politics, and that its closest links in Iraq were to two large Shiite factions that happened to support the US-backed government, while the Iranian government engaged in wide-ranging negotiations with the Iraqi government of Prime Minister Nuri al-Maliki on trade, diplomacy and military training. Juan Cole noted that the terrorist group "Al-Qaeda in Mesopotamia" had announced that its policy was to kill as many Shiites as possible, thus making it highly unlikely that Shiite Iran would support their cause. In addition, as Gareth Porter noted on February 14 in *Truthout* (cited by Media Lens, 2007) most weapons can be "purchased by anyone through intermediaries in the Middle East." Porter cited evidence that the equipment to make roadside bombs could easily be manufactured in Iraq. To its credit, the *Los Angeles Times* noted that US and British military officers had seen no evidence to support allegations of arms smuggling and that the USA had declined to present the evidence that it claimed to possess.

Notwithstanding the considerable doubts surrounding such allegations, the *Daily Telegraph* on January 16, 2007, editorialized that "It has been clear for many months that Iran has been actively involved in the Iraqi insurgency: by supplying arms and manpower to the militias who target American and British forces, and inciting sectarian violence, it has helped to maintain the state of chaotic instability which has persisted in spite of all attempts to bring order to the country" (cited by *MediaLens*, February 21, 2007). Thus the *Daily Telegraph* attributed to Iran – which had absolutely nothing to do with the US invasion of Iraq – culpability for the terrorization of the population that was directly attributable to that invasion. Over the space of 12 months, noted MediaLens, the *Telegraph* carried 16 articles containing similar allegations against Iran.

Presuming that official sources tell the truth: (2) Iran in Syria

In 2012, a *New York Times* article by Michael Gordon, Eric Schmitt and Tim Arango argued that "the American effort to stem the flow of Iranian arms to Syria has faltered because of Iraq's reluctance to inspect aircraft carrying the weapons through its airspace." The propaganda value of this story lay essentially in its combining of "negatives:" Iran and Syria and the opportunity to link Iran with another official object of American hate, namely the "Lebanese Islamist movement Hezbollah." The information was attributed to "American officials," swinging wildly at the US puppet government of Iraq for its apparent shortcomings in checking the imagined flow of arms to the Assad regime – an inspection process to which Iraq had apparently committed through the person of Iraq's foreign minister less than three months before the story was written. Apparently only two flights between Iran and Syria had been inspected and one of those was returning to Iran from Syria: no weapons were found. The story makes one other reference to an inspected flight, one that was found to be carrying only humanitarian supplies – a negative result that was allegedly indicative of collusion between Iranian and Iraqi operatives – but it is not clear whether this was one of the two flights specifically mentioned early on in the story. The premise that was uncritically accepted was that there was indeed a flow of Iranian arms to Syria, although there was no proof of this whatsoever, merely smoke principally emanating from US anonymous sources. The main thrust of the story and, significantly, all assertions that were critical of Iran, Iraq or Syria, was based on anonymous sources: American officials, western intelligence officials, senior American officials, American intelligence analysts, Iraqi officials, one former Iraqi official, American intelligence assessments, "American, European and Israeli officials," and so on and so forth.

"As though" journalism: pretending that the reader has not been paying attention

The purpose of this strategy (named as such by Boyd-Barrett, 2007) is to convince readers that they have been daydreaming, that what they thought they had been told wasn't real, and that now things are back to "how they have always been." *MediaLens* drew attention to a January 2006 article in the *Guardian* by Timothy Garton Ash, in which he wrote "Now we face the next big test of the west: after Iraq, Iran," as though Iraq had really been a "test" and that Iran was equally as much a "test" (notice the seductively vile "we"). He and the *Guardian*'s Polly Toynbee "unblushingly presume to tell us that soon Iran (or, rather, the 'mad mullahs') will have (nuclear) bombs."

Presumption of the worst

At least up until a possible resolution between Western powers and Iran in 2014, mainstream western media operated from the default presumption that pretty much anything that Iran did was nefariously related to the development of nuclear weapons. Through all the years when there was no evidence of Iranian possession of, or indeed capability of, making, nuclear warheads – an absence of evidence that was continually confirmed by the IAEA, NIE, CIA and other western intelligence reports and spokespersons – many western media contributors and journalists presumed either to directly claim or otherwise to lead their readers indirectly to the conclusion that Iran actually did have them, or would soon have them, or badly wanted them and would do anything to get them.

Mike Whitney (2006) cites a *Times* editorial of February 8, 2006, asserting that Iran was developing nuclear weapons. Justin Raimondo, writing in late November 2008, noted that the mainstream western media were getting themselves into a lather about a UN report that claimed Iran was planning on building 3,000 new centrifuges (which would be necessary to enable them to enrich uranium to the low grade of purity necessary for peaceful nuclear energy) and predicting that the country would have the bomb within a year (by 2013, only 700 of the 3,000 advanced centrifuges that Iran had acquired appeared to be operating).

When mainstream media were not predicting nuclear bombs they were agonizing over the apparent lack of communication between the IAEA and Iran about a nuclear weapons program that had ended in 2003, evidence of which had been indicated in documents, possibly forged, obtained by the USA from the terrorist organization Mujahideen-e-Khalq (MEK). The USA had refused to completely divulge the details to the IAEA, let alone to Iran. The laptop from which the documents were taken, according to Sahimi (2009), has "never been analyzed for its digital chain of custody to reveal the dates at which the documents were stored in it." Ritter (2006) has described the laptop as a "product of joint cooperation between the Israeli intelligence service and their German counterparts." Then Director of the IAEA, El Baradei, told *The Hindu* that there was a major question of authenticity concerning the documents (Symonds, 2009). Porter (2014) indicates that at best the activities to which the documents, forged or otherwise, alluded were unauthorized scientific studies and not physical preparations.

Making it up

Presuming the worst can convert into unreflecting certainty of the worst, even in the face of contrary evidence. FAIR (2012) called attention to misleading articles in the *New York Times* on May 1, 2012. On the front page, an article by Steven Erlanger reported that "The threats from Iran, aimed both at the West and at Israel, combined with a recent assessment by the International Atomic Energy Agency that Iran's nuclear program has a military objective ... " FAIR correctly pointed out that there was no such IAEA assessment. The IAEA has raised questions about the status of the Iranian program and presented old evidence pertaining to something that might or might not have been the case prior to 2003, evidence whose authenticity has been called into question. *MediaLens* (2012) took note of a BBC *News at Ten* bulletin that included in its headlines the assertion that "The Iranians delight in the latest advances in their nuclear programme." But when the corresponding news report was introduced "nuclear program" had now miraculously become a "nuclear weapons program."

Canada's *National Post*, the *New York Post*, and the *Jerusalem Post* ran a story in May 2006 that falsely reported there was new legislation in Iran that would require Jews and other religious minorities to wear distinctive colored badges. The article was written by US neoconservative and Iranian-American Amir Taheri, a frequent contributor to the *Wall Street Journal* (Lobe, May 23, 2006). Taheri had also been a long-time editor of the French publication *Politique Internationale*, a publisher of many stories by Alexis Debat that were based on fabricated interviews with leading US politicians.

AP engaged in similar scare mongering when in February 2010 (Ditz, 2010) it reported that Iran had moved closer to "nuke warhead capacity," "when in point of fact Iran had merely informed the IAEA that it was planning to begin efforts for production of less than 20 percent enriched uranium. AP claimed that this was 'just below the threshold for high enriched uranium.'" Actually it was well short of the 90%-plus needed for weapons grade material. Iran's motive was that it wanted to produce fuel rods for its US-built Tehran reactor, needed in the creation of medical isotopes for cancer patients.

In March 2010, *Fox News* ran an item claiming that the CIA had asserted that Iran was still working on building a nuclear weapon despite some technical setbacks, and that the Pentagon was still concerned about Iran's intentions. *Fox*'s claims, as noted by George Maschke and cited by Glenn Greenwald (2010), were categorically false: the actual CIA report said no such thing, rather the opposite. The news agency Reuters has carried similar deceptive reports, claiming that the IAEA had said that Iran may be working to develop a nuclear armed missile whereas, as Juan Cole observed (also cited by Greenwald, 2010), the IAEA continued to certify that none of Iran's nuclear material had been diverted for military uses, although it could not give 100% assurance on this since it had not been allowed complete access.

Boosting war sentiment, blaming Iran, while celebrating western war plans

US mainstream news media lend themselves willingly to official US propaganda aims. Solomon (2006) describes how on September 25th of that year *Time* magazine devoted five pages "scoping out a U.S. war against Iran," and headlined its cover-story interview with Iran's president, Mahmoud Ahmadinejad, "A Date with a Dangerous Mind."

Early in 2007 media reports appeared to be lending credence to a story that Iran was responsible for downing a US helicopter in Iraq by means of advanced weapons. A critique of the relevant White House briefing from Larisa Alexandrovna complained that none of the experts and analysts would "provide their names, background, or any identifying information – even off the record … In other words, the sources were not vetted and unknown." In addition, the allegations were based on a set of photographs of unknown origin, date, time, or any other contextual information that could be confirmed or debunked. In other words, the facts of the story were unsupportable and could not be in any way explored.

US mainstream media exercised little restraint in lauding the efforts of their own and other nations' aggressive intentions and actions towards Iran. These included the assassinations of Iranian nuclear scientists and the launching of computer malware ("Stuxnet") whose purpose apparently was to create a setback to Iranian progress but which also threatened to contaminate computers around the world and might have provoked Iran to counter cyber-attacks. *MediaLens* (2012d) observed how the fourth assassination of an Iranian scientist "generated minimal outrage in the press." The *Sunday Times* published a meticulous account of the attacks by a source supposedly knowledgeable about a covert Israeli operation inside Iran. *MediaLens* could find only one media outlet that was prepared to refer to the assassination as an act of terror. These same outlets had no qualms about describing an (entirely phony) story about a supposed Iranian plot to assassinate the Saudi Arabian ambassador to the USA as "terrorism."

As we have seen, journalists routinely assume that Iran has a nuclear weapons program even though it does not. Given such a presumption, it is easier for them to give uncritical coverage to attack plans that the USA and/or Israel are prepared to launch on the pretext of Iran's having or potentially developing nuclear weapons at some point in the future. One such instance, an article by Defense Correspondent Jonathan Marcus (2012) for the BBC, was identified by *MediaLens* (2012a). In his piece Marcus listed Israeli aircraft that would be involved in a presumed upcoming attack on Iran, and identified the potential targets. He assigned the "task" for each aggressive Israeli weapon system, but chose the word "threat" in relation to Iranian defenses. He also asserted that the nuclear enrichment plant at Natanz would be a clear target and that because it was underground "bunker-busting" munitions (which can be conventional or nuclear) would be essential.

No consideration was given to consistent IAEA reports showing no evidence of the high nuclear enrichment that would be required for nuclear weapons manufacture. *MediaLens* commented that the article provided no discussion of the legal issues that would be raised by an Israeli attack, nor did it concern itself with the possibility of major civilian casualties. The military site at Parchin was identified as a likely target for Israel on the grounds that "IAEA inspectors were prevented from visiting the site" that month. An investigation by Gareth Porter corrected this view of Parchin, noting that the Iranians did not object to the IAEA visit to the base in principle, but refused access for as long as no agreement had been reached with the IAEA governing the modalities of cooperation (Porter, 2012d). Porter quoted the Iranian ambassador to the IAEA:

> Soltanieh referred to two IAEA inspection visits to Parchin in January and November 2005 and said Iran needs to have "assurances" that it would not "repeat the same bitter experience, when they just come and ask for the access." There should be a "modality" and a "frame of reference, of what exactly they are looking for, they have to provide the documents and exactly where they want [to go]," he said.

QUESTIONABLE SOURCES FOR QUESTIONABLE JOURNALISM

Unholy alliances between particular journalists and particular sources are struck in which both journalists and their sources appear to collaboratively engage in propaganda. These "disinformation dyads" acquire a triadic dimension when the resulting propaganda reports are given clearance by the top editors or owners of mainstream media.

George Jahn, Bureau Chief, Austria and Eastern Europe, for AP, has frequently incurred criticism for alarmist reports on Iran, sometimes based on anonymous sources, possibly on behalf of Israel. Nima Shirazi (2012) described Jahn as the "Associated Press' favorite conduit for pathetic Israeli garbage." He instanced one of Jahn's stories (Jahn, 2012b) entitled "Graph suggests Iran working on bomb." Shirazi was critical that the supposed graph had been released by anonymous agents of an unnamed country that was opposed to Iran's nuclear energy program and considered it obvious that the graph had been released to AP for propaganda purposes. Jahn's main named sources were known anti-Iran nuclear alarmists David Albright of the Institute for Science and International Security, and former IAEA inspector Olli Heinonen with whom Albright was said (Sahimi, 2009) to be close, and who in 2009 was IAEA's deputy director for safeguards in charge of the current inspections in Iran and likely to be Albright's principal source. Shiraz debunked the graph as:

> ... not only weirdly crude, but also undated, unsourced, and unexplained. The Persian text at the bottom, as translated by AP, mentions nothing about nuclear weapons or an atomic payload for a bomb. It just reads, "Changes in output and in energy released as a function of time through power pulse." To call this graph "dubious" would be generous; to tout it as "proof" of anything is simply embarrassing. It literally means nothing, except perhaps that math exists. The graph shows nothing more than a probability density function, that is, an abstract visual aid depicting the theoretical behavior of a random variable to take on any given value.

> Beyond that, theoretical physics professor Dr. M. Hossein Partovi, who teaches courses in thermodynamics and quantum mechanics at Sacramento State, noting that the graph is plotted in microseconds, explains that "the graph depicted in the report is a nonspecific power/energy plot that is primarily evidence of the incompetence of those who forged it: a quick look at the energy graph shows that the total energy is more than four orders of magnitude (ten thousand times) smaller than the total integrated power it must equal!" Partovi added that the actual discrepancy is closer to 40,000 times smaller."

Other media critics rallied to dissect Jahn's graph story. These included Richard Silverstein (2012) at *Tikun Olam*, who considered the document was actually a Mossad forgery, and Glen Greenwald for the *Guardian* (2012), who wrote that it was

> ... completely reckless for AP to present this primitive, error-strewn, thoroughly common graph as secret, powerful evidence of Iran's work toward building a nuclear weapon, a graph that had been handed to it by a country which AP has acknowledged is seeking to warn the world about the dangers of Iran. This is worse than stenography journalism. It is AP allowing itself, eagerly and gratefully, to be used to put its stamp of credibility on a ridiculous though destructive hoax.

Gareth Porter quoted former senior IAEA inspector Robert Kelley as saying, "It's clear the graph has nothing to do with a nuclear bomb" (Porter, 2012a). Porter (2012b) later wrote that the graph appeared to have been adapted from a scholarly journal article published in 2009 and available on the Internet. He also cited John Glaser at Antiwar.com and nuclear physicists Yousaf Butt and Ferenc Dalnoki-Veress in the *Bulletin of the Atomic Scientists* who concluded that the diagram "does nothing more than indicate either slipshod analysis or an amateurish hoax." Jahn's own admission that the graph was flawed was followed by an explanation proffered from his original source (almost certainly Israeli), making the unlikely claim that the graph was deliberately simplified for the benefit of Iranian officials. Jahn tells us that "one of the diplomats who spoke comes from a country critical of Iran's nuclear program while the other is considered neutral, and both spend much of their time probing Iran's nuclear activities." We can assume that the first is Israel and that the second is the USA or a US ally – in other words, not at all "neutral." Jahn claimed that the sources demanded anonymity because they were not authorized to discuss confidential information about IAEA inspections. This recalls an observation from Greenwald the previous year, namely that when such sources are clearly operating for propaganda purposes and their information has previously been found highly suspect then there no longer exists any journalistic obligation to protect them but, on the contrary, an obligation to expose them for the protection of the public.

One named source for the Jahn graph was, once again, David Albright, founder of the private Institute for Science and National Security, prompting expert Mark Hibbs to raise the issue in *Foreign Policy* as to whether the IAEA was becoming over reliant on evidence supplied to it by others, of which some, like the now-notorious graph, would be highly deceiving. Yousaff Butt in the *Christian Science Monitor* worried that:

> ... the AP story said that this amateurish and technically incorrect graph even made it into official reports from the International Atomic Energy Agency, specifically one from November 2011 citing indications that Iran was trying to calculate the explosive yield of potential nuclear weapons. This raises another interesting issue: What if Iran is right when it says that the IAEA is confronting it with fabrications? And if this graph is a hoax how exactly is Iran supposed to come clean?

The graph was obviously not the work of a real Iranian scientist – much less someone working in a top secret nuclear weapons research program – but of an amateur trying to simulate a graph that would be viewed, at least by non-specialists, as something a scientist might have drawn. Other evidence involving Jahn came from an official Iranian source, namely Iranian nuclear chief Fereidoun Abbasi, who was quoted by the semi-official Fars news agency as saying that more than 3,000 high-tech centrifuges had already been produced and would soon phase out the more than 12,000 older-generation enriching machines at Natanz. The statement undermined suggestions of Iranian "secrecy" but was declared by Jahn to be evidence of an Iranian "evasion" of sanctions. More likely it was an indication of increasing Iranian self-sufficiency in the face of concerted US sabotage. The new centrifuges were said to enrich faster, which Jahn and his sources appeared to want to confuse with the idea of enriching to a greater percentage of purity – not the same thing at all.

Jahn continued his role in 2013 with another AP story based almost entirely on anonymous sources. This attempted to spike up the "threat" of Iran having tripled its installations of "advanced" centrifuges to something approaching 600. Iran's nuclear authorities, as we have just seen, had already disclosed that Iran had produced 3,000 such centrifuges to replace 12,000 older machines. Further, as Jahn's story reluctantly acknowledged, the "advanced centrifuges were not yet producing enriched uranium, and might only be partially installed." All of the reported activities fell within Iran's continuing right to enrich uranium for peaceful purposes, including to around 4% for the generation of power or 20% for medical isotopes. Western intransigence in providing Iran the isotopes that it needed, and in reaching agreements that would make Iran less dependent on indigenous enrichment, appeared to have impelled it to greater independence and self-sufficiency.

CONCLUSION

Western public opinion about Iran, with particular reference to the issue of the country's pursuit of nuclear energy, but also with reference to the history, culture and polity of Iran itself, indicates its vulnerability to a very high level of disinformation. For this, the media and the privileged access they allow to a select range of powerful political, military and corporate sources must carry considerable blame. That it is sometimes a difficult and complex subject, requiring at least some insight into a dialectical history of several decades' duration, should be no excuse. I have found evidence than something more than "mere" incompetence in the reporting of matters of extreme gravity is at issue here. Not only are the most relevant contextual facts of this one case frequently missing, but there is an element of complicity between western journalists and extremely partial sources. In addition we find evidence of the kinds of propagandizing of western media that are familiar to any students of Herman and Chomsky's propaganda model, namely a dangerous dependence on selective official or authoritative sources, one that reveals an indefensible presumption that these are "telling the truth." Simply because the word "negotiation" is used in the context of imposing institutions such as the IAEA or UN Security Council does not necessarily mean that parties to the negotiation are acting in good faith. Mainstream media propagate a view of Iran as aggressor when frequently, if not typically, it is the western parties who are the aggressors. The very behaviors that cause such apparent outrage when they are undertaken by Iran seem to merit hardly a mention if they are undertaken by nations (Brazil and India, for example) that have not been singled out as special enemies of the empire. At the very root of the problem in this and in so many other areas of US foreign policy, is an overweening presumption of American exceptionalism, of an American right to dictate the terms of power in the Middle East and around the world – a presumption that is driven less and less by any meaningful ideology of public good and more and more by an odious fusion of political ambition, corporate greed and the perpetuation of the military-industrial incubus.

8 Towards Digital Media Empires

ASIA RISING

Reorienting the media imperialism tradition away from earlier presumptions as to who were the most evidently pro-active agencies of media imperialism, recent research (e.g. Thussu, 2008; Curtin and Shah, 2010) refocuses on strong production and export activity from countries of the South, including China, India, Hong Kong, and South Korea. Some of these forces are commercial, others take the form of state-subsidized "soft power" initiatives (as in the case of China's Xinhua, and CNC World – see Chapters 9 and 10 – or South Korea's K-Pop). Other candidates for the status of media imperialist include (a) lesser centers of media production as in Beirut, Cairo, Caracas, Dubai, Moscow, Qatar, São Paulo, that achieve either or both regional (e.g. Telesur) and global reach (e.g. Al-Jazeera); (b) centers for the manufacture of a pan-Asian or pan-Chinese media product (e.g. Seoul for 'Korean Wave' television dramas, computer games, music, and movies or Hong Kong for informational and entertainment television and movies, all widely exported throughout East Asia and beyond; and mainland Chinese media centers in Beijing and Shanghai for China and the Chinese diaspora); and (c) niche centers of production defined by ethnic, geo-political or generic type (e.g. Lagos for video dramas – "Nollywood" – distributed throughout continental Africa and its diaspora; Brazil and Mexico for telenovelas, distributed mainly but not only to Latin audiences; Moscow for print and broadcast media distributed throughout the former Soviet Union).

In addition powerful electronics and digital giants have also emerged from the South. To the longstanding global presence of Japanese companies such as Sony, Panasonic, Toshiba, Sanyo, Sharp (many not performing robustly in 2013), reflecting Japan's slow adjustment from mechanics to software production, and to new competition from the USA, South Korea and Taiwan (Wingfield-Hayes, 2013), more cutting-edge Japanese software companies such as Softbank are doing better), should now be added companies such as Samsung and LG Corp of South Korea; Alibaba (including Tencent), Huawei Technologies Co., Lenovo and SinaCorp (includes Weibo) in China; Acer, Foxconn and HTC of Taiwan. Many such new arrivals have benefited from strong state backing. Many have also adapted software and computing language deriving from the USA (including Google's open-source Android) and Sun's Java language (now owned by Oracle).

EMPIRE

I do not discount the possibility of a new media order reflective of the escalating power and influence of China and the corresponding relative decline of the USA. But my main purpose here is to monitor the continuing strength and influence of the global media, information and communication industries, from print to digital, up to the 2010s. In considering the newer models of imperialism to which I have just alluded, I shall still take into account that alongside globally or regionally hegemonic or merely locally-influential nation states is the still evolving formation under US leadership of a world economic order (NLWEO or the "Empire" – I find Hardt and Negri's [2001] formulation helpful here) that we may think of as a form of neoliberal, corporate, capitalist network of interests (not free of internal conflict), more intensely present in and reflective of some territories, groups and cultures than others, closely allied to plutocracies almost everywhere, and working in an uneven partnership with nation states (and the global regulatory organizations through which these negotiate), some of which we may consider to have been entirely coopted by the NLWEO.

While "Empire" does indeed appear and to some extent is supra-territorial, it has been engineered by the aggressive, missionary propagation and embrace of the Chicago School's ("Friedmanesque" or "monetarist") economics of both the Reagan (USA) and the Thatcher (Britain) regimes of the 1980s (see Klein, 2008). Recent manifestations involve the unfettered opening to international capital of national markets hitherto principally manipulated or shuttered for the benefit of local plutocracies, ethnic groups or the military. These include the US invasions and occupations of Afghanistan and Iraq, the consequent destabilization of Pakistan and adjacent areas of Central Asia, and throughout 2010 to 2012 the so-called "Arab Spring," involving Tunisia, Egypt, Libya and Syria, and the constant stream over several decades of western invective against Iran, and in February 2014, NATO support for the protestors who seized power in Kiev and its subsequent opposition to Russia and to Crimea's vote in support of annexation by Russia. For chronicles of post-World War Two US imperialism see Blum (2004), Gonzalez (2002),

Johnson (2004), and Kinzer (2007). These considerations call for a reaffirmation of the role of media in broader historical processes of imperialism conceived as a form of subordination of smaller or weaker nations to the will of larger or stronger nations (Boyd-Barrett, Herrera and Bauman, 2010).

MEDIA AND GLOBALIZATION

Media, information and communications industries interrelate with processes of globalization in seven important ways: (1) they provide the enabling physical infrastructure for global communications (e.g. overland and undersea cables, satellites and satellite delivery systems, and wireless stations for wired and wireless communication, including internet and telephony); (2) media and communication hardware and software industries are themselves significant domains for international capital accumulation, frequently acquiring the form of large multi-media conglomerates operating internationally, and as such are full-blooded corporate members of what is sometimes described as a neoliberal world economic order; (3) they provide vehicles for the advertising (on which many if not most media systems are substantially dependent for revenue) of goods and services produced by member states and corporations of this order, most of whom are signatories to the World Trade Organization; (4) through their content and its representations of lifestyles, they trigger a "demonstration" effect that stimulates a continuing demand for goods and services, positive for consumerism; (5) many media service the global financial and commercial order through informational infrastructures that are increasingly essential to the operation of modern capitalism, comprising sophisticated, interactive instruments for the interrogation of massive financial, commercial and corporate data-bases and that sometimes constitute electronic market places for trading activity; (6) media police the ideological boundaries of tolerable expression at national and international levels, promoting content that increasingly serves the interests of neoliberalism (mainly having to do with the progressive abolition of national restrictions on the trade in goods and services), marginalizing, suppressing or excluding content that does not; and (7) these industries provide critical support to the development of the "surveillance society," or in other words, to the centralized collection of ever more intimate, instantly accessible intelligence (to those few who control or pay for it), to a degree unparalleled in human history and in a manner that is increasingly and literally "weaponized," in the form of drone and other forms of robotic warfare.

NEWS

Notwithstanding significant permutations since the 1960s–1970s, classic manifestations of unidirectional, power-inflected media imperialism have persisted into the 2000s and have even been accentuated in parallel with considerable concentration of ownership and control of media industries in most locations globally. In the business of wholesale global news-gathering and distribution, mainstream media everywhere continue to be highly dependent on a narrow range of enterprises for print, electronic and video news whether general or specialized. The market is strongly dominated by the Associated Press (AP) and its video news subsidiary APTN, as well as Thomson Reuters and its television subsidiary Reuters Television. With the notable exception of Agence France Presse (AFP), and its video subsidiary (AFPTV), based in Paris, the bedrock of international news reporting by the news agencies is headquartered in North America (AP, Bloomberg, the News Corporation – which owns the Dow Jones news wires and the *Wall Street Journal* – and Thomson Reuters), seconded by London which hosts the video newsrooms of APTN and Thomson Reuters (Boyd-Barrett, 2010). CNN, a major wholesaler and retailer for television and online news generally, frames international news in ways that are friendly to the USA (Thussu, 2008; Boyd-Barrett, forthcoming), and its nearest competitor, BBC Worldwide, similarly frames events in ways that are compatible with British and NATO interests. Often celebrated for its contribution to diversity in television news, Al Jazeera has direct ties to the interests of one (small) state, Qatar, whose foreign policies are influential in the Arab world. Al Jazeera helped provide considerable news exposure to the "rebels" in Egypt, Libya and Syria, 2010–2012, and appears far more copasetic with the foreign policies of the USA and its major allies in 2013 than in 2003 (Kellner, 2011). Most international television news operations, including those of China, France, Germany and Russia, constitute classic examples of state-supported soft power.

MOVIES

In terms of revenues the international movie industry continues to be dominated by the six principal studio-distributors of Hollywood and the multinational conglomerates that own them. These are News Corporation's 21st Century Fox, Viacom's Paramount, Sony's Sony Pictures, GE and Comcast's NBC/Universal, Walt Disney, and Time Warner's Warner Bros. Some other production centers, such as Mumbai (Bollywood) in India and Lagos (Nollywood) in Nigeria, make more movies and reach even larger audiences. Yet almost 40% of the revenue for global movie production and distribution (worth $86.7 billion in 2012) is generated from North American audiences, followed by Europe with 23.5% (IbisWorld, 2012). While MPAA studios and studio subsidiaries accounted for a modest number (141) of films released in 2011, most film-makers collaborate with these giants to acquire finance and/or distribution. Of the top 25 films in terms of 2011 box office revenues, 24 came from the big six.

In the USA/Canada, where 607 movies were rated by the Classification and Ratings Administration (CARA) for release to theaters in 2011 (758 were rated in total, including non-theatrical movies), this market accounted for approximately one third ($10.2 billion) of global box office ($32.6 billion), primarily consuming US products. Out of a world box office market valued at $34.7 billion in 2012 the USA accounted for $10.8 billion, followed by China ($2.7 billion), Japan ($2.4 billion), the UK ($1.7 billion), France ($1.7 billion), India ($1.4 billion), Germany ($1.3 billion), South Korea ($1.3 billion), Russia ($1.2 billion), Australia ($1.2 billion) and Brazil ($0.8 billion). In many of these countries total box office includes large proportions earned by the sale of foreign, primarily US, products. Whereas box office revenues on the US market were earned almost entirely by US movies, the national market accounted for only 57% of revenues in Japan, 36% in the UK's, 40% in France, 51% in Germany, 24% in Australia and 11% in Brazil (MPAA, 2012). US box office revenue climbed to $10.9 billion in 2013. China showed strong growth in 2013 when box office revenues surged 27% to $3.6 billion in 2013, from 18,000 screens. Chinese movies dominated the list of the 10 highest-grossing films on the Chinese market, with only three Hollywood productions making the list – and each of these three contained strong Asian elements. Small and mid-budget Chinese movies did particularly well (Makinen, 2014). The Chinese government imposes a quota on the number of foreign movies for theatrical realease in any year – 20 in 2013.

TELEVISION

Even were it a sensible claim that media imperialism theory was mainly about television content and its consumption, which of course it is not, then in the 1960s and 1970s it was certainly correct to point to the dominance of the USA as a source for television imports throughout many countries of the world, and to the impact of such imports on prime-time programming (Nordenstreng and Varis, 1974). The significance of such imports was all the greater in as much as consumers of television in many countries had only one or two sources of television supply to choose from, and bearing in mind that in many of these countries, especially in the developing world, radio was the most consumed medium. In the succeeding 40 years or so a great deal has changed: there are considerably more television outlets in most countries; there is much higher consumption of television; television production technology costs have fallen, so that in most countries there has been a considerable increase in local productions – which are preferred by consumers, other things being equal – particularly in primetime hours. So a simple argument of US-based media imperialism that is founded on a criterion of the proportion of local programming imported from the USA for primetime viewing no longer has much meaning for most countries (although it is still quite high when all viewing of motion picture entertainment is factored in, regardless of source, whether terrestrial television, satellite or cable, recorded programming, computer or mobile downloaded). And we may wonder about the significance of the fact that the USA, which continues to export so much, imports relatively little. None the less we should note that of total revenues represented by the global television market (from advertising, subscription and public funding), North America had the largest share in 2009, accounting for 39% of almost 270 billion EUR, followed by Europe (31%), Asia Pacific (21%), Latin America (8%), Africa and the Middle East (2%)(International Television Expert Group, 2010).

MUSIC RECORDING

The international music recording industry in 2014 was dominated by three players. These were Sony BMG, Time Warner's Warner Music Group, and Vivendi's Universal Music Group. A fourth, EMI, was sold off to Sony and UMG in 2011. The USA is the top national market, accounting for $4.37 billion in 2011, ahead of Japan ($4.09 billion) and Germany ($1.47 billion) (International Federation of the Phonographic Industry (IFPI), 2012). A long period of industrial contraction, reflecting the impacts of digitization and piracy among other factors, continued into 2013.

VIDEO AND COMPUTER GAMES

The global video and computer games industry manifested considerable concentration of ownership and control, notably in Japan and the USA. This impacted video games (fixed and handheld consoles), video games packs for consoles and PCs, and downloadable games for computers, phones and tablets. Like so many other media industries, this experienced a rapid transition as it coped with the evolving impacts of digitization. Sales of video game discs and consoles dropped 22% in 2012, following a 9%

drop in 2011, as competition intensified from the less lucrative download-able and mobile games industry. Games developers and publishers (principally Japanese, French and American) were producing fewer games at higher prices, concentrating on high-investment blockbusters. The top ten games accounted for 46% of spending in December 2012 (Gaudiosi, 2012; Entertainment Software Association, 2013).

In the early days of video games, the consoles market was dominated by three Japanese companies, Sony, Sega and Nintendo, whereas by the late 2000s the big three comprised Sony, Nintendo and Microsoft (Sega was still a substantial company with $5 billion sales in 2011). US games companies such as Entertainment Arts and the French-owned (but US-based), Activision Blizzard have enjoyed spectacular global success. Entertainment Arts was a major player in also extending console gaming to the personal computer, a market later undermined by downloading through services such as Steam.

The global video game industry was worth almost $60 billion in 2011 sales, of which Microsoft's Xbox 360, Nintendo's Wii and Sony's PlayStation accounted for almost half ($27 billion). Console gaming accounted for 42% of the global video games market. Other markets comprised personal computers ($12 billion), mobile/tablet ($10 billion), social/browser ($8 billion), and handheld devices ($1 billion). In terms of units, Microsoft's Xbox 360 led with the sale of 66 million by the end of 2011, followed closely by PlayStation3 with 63 million, and Nintendo Wii (global total unavailable: 4 million units sold in the USA in 2011). Geographically, in 2011 the Asia-Pacific market accounted for $24 billion; Europe, the Middle East and Africa for $18 billion; North America for $15 billion; and Latin America for over $1 billion (VG Sales Wiki, 2013).

A new wave of Asian activity in the games market was apparent in the 2010s, especially in "free-to-play" mobile games, whose business model is to provide games cheaply or free, and then profit from in-game purchases, advertising and other add-ons. In one month of 2013 (September), Japan and South Korea accounted for 62% of worldwide revenues from games on the Google Play mobile application store. The role of Google, a US corporation, as the delivery channel here bestows an important gatekeeping power, as does Google's contribution of Android to many of the smart screen devices on which many games and apps are played.

COMPUTING HARDWARE AND SOFTWARE

Despite significant growth in China and India, global computing hardware markets continued to be dominated by US-based corporations such as

AMD, Apple, Cisco, Dell, Hewlett-Packard, IBM, Intel, and Oracle – now owner of Sun Microsystems and Java. US-based corporations remained exceptionally strong in computer software and Internet services (including Microsoft, Amazon, Apple, eBay – which owns PayPal – Facebook, Google, and Twitter), nurtured as many of these are by the concentration of talent and capital in San Jose's Silicon valley, California (Boyd-Barrett, 2006).

In the field of Internet and social media by 2013, China's Alibaba – 24% owned by Yahoo! (Yahoo! previously held a 40% stake) and operating through sales platforms Taobao and Tmall – challenged Facebook in terms of market value. Alibaba was assessed at $190 billion as against Facebook's original IPO evaluation of $104 billion. Each company earned around $7 billion annually. Amazon, more directly comparable with Alibaba, earned $61 billion in revenues. The value of merchandise that these companies shifted through their respective advertising and marketing activities stood at $160 billion in the case of Alibaba, well exceeding Amazon ($86 billion) and ebay ($68 billion) (Yu, 2014). In 2013 Alibaba acquired an 18% share in Sina Weibo. Sina Weibo earned most of its revenue from advertising on microblogs, heading towards $176 million in 2013 (Oreskovic and Carsten, 2013). Total revenues for parent Sina Corp were close to $700 million. China's largest Internet earner was Internet portal Tencent, also owner of instant message service WeChat, whose total revenues in 2013 approached $8 billion. Among search engines, China's Baidu struggled towards annual revenues of $4 billion as against Google's $60 billion. While the speed of China's growth on Internet markets was impressive, Chinese Internet influence was more concentrated inside China than the concentration of US competitors within the US market.

China unveiled the world's fastest supercomputer in 2010, but most of its chips and components were built by Intel (USA) and NVIDIA, a US computer animation company. Many experts estimated that China's best chip manufacturers were still two or three generations behind companies like Intel (Shambaugh, 2013: 161). Although China was the world's largest manufacturer of personal computers by 2014, almost all firms manufacturing in that field in China were foreign in origin. Lenovo was the major exception: it bought IBM's worldwide personal computer division in 2010 and was soon China's top-selling computer brand (earning 46.4% of its earnings from China) and the world's third largest vendor of personal computers, with a global market share of 10.4% in 2010 (rising to a 17% share and number one placement of an overall shrinking market by 2014, just ahead of Hewlett Packard). Hit by the 2008 economic recession it focused more on the demand in developing economies, while designing products to counter Apple's iPhone and iPod (Shambaugh, 2013: 199).

China is home to a top telecommunications equipment manufacturer and computer producer, Huawei, which reported revenues of $32bn in 2011 from operations in 140 countries. Shambaugh (2013: 194) finds that its corporate structure and accounting remain opaque: 75% of its revenues come from Asia, Africa and Latin America, and the company supplies many European telecom operators.

Top Internet Service Providers (ISPs) globally in terms of 2012 revenues were US corporations Comcast Cable (7.15%), Road Runner (4.58%), AT+T (2.5%) and Verizon FiOS (2.15%). Global desktop browser markets were dominated by Microsoft's Internet Explorer (55% of the market in 2012), Mozilla's Firefox – affiliated with Time Warner's Netscape (21%), Google's Chrome (17%), and Apple's Safari (5%) (Netmarketshare 2012).

IT GOODS AND SERVICES

In 2014, by far the largest national market for information technology goods and services (government and business spending, excluding corporate tele-communications services and consumer spending) was projected by Forrester Research to remain the USA, accounting for $877.2 billion dollars. Trailing a very long way behind was Japan in second place ($211.4 billion), China in third ($124.5 billion), Britain in fourth ($100.2 billion), and Germany in fifth ($95.6 billion). China's growth over the year was projected at 10.5% over 2013, but it would still be only the third fastest growing market among emerging economies, behind Brazil and Mexico. As a group, China, India, Brazil, Russia, Turkey, South Africa and Mexico would account for 13% of the global technology market in 2014 (Perez, 2014).

WIRELESS

Microsoft has long enjoyed over 90 per cent control of the global desktop operating system market for PCs (91.5% in 2012), followed by Mac (7.3%) and Linux (1.25%) (Netmarketshare, 2012). In the mobile/tablet market, dominant operating systems were Apple's iOS with 61%, followed by Google's Android (28%) and Oracle's Java ME (7%). Google had a global share of over 84% of the desktop search engine market, followed by Yahoo! (8%) and Microsoft's Bing (5%). Google's lead was even stronger in the mobile/tablet market at 91%, followed by Yahoo! (6%) and Bing (2%). In the more diverse world of mobile telephony market share, Nokia, Samsung, LG Electronics and Apple dominated in 2012, and similarly in smartphone manufacture where the dominant names were Nokia (swallowed by Microsoft in 2013), Apple, RIM

(Canadian) and HTC (Taiwanese). Of the top 10 global mobile operators, five were Asian and four were US /West European. But the mobile phone operating systems were dominated by Google's Android (72%) (Android is open source, but substantial revenues are earned from applications that are based on Android), Apple (14%) and Nokia's Symbian (3%) (mobithinking.com).

ADVERTISING

Advertising is fundamentally important because it finances a great deal of media activity: up to three quarters of the revenue earned by US newspapers, for example, over 90% of the revenue earned by US broadcast networks, and approximately 50% of cable television revenues. In addition, visual entertainment in movies and television looks increasingly to product placement to help finance productions. One consequence of media deregulation and privatization globally has been both the proliferation of television channels and the intensification of television's dependence on advertising as a source of revenue. Among new media the sustainability of websites depends increasingly on their ability to host advertisements through proxy brokers – a market in which Google dominates – or to promote their own goods and services. One of the primary drivers of Internet use is the search engine whose revenue is almost entirely based on various forms of advertising. Google is paramount among search engines globally. Increasingly, Google's television arm, YouTube (earning $50 billion by 2013), is seeking to establish its business model on the sale of advertising prior to or during programs. Other core Internet services such as Amazon and eBay are fundamentally in business to sell goods and services.

Advertising provides funding to media institutions for the creation of content. Countries and corporations that attract significant shares of total advertising expenditure have a privileged place on the market and accumulate the capital they need to win in the battle for the attention of users and consumers. Advertising determines which media products will thrive, and therefore whose voices will get to be heard and how loudly. Advertising directly shapes media content. Newspaper content among the wealthier countries of the world chases an essentially middle-class market of households with sufficient disposable income for the purchase of consumer goods. Newspapers fashion their products to attract the markets that are of interest to advertisers. They seek to create a reading environment that is conducive to selling, specifically, and to capitalism, generally. This is the ideology that envelops all those who work within the industry, the one that they live and breathe.

The development of special, niche sections over recent decades for, say, particular demographics (e.g. fashion and shopping for women, sports and finance for men, property and travel for families) has been all about creating innovative product vehicles that will appeal to the needs of advertisers. Creators of television series typically consult with advertisers as – or even before – the series are shot, and even allow advertisers to participate in the process of development so as to make the series' success more probable and to enhance their usefulness to advertisers. Many corporations have established offices in Los Angeles to facilitate their prompt and productive consultation with studios and producers who are seeking product placement income to help support their creations. Advertising shapes content, both in general and in very specific ways. The more advertising that media content carries the more the substance of the content itself is coopted for the purpose of selling goods.

The symbiotic ties of media to advertising are specifically an American invention. It is hardly surprising therefore that more money is earned from advertising in the USA than in any other country in the world. In 2012 it was the single largest beneficiary of advertising expenditure from all forms of advertising at $154.1bn. This was over three times as much as the next largest market, Japan, at $49.9bn, which in turn was considerably ahead of China's $32.3bn, Germany's $25.6bn, the UK's $19.2bn, Brazil's $16.8bn, France's $13.8bn, Australia's $12.8bn, Canada's, $11bn, and South Korea's $10.2bn. (Zenithoptimedia). Relative rankings were not expected to change considerably even by 2014. Indeed, the relative US lead over Japan was projected to increase to $174bn, compared to Japan's $53bn. The value of the US market relative to Japan's would increase from $104.2bn to $121bn. Notwithstanding the heralded rise of China as an economy and as an advertiser, the situation by 2010 was that the USA, accounting for 5% of the world's population and 20% of global GDP, attracted 34% of total worldwide advertising, whereas China, accounting for 20% of the world's population and 13% of global GDP, attracted just 5% of total worldwide advertising (AdAge.com). In regional terms, the North American lead was still considerable in 2011 at $165.1bn, followed by Asia/Pacific at $132.2bn and Western Europe at $108.7bn. The US lead was projected to increase to $186.3bn in 2014 as against $157.2bn for Asia/Pacific and $112.6bn for Western Europe. The US lead over Asia/Pacific was projected to diminish 11.6% from $32.9bn to $29.1bn, whereas, contrasted with Western Europe, the US lead was projected to expand 30.7% from $56.4bn to $73.7bn (Zenithoptimedia). The major medium benefiting from advertising expenditure worldwide in 2011 was television (40%), followed by newspapers (20.2% but projected to decline to 16.8% by 2014), the Internet (16%, projected to increase to 21.4%), magazines (9.4% but projected to decline to 7.9%), radio (7.1% but projected to decline to 6.7%), outdoor advertising (6.6% but projected to decline to 6.3%) and cinema (0.5%).

In the entertainment and media niche, global advertising spending was projected by McKinsey and Company (2013) to reach $473bn by the end of 2013, with $168bn contributed by North America, followed by Asia Pacific ($149bn), Europe, Middle East and Africa ($127bn) and Latin America ($32 bn). Projections for 2017 were for a total of $617bn, with the USA contributing $207bn, followed by $214bn from Asia Pacific, Europe, the Middle East and Africa ($148bn) as well as Latin America ($47bn). McKinsey notes that 63% of the growth in global advertising in the period 2013–2017 would be generated in Latin America, Asia Pacific, and Central and Eastern Europe; however, two of these regions would be starting from a low base.

In terms of consumer media spending a process of flattening does become more apparent, as in 2013 consumer media spending in North America ($271bn) would be outpaced by Asia-Pacific ($369bn) and Europe, the Middle East and Africa ($357bn), but with Latin America ($63bn) still trailing. By 2017 the disparities in consumer media spending would broaden, with Asia Pacific leading ($484bn), followed by Europe, the Middle East and Africa (U$430bn), and North America ($325bn). Broadband was expected to generate the most growth in global consumer media spending. Of a total trillion dollars, McKinsey forecast that in 2013 $390bn would be spent on broadband, followed by $269bn on in-home video, $109bn on consumer and educational books, $75bn on newspapers, $66bn on audio, $64bn on video games, $40bn on consumer magazines, and $35bn on cinema. By 2017, total global expenditure was expected to reach $1.3 trillion dollars, of which broadband would account for $558bn, followed by in-home video ($345bn), consumer and educational books ($108bn), video games ($85.5bn), newspapers ($79bn), audio ($75bn), cinema ($42bn), and consumer magazines ($40bn).

Which industries did all this advertising promote? In 2009, personal care accounted for 24.4% of advertising expenditure worldwide; automotive products 20.3%; food 15.9%; entertainment and media 8.5%. All other categories represented a total of 27.8%. The percentages of this money that were spent in the USA ranged from 22.4% in the case of personal care, to 68.6% in the case of pharmaceuticals.

These figures demonstrate the continuing importance of the US market to the manufacturers of these commodities, and the US market is very likely to influence how the products are promoted. The top global advertisers still invest 39% of their measured-media budgets inside the USA (Ad Age Global

Marketers). Among the 46 of the top 100 marketers in 2009 who were US based, only 12 spent more than half of their expenditure abroad. Among the 54 non-US companies, six spent more than half of their marketing budgets in the USA. The top 30 marketers in 2011 were principally US, West European and Japanese: Proctor and Gamble, Unilever, L'Óreal, General Motors, Nestlé, Coca-Cola, Toyota, Volkswagen, McDonalds, Reckitt Benchiser, Fiat, Kraft Mars, Johnson and Johnson, Ford, Comcast, PepsiCo, Sony, Pfizer, Nissan, PSA Peugeot/Cit, Time Warner, Glaxco, Honda, Disney, Yum (which owns Kentucky Fried Chicken among other things), Ferrero, Danone, Deutsche telekom, and Bierrsdort/Tchibo (which manufactures Nivea, among other things) (Allbrands.com). Their advertising is channeled through five principal advertising, marketing and public relations holding companies which are Dentsu (Japan), earning $14bn in 2012, 50% of it from North America; WPP (UK) earning $16bn, with 33% from North America; Publicis (France), earning $9 bn, 34% from North America; Havas (France), earning $2bn; and Interpublic (USA), earning $7bn, 57% of it from North America.

COPYRIGHTS AND PATENTS

Millien (2010) notes that due "to the lack of legal reporting requirements in the United States (and in most other countries), there are currently no reliable national or international figures that can adequately report the size of the IP marketplace," but the International Monetary Fund (IMF) findings report that the global intellectual property marketplace was worth US $173.4bn in 2009 and in the USA $84.4bn – half of the global total. In 1997 royalties and license fees constituted 29% of overall US trade surplus in services, representing 14% of service exports and only 6% of service imports (US International Trade Commission, 1999).

By 2007 the intellectual property trade accounted for 60% of US exports (totaling $900bn) in a country whose GDP was approaching $14 trillion. The total value of global trade in information and communication technology (ICT) was $4 trillion in 2008 (Slater, 2011). The Internet economy alone amounted to 4.1% of GDP across the G-20 nations ($2.3 trillion) in 2010. Slater (2011) also records that intensive IT-using industries accounted for 25% in GDP and 25% of economic growth, whereas IT-producing industries (semiconductors, computers, communications, software) accounted for 3% of GDP and 25% of economic growth. In 2007, the USA spent 2.67% of its total GDP on R&D, or $374.11bn.

Consulting firm IBISWorld estimated that the 2010 US domestic intellectual property licensing and franchising market alone was valued at $27.5

billion, with 20.3% of that total (or $5.58 bn) attributed to patent and trademark licensing royalty income. Millien (2010) cites the *Economist* (October 22, 2005) for evidence that the broader market of technology licensing accounted for an estimated $45 billion annually; worldwide, the figure was around $100 bn. In 2009, nearly 81% of the value of the companies comprising the S&P 500® stock index came from intangible assets – the largest component of which was IP (Ocean Tomo, cited by Millien, 2010). In 2005 alone IBM was awarded 2,941 US patents, and in 2007 earned about $1bn annually from its portfolio.

ICT INDUSTRIES

Total US revenue for publishing, film and sound recording, telecommunications and Internet industries in 2009 exceeded one trillion dollars. Telecommunications accounted for almost half ($494bn); publishing for a quarter ($264bn), Internet service, web services and data processing less than a tenth ($103bn), broadcasting a little less ($99bn), and motion pictures and sound recording less still ($91bn), with the remainder accounted for by Internet publishing and broadcasting ($20bn) and "other" ($7bn). (US Census Bureau, Statistical Abstract of the United States, 2012: 710).

Global added value of the "knowledge and technology-intensive" industries (KTI) totaled $18.2 trillion in 2010, representing 30% of estimated world GDP. Global value-added by ICT industries (semiconductors, communications equipment, computers, communications, computer programming and data processing) more than doubled from $1.2 trillion in 1995 to $2.8 trillion in 2010 (suggesting that the US contribution to this figure is not less than one half), and that by 2012 the ICT industry accounted for 6% of global GDP (National Science Board, 2012). Of the total, the USA alone accounted for 26%. Asia as a whole, including Japan, China and the "Asia 8" accounted for 33% and Europe 22%. The USA had the highest ICT share of fixed capital investment (26%) among the large OECD economies, with the UK a close second. The USA was the leader in ICT business infrastructure. Half of all global flows in finance, knowledge industries, manufactures, and personnel were accounted for by knowledge industries in 2013, and these were heavily concentrated in the developed economies (McKinsey, 2014).

INTEGRATING WITH GLOBAL CAPITAL

Conventional thinking asserts that US media imperialism peaked long ago, but evidence indicates that it has intensified considerably in recent decades.

In most countries, including those that were formerly Communist (e.g. the former Soviet Union) or countries that still are Communist (including China), together with countries like Britain or France that are social democracies, mainstream television was either highly propagandized or guided by state-regulated or state-governed principles of public service broadcasting. But mostly these have experienced rapid proliferation of television outlets, usually advertising-driven or, increasingly, driven by subscription revenue for multi-channel cable or satellite delivery (expected by ITVE 2010 to have exceeded television advertising worldwide by 2013) and intense commercialization. Commercialization impacts channels that are still ostensibly governed by the logic of public service yet must demonstrate their ability to compete for large audiences so as to justify the state subsidies or state-sanctioned license fees on which they depend.

In India, the apparent profusion of indigenously controlled media since Indian independence and, in particular, since the neoliberal drive towards the deregulation, privatization and commercialization of media occurred in the wake of IMF bailouts in the late 1980s and early 1990s (Thomas, 2010). This masked a profusion of alliances between domestic and international capital, and increased Indian dependence on the vagaries of the global and in particular the US economy. Thomson argues that while liberals hail a flattening of media power in the age of "convergence culture," the evidence points to greater inter-linkage between Indian and global enterprise in the domestic entertainment and media market, together with more intense market concentration and tiered ownership. India's entertainment and information media have been concentrated into conglomerates (such as Bennett Coleman, owner of the Times Group; Ananda Bazar Patrika; News Corporation's Star Network – which also holds 20% of Tata Sky; Infosys – the largest software exporter in India; the Sun TV Network – supporter of the regional Tamil party DMK in Southern India; Ramoji Rao, supporter of the Telugu Desam Party in Andhra Pradesh; Network 18; HT Media; Zee; and Reliance Adlabs). These have had close ties, variously, with plutocratic families (including the Tatas, Birlas, Goenkas), real estate (including the Alliance Group, Hathway, Maytas Properties), political parties, politicians, and even criminal elements.

Thomas is skeptical of the quality of the "flattening" that is alleged to have occurred: " … the structuration of international economics and politics remains key to the understanding of a global and local political economy of communications." The Indian animation industry, for example, is basically an off-shore outshoot of the dominant animation industries associated with Hollywood which knows that costs per film may be only one seventh in India as in the USA. In telecommunications, major Indian companies, faced with a raft of problems such as the deterioration of cell phone services, mismanagement of spectrum, a lack of investment in value added services, clumsy regulation etc., are trying to sell equity to foreign investors. Indian software outsourcing has merely strengthened links between the center and periphery, tying software hubs to the export markets.

What this amounts to, in the context of television, is the global extension of a model of broadcast regulation that was developed in the USA and ratified by Congressional legislation in the 1930s, and whose primary characteristic was the free distribution of publicly owned airwaves to the capitalist enterprises who could best show means and intent to exploit them for the purposes of making money through the sale of advertising. By common consent this model has tended to produce cheap television that is entertainment driven or, when dealing with news and real world events, seeks to entertain more than inform (infotainment). It is formulaic, undemanding, repetitive, and easily manipulated for state and capital propaganda. Its primary purpose was and continues to be to capture audience attention for as long as possible and, in effect, to sell that attention to advertisers.

The global extension of this model is hardly a matter of mere academic interest. Broadcasting has been the single most important source of popular information throughout most of this period, yet the substance and quality of that information in terms of its suitability as a basis for considered action – as would be required in a properly functioning democracy – are abysmal by almost any standard. By 2010 the subscription-driven paid television market, primarily cable and satellite, had begun to draw level with that of the advertising-based market. But this too was a form of television that originated mainly out of the USA and was driven by US telecommunications and television industry interests, including big corporate names such as AT&T, Comcast and Time Warner.

Pay television is not antithetical to advertising: the most watched channels on pay television in the USA are the major networks and their local affiliates which carry abundant advertising as do many channels made solely for cable and satellite distribution, including shopping channels. The business genius of pay television is that it has persuaded consumers to spend far more on television services than they once did in return for a greater multiplicity of channels (although using compression technology these could now be provided terrestrially if desired) – an average of 118 in 2008 – even though most viewers regularly watch only a very small cluster (16 or 13% on average). This had led to an overall increase in US adult viewing time from around four hours a day in 1988 to five hours a day in 2011 – more than any other nation (Television Bureau of Advertising, 2012), even before factoring in cellphone and computer viewing. This in turn is indicative of additional exposure to advertising. The arrival of digital television, which has penetrated the USA (83% in 2010) to a far greater degree than in other world regions, has merely amplified these features, enhancing the flexibility of individual access to programming.

Critics of media imperialism routinely take earlier proponents of media imperialism to task for their apparently simplistic fears of a monolithic US dominance of television worldwide. Yet that is precisely what has happened, not in the form of television products imported from the USA (although by far the strongest leaders of television program format sales worldwide are the UK and USA, followed some way behind by the Netherlands [ITVE, 2010]), but in the form of the global adoption of an approach to television that was invented by US media corporations and that in many countries looks rather like US television – soap operas, celebrity features, reality shows, game shows, US news formatting, heavy presence of advertised global brands, and so on.

Critics of the earlier proponents of media imperialism are equally scathing about fears of the cultural and other consequences of a putative US-based television universe. They justified their ridicule with references to ethnographically-based reception studies that demonstrated, quite reasonably, there is rarely any such thing as a hypodermic needle model of media "effect," and that through processes such as selective attention, perception and retention (Klapper 1960), television is more likely to reinforce existing attitudes than to change them. This is an important and complex debate, yet we should not overlook how, since it began, global space and time have contracted, largely because of US and western-dominated systems of communications hardware and software, and that the officially enshrined values of the largest economies of the world (principally the USA, followed by Europe, the former Soviet Union, India, China, Brazil, Indonesia) look every day more similar, and more like the values propelled by US elites and associated with the philosophy of neoliberalism: a philosophy of the "free" market executed through unregulated monopolistic or oligopolistic capitalist production and exchange, consumerism and individualism. These values make little sense on even the most fundamental of criteria – sustainability. With accelerating speed they are destroying the planet through global warming, the exhaustion and pollution of world resources including its earth, forests, rivers and oceans, and the annihilation of a substantial proportion of all living species. We need pay little heed to the hypocrisy with which these values are celebrated by capitalists who prefer monopoly and oligopoly to competition, and whose own scandals, criminality and incompetence (as in the crisis of the global financial and banking system that erupted in 2008 and continues unabated, or even intensified, into 2014) are assuaged by the egregious state generosity of a system of socialism-for-the-rich that they control. They preach free capital flow yet resist freedom for the international movement for labor, and apply intense pressure on smaller nations to open up their markets while protecting their own domestic producers in agriculture and other favored domains. What is most important and significant here is that every day the lords of the major economies of the world, dancing to the music of "freedom" while subjecting their populations to intensive surveillance and control, converge upon an ideology of the "free" market while continuing to indulge protectionist hypocrisies in practice.

CONCLUSION

Some critics of media imperialism have seemed oblivious to the original connections identified by scholars such as Harold Innis (2007 [1950]), Marshall McLuhan (1967) and Herbert Schiller (1992 [1969]) (ideologically different though they were), and picked up on by Daya Thussu (2006) in his textbook on *International Communication*, between the rise of new media forms and the emergence, shaping and consolidation of empires. Schiller (1992 [1969]) was among the first to integrate the analysis of media hardware (including satellite) and software (both manifest content and advertising) with the various economic and political needs of the United States for industrial growth at home, the penetration of foreign markets and the consolidation of superpower status. While not so often explored with specific homage to concepts such as media imperialism, many scholars have continued to explore these connections in the strong parallelism between media representations of the world and the foreign policies of their home governments. Others have considered the case of global media such as the international news agencies or international 24-hour television news channels in the context of the formation of a globalized mediatized ideology of neo-liberal deregulated global capitalism. Additionally there are national media that also enjoy a considerable international following, where these are found to serve as conduits of propaganda on behalf, variously, of their home governments specifically, or in more cases than not of a generalized neoliberal commercial, corporate and financial world order.

Theories of agenda-setting (Weaver et al., 1997), framing (Entman, 2003), indexing (Bennett et al., 2008), hierarchy-of-influences (Shoemaker and Reese, 1995) and the "propaganda model" (Herman and Chomsky, 2002 [1988]) significantly converge in their relevance here, even when they do not reference one another. Media scholars are confronted with the challenge of unpicking the ways in which mainstream and alternative me across all modes or platforms, "frame" stories to align with particular interests. Much of this activity justifiably falls within the context of discourses of imperialism, especially in countries or regions, as in Central and South America, Iraq, Iran, Libya, North Africa, Pakistan or Palestine, that have long been subject to the depredations, intimidations, and manipulations of hegemonic power and imperial ambition.

Several scholars have concentrated on ways of thinking about cross-cultural media flows that do not seem so much dependent on relations of power but foreground mid-range variables such as geographical, cultural and linguistic proximity and cultural discount (see Sinclair et al., 1996). Ultimately these confirm the vitality of regional and local centers of media influence but they do not undermine the significance of the continued exertion of media influence on local or regional centers from imperial or ex-imperial powers. Relating to Castells' (2000) proposition of a new world order that is definable in terms of networks, Straubhaar's (2007) research has contributed sophistication to our understanding of media flows, acknowledging the co-existence of several different kinds of flow including classic unidirectional flows from more to less powerful countries. His work also reasserts a persistent criticism of media imperialism theories, namely the relative absence of sophisticated audience/reception research and of the role of "active" viewing or reading. While this is a key charge, media are significant not simply because they might or might not have been persuasive in the ways that producers intended or that interpreters may fear or suspect. They also represent a resource of "media space." When this is commandeered by a small number of voices, there is less space, time and opportunity for others to give voice and be listened to. A form of media imperialism is in play. One can question whether critics can afford to be sanguine in their presumptions about the inherent democracy of individual "meaning-making." Newer iterations of media effects, reception, uses and gratifications research demonstrate the powerful influences that mainstream media texts exert, and whose constructions of reality are socially validated by the prevailing coalition of power in any society on the grounds of their presumed "authoritativeness" and "detachment."

The passion for social justice that inspired the original theories of media and cultural imperialism has been enveloped by a newer generation of critical post-colonial assessment of so-called processes of globalization. Some contributions deepen our appreciation of ideas of culture in relation, particularly, to formal ideologies of the nation state, ethnicity and identity (Appadurai, 1992). They have helped expose the complexity of relations between the ▸bal, national and local (sometimes prematurely understating or even 'dis-▸aring' the nation state – see Sparks, 2007), and through the use of

its close allies, as well as the mainstream media of many of the more servile states, support, by omission or commission, the status and strategies of the imperial power. Another, not unrelated, has to do with inequalities between media systems of different nation states and the variable subjection of some media systems to the interests and strategies of the media systems of more powerful nations. For this latter form, I have referenced, as examples, the market penetration of less powerful countries by the media of more powerful countries, without proportionate reciprocation of influence, and the dominating influence of certain media of the most powerful countries on the media framing of issues in some or most other countries. As discussed in Chapter 8, these examples have included the global news agencies based in North America and Western Europe, "Hollywood," the recording industry, the advertising industry, and many areas of the new information and communication technologies, from hardware (e.g. satellites, computer servers, cable desk-top boxes) to software (e.g. Internet search engines and browsers, social media). Some of this influence may appear to have declined in proportion to the market activity of local or regional corporations, but in 2014 the USA still represents the single largest concentration of communications capital in the world. This has been extensively leveraged for the purposes of political, economic and military surveillance, control and profit.

Gradations of media power exist not just between major and smaller powers, but also between middle-sized powers and smaller powers. Tunstall (2007) notes that this is particularly true of small-population countries whose markets are not sufficiently viable to enable them to compete with larger, foreign corporations, the costs of whose products might already have been recovered from their domestic markets and who can benefit from economies of scale unavailable to local companies. Unequal advantage may be intensified where the countries in question share geographical and/or cultural/linguistic proximity.

Approaching the issue of "other media imperialisms" I identify a variety of different – though not mutually exclusive, nor exhaustive – manifestations. The development of media empires can be defensive as well as offensive, and not infrequently a mixture. The development of Chinese media soft power, for example, is both about buffering the sovereignty of China from western media penetration and about exercising a cultural influence on the world that is commensurate with China's political and economic power. The line between "other media imperialisms" and efforts to *resist* the media imperialism of global or regional hegemons is sometimes fuzzy.

THE POST-IMPERIAL MODEL

This model is represented, among others, by the United Kingdom (UK), France, Spain and, of course, the USA, all of whom enjoy a significant media presence not only in the media markets of countries that were once their colonies, but also regionally and worldwide. These countries host many of the world's major global media conglomerates. To their list Japan should be included, ranking as an ex-imperial power whose economy was resuscitated under US supervision following its military defeat in 1945, and which is host to Sony.

Post-Soviet Russia exercises substantial media influence in the former Soviet territories, especially those with significant Russian-language speaking populations. As outlined in a survey by David Satter, this includes the strong presence of Russian-owned television station PBK – a high proportion of whose content comes from Russia's Channel One and REN networks – and the website regnum.ru – in the Baltic states (Satter, 2014). PBK is viewed by four million people. It has contributed to the campaign against energy independence in Lithuania, and supports the Centre Party in Estonia. A former PBK news editor became mayor of Riga, capital of Latvia. In the Ukraine, up until the 2014 western-backed coup, major Russian television channels were available on cable networks. Russian interests helped to engineer the centralization of control over the Ukrainian press. Russian media such as Channel One, Rossiya and NTV dominate the media of Belarus, and have supported Russian interests in their critical coverage of President Lukashenko. Likewise, Russian media dominate in Moldova. Other countries exposed to significant Russian media influence include Armenia, which enjoys close ties with its former Soviet hegemon. In Kyrgyzstan some ten Russian television channels are available, and Russian media collaborated in a campaign to unseat Presdient Bakiyev over his support for an American air base in Manas. In Kazakhstan, 50% of the population view Russian television, and a strong majority of all periodicals are in Russian.

The UK is a significant center of media production and export activity, especially in the fields of film, radio and television entertainment and news, and in newspaper, magazine and book publishing and, not least, digital content. This gives UK producers access to the media systems and cultures of many other countries. This is in some cases substantial and the UK thereby acquires a privileged "voice" in the realm of communications space. The UK's export success relates to its status as an ex-imperial power (once the world's largest) with extensive, continuing political, cultural and economic ties with many countries around the world, and to the fact that most of its products are in English, which has come to dominate international diplomacy and commerce and which is also the language, or one of the official languages, of several other major centers of media consumption, including the USA, India, Australia and New Zealand. The principal overall motivation for its media production is directly economic, to make a profit through sales and advertising, but this economic benefit is widely acknowledged to have political or "soft power" value, helping to cultivate positive images of the UK, its political system and culture, and also of its capacity for allegedly impartial news reporting, in other countries.

Take Reuters: the for-profit global news agency serves wholesale general print, television and online news services to news media worldwide, and economic and financial news to corporations, brokers, banks and investors. Headquartered in London since its inception in 1850 this is still the company's preeminent news center, although in 2008 it was acquired by Thomson to become Thomson Reuters, a Canadian-owned company headquartered in New York, and quoted on the Toronto and New York stock exchanges. Its global strength is rivaled only by Bloomberg, which is both an economic and general news agency, headquartered in New York. Thomson and Bloomberg are far stronger, financially, than the other two major international news agencies, Associated Press (AP)(USA) and Agence France Presse (AFP) (France). Through Reuters, the UK has shaped global ideas as to what is important in news. In periods of war (including World Wars One and Two), and in post-war periods of crisis, Reuters was co-opted in various ways into British imperial propaganda strategy, although for some decades it has been safe to regard Reuters first and foremost as an entrepreneurial enterprise that has incidentally yielded "soft power" benefits to Britain. In some cases, notably that of the BBC, we can say that the reverse relationship obtained, namely that the BBC's external or overseas services were originally intended to serve a "soft power" function for British interests, both political and economic, and that this success in "soft power" contributed to the development of for-profit activity as in the case of BBC Worldwide, which today shares with CNN the status of being one of the world's two strongest international broadcasters.

STRONG-WEAK MEDIA MARKET MODEL (UNITED KINGDOM AND IRELAND)

The strong-weak media market relationship has long been true of relations between the UK and its one-time colony – part of it still colonized – Ireland. This model exemplifies the inequality of media relations between any given two countries, but needs refinement on at least three counts. Firstly, "invading" media systems are often also active not just in their country of origin, but also in other parts of the world – they rank among global media conglomerates and might be considered global media imperialists in their own right. In the case of Ireland even the "invaded" camp can boast one such conglomerate. Secondly, the model highlights the symbiotic character of the dependence of the domestic media system on the media system of another country, but the media entities of both "invading" and "invaded" countries may themselves depend on media imports from other countries. In both Britain and Ireland, for example, Hollywood movies command far greater revenues at the box-office than do domestic film industries, their television systems consume significant quantities of product from the USA, and their computing and online markets are significantly Americanized through corporations such as Apple, eBay, Facebook, Google and Microsoft. Thirdly, the transnational dimension of media inequalities should not be considered intrinsically or necessarily more significant than phenomena of domestic media imperialism which occurs wherever – and this applies to most countries of the world – domestic media markets show evidence of monopoly, oligopoly, or severe concentration of ownership. In a globalized world, media imperialism is is about the colonization of consciousness both within and across national boundaries.

Following the limited home rule established in the Irish Free State (1922–1937) following the War of Independence, an early historian of the Irish press (Brown, 1937) commented that "the British press constitutes a perpetual menace to Ireland owing to its wide diffusion in this country." In the early 2000s, a third of the daily newspapers sold in Ireland were British. These were mainly controlled by (1) the News International group – owner of the *Irish Star*, the *Irish News of the World*, and the *Sunday Times*; (2) Associated News, owner of *Ireland on Sunday*, and *Metro Ireland*, (3) Trinity Mirror, owner of the *Irish Daily Mirror*, *Irish Sunday Mirror* and *People*. English or Scottish regional newspaper groups also operated in Ireland; these included the Johnston Press, Scottish Radio Holdings, Dunfermline Press, and Alpha Group Newspapers. The share of national readership controlled by British newspapers was increasing rapidly, facilitated in some cases by price wars that Irish newspapers were unable to withstand. Having much smaller markets than their British rivals, Irish newspapers typically cost more. British influence extended beyond mere ownership to affect the business model and style, reflected in the tabloidization that has afflicted both British and Irish newspapers, a trend that is especially compelling because Irish "quality" papers are very constrained in circulation size.

The Irish case highlights the danger of identifying media imperialism solely in turns of domestic autonomy and foreign invasion. At the root of media imperialism lie anxieties about limits on the potential diversity of voices in the media. Foreign-owned media are hardly the only threats. As have many countries Ireland has experienced intensifying consolidation of ownership and control across both domestic and foreign media: 60% of daily newspaper sales in Ireland in the early 2000s were controlled by Murdoch's NewsCorp, owner of the *Irish Sun*, and by Irish media magnate Tony O'Reilly, owner of the Independent group, which also owned the *Belfast Telegraph* and, like NewsCorp, is a global media conglomerate.

Domestic concentration presents a challenge to diversity hardly less worrying than its foreign equivalent. Even following the establishment of state television broadcaster RTE in 1960, Ireland was subject to considerable influence from the overspill of BBC signals from both England and Northern Ireland. The British influence has not disappeared but it has fractured with the privatization of television in both Britain and Ireland and with the introduction of cable and satellite broadcasting. More than half of Irish households subscribe to multichannel television networks. Today, the BBC and British independent terrestrial and satellite channels account for 20% of total viewing. At least a similar proportion is accounted for by channels from other foreign sources (Mercereau, 2005).

STRONG-WEAK MEDIA MARKET MODEL (AUSTRALIA AND NEW ZEALAND)

New Zealand's media are heavily penetrated by Australia's media, primarily. A 2011 report (Myllylahti, 2011: 1) concluded that "New Zealand media companies are increasingly dominated by global and pan-regional media corporations and ... are vulnerable to commercial and shareholder pressures" with declining government financial support for public service media, even as government finance has bailed out a privately owned media conglomerate, MediaWorks. The situation had not changed considerably since a similar report in 2008 (Rosenburg, 2008) which concluded that New Zealand media were essentially controlled by four corporations, all of them foreign owned by a mixture of international financial institutions and media moguls, namely: APN News and Media, whose largest shareholder was the Irish Independent News and Media group, associated with Tony O'Reilly; Fairfax Media (Australian), in which Australian billionaire Gina Rinehart held a modest stake; MediaWorks (owned by an Australian investment group Ironbridge); and NewsCorporation/Sky (USA), associated with Rupert Murdoch.

New Zealand retains a substantial free-to-air television service, now managed by Freeview. This carries government-owned channels of

Television New Zealand, 90% of whose funds are commercially generated. The government lifted the charter obligations on TVNZ in 2008 to encourage reliance on advertising and payment of a dividend to the government. At the same time it closed down public service channels TVNZ7 – a public 24-hour television service – and TVNZ6, which was sold to a commercial, advertising-driven enterprise called U. Freeview also transmits public service Radio New Zealand, and Maori Television, as well as the Australian owned Ironbridge, owner of MediaWorks. MediaWorks is owned by Ironbridge Capital – a group of Australian investors – and in turn owns TV3, C4 and 10 radio networks. The company went into receivership in 2013. Australian Provincial Newspapers (APN News and Media Ltd) is part owned by Irish group Independent News and Media, and owns six New Zealand newspapers, including the *New Zealand Herald* and the *Herald on Sunday*, as well as eight radio networks. The Radio Network is a division of the Australia Radio Network, which in turn is a partnership between Clear Channel (of the USA) and APN News and Media Ltd, and owns eight radio networks in New Zealand and 100 radio stations. A major shareholder in Sky from 1987 to 2013 was NewsCorp. NewsCorp sold its 44% holding in 2013. Sky enjoyed a monopoly in subscription television services, reaching 53% of the New Zealand population in 2011. It owns Prime TV, and a low-cost television service, Igloo, in partnership with TV New Zealand, along with 14 mobile television channels through Vodafone. Fairfax New Zealand Ltd is owned by Australia's Fairfax Media, and runs more than 70 newspapers in New Zealand.

The heavy Australian representation in the New Zealand newspaper industry coupled with long-standing rivalry between the newspaper interests of Fairfax and APN, destabilized New Zealand's 130-year-old cooperatively owned national news agency, the New Zealand Press Association (NZPA), which closed its doors in 2011. Fairfax had owned 60% of NZPA, APN 40%. The rival conglomerates came to view NZPA as a competitor to their proprietorial, commercial news services. Three different services emerged to replace NZPA, all of them foreign owned: APN News and Media's APNZ, New Zealand Newswire (owned by the Australian Associated Press, AAP), and Fairfax New Zealand News (FNZN).

PAN-REGIONAL MODEL (ARAB WORLD)

Intensifying privatization and commercialization of media has placed a premium on regional media production so as to capitalize on economies of scale in regions that share a common language and/or culture. This applies to the 17 national markets of the Arab World.

Major media of the Arab World in 2011, measured by advertising revenue (worth $1.8billion in television), were television (40% of expenditure) and the press (31%) with digital expenditure rising to 10%. The dominant medium was free-to-air television (of which terrestrial constituted 38% and satellite 63%), through 540 channels: nearly half was accounted for by three countries, Egypt (18%), Saudi Arabia (17%), and the UAE (14%).

The region is characterized by high interest in local (national) content, in a market of which some 50% of the audience is aged 25 or under. But producers are more interested in supplying pan-Arab content even if this requires some tailoring for local markets. The region therefore combines a high incidence of pan-regional programming, significant importation from outside of the region, growth in local production, and local concentration.

The report of the *Arab Media World* for 2012 (p. 9) notes that "imports continue to dominate the Arab television landscape in terms of audience with Turkish series as popular as ever and with the success of local versions of international talent shows such as Arab Idol." A Saudi platform, MBC, accounted for 16 out of the 40 most popular channels watched in four markets (Egypt, Morocco, Saudi Arabia, the UAE), followed by Qatar's Al Jazeera (3), and Saudi Arabia's Rotana Cinema. In Saudi Arabia, MBC accounted for Nos. 1, 3, 5, 6 and 9 of the ten most popular channels; whereas in Egypt, Egyptian Al Hayat accounted for Nos. 1, 2, 3 and 5 of the most watched channels.

In the Pay-TV market (accounting for 22% of total advertising revenues in 2011) dominant suppliers included western-focused OSN (representing a merger between US-based Orbit and Showtime platforms), with 45% of the market in Egypt, 11% in the UAE, 19% in Kuwait; and Al Jazeera Sport (accounting for 26% of sales in Egypt, 64% in Morocco, 14% in the UAE, and 57% in Kuwait). Sports dominate Pan-Arabic Pay-TV (63% to 93%). Additionally there is a high rate of piracy; 50% of pirated movies come from major US studios.

In sports broadcasting, the logic of monetization favors international leagues, especially in Egypt and the Lebanon. Pan-Arabic broadcasting dominates the preferred channel list in major markets such as the UAE, Morocco and Saudi Arabia, although local is preferred in populous Egypt, which is the region's strongest producer. Among magazines, women's accounted for 75% of total sales of which a strong majority (47%) were for Pan-Arabic audiences. The report notes a rising number of joint ventures between regional and international groups, including News Corp's investment in *Rotana* (owning 15%); the BBC's Arabic version of *Question Time*;

Sky News Arabia; and Sony Pictures Television's Arab language versions of its popular US productions.

The most prominent international influences in television arrive in the form of licensed formats, accounting for 24% of reality series in the region, dubbed content (especially in the case of Turkey's *Nour*, provided by MBC and whose popularity is helped by being dubbed in colloquial Syrian Arabic, and the Arab version of TBS's *Cartoon Network Arab*). In movies, regional film production is concentrated in Egypt. Quotas have helped contain the pressure of imports from Hollywood and Bollywood.

International penetration is further extended by new media: 78% of the Saudi market has bought into foreign importation of laptops, 68% of smartphones, 48% of desktops PCs, and 15% of tablets, Smart or computer TV. Facebook had signed up 54% of the population in the UAE, 38% in Qatar, 34% in Kuwait, and 33% in Lebanon. Facebook and Twitter dominated the social media landscape. These two sites alone drove significant traffic to regional content websites such as *Al Arabia.Net*, *Vodafone Qatar*, *Koora.com*, and *Nawras*. Google was easily the most preferred search engine. Between them, Google and Yahoo! accounted for 83% of online search. Yahoo! also owned *Maktoob*, a popular online portal in Algeria. Major pan-regional online portals included Egyptian *Koora.com* for sports, Jordanian-backed *Souq.com*, Qatar-backed *Al Jazeera.nt* and *Maktoob.con*. The smartphone market was dominated by Nokia, Apple iPhone, REM-Blackberry, Samsung and HTC. The strongest regional advertising agency, Flip Media, had been acquired by the Number 2 of the three global advertising and marketing behemoths: Publicis.

PAN-REGIONALISM AND THE "KOREAN WAVE"

The Korean Wave (or "Hallyu") emerged from the late 1990s and is sometimes also cited as a successful application of "soft power" (see below). The term denotes South Korean exports of popular culture products, principally to other Asian countries including Japan, China, Taiwan, Hong Kong, and Singapore, as well as further afield (Kim, 2013) and to the Korean diaspora in Europe, North America and elsewhere. Sung (2013a: 135) notes that although the Korean Wave has reached international audiences around the world, "its main consumers are East Asians, who create a transnational consumer group and play a significant role in circulating the Korean Wave in various local settings." It may be regarded, Kim (2013a: 15) argues, as a "counterweight to Western cultural influence," a mixture of regional hegemony that co-exists with Western media domination and unequal power relations and even with an intensification of US influence "through the flows of cultural products and capital in the form of joint ventures, direct investment and program affiliations" (Kim, 2013: 16). Iwabuchi (2013: 50) advises that the "rise of East Asian media cultures does not fundamentally challenge West-centered power configurations but has been formulated under and incorporated into imbalanced globalization processes." With reference to films and online gaming, Jin (2013: 148) argues that these two genres have "vehemently developed hybridization strategies" through production, storytelling, special effects, and hiring local staffs to adopt local cultural taste.

The Korean Wave concept indicates intra-regional, multidirectional flows and the remaking of successful TV dramas and films from other parts of East Asia including Japanese, Korean, Hong Kong and Taiwanese texts (Iwabuchi, 2013). The hybridization of cultural products creates new spaces and resources for new constructions of identity that also penetrate, to varying degrees, hegemonic markets. But the Korean Wave may also be regarded as a form of cultural nationalism that "can ironically generate a new version of cultural imperialism that is deeply embedded in cultural nationalism and its ideological position going against cultural diversity and soft power of attraction" (Nye and Kim, 2013: 41). Iwabuchi (2013: 50) notes that

> the kinds of media texts that are promoted to circulate are chiefly commercially and ideologically hegemonic ones in each country, which tend not to well represent socio-culturally marginalized voices within the nation (except those of tokenized multicultural commodities).

Yet they satisfy what Kim (2013b: 86–7) identifies as "Asia's yearning for an independent cultural force, a particular speaking position in the struggle for national cultural identity amidst the threatening presence of the mediated space of the West now that the borders of the nation are becoming increasingly vulnerable to Western hegemony of globalization." An alternative view is provided by Suk-Young Kim (2013) whose analysis of *Boys Over Flowers* suggests that Korean Wave texts also serve to normalize, positively valorize and commercialize (through product placement) the neoliberal, materialist removal of restraints on corporate power, and the concomitant reduction of state power, the subordination of social relationships to the plutocratic acquisition of wealth, and submission to class and wealth inequalities.

Development of the Korean Wave was aided by satellite broadcasting in the 1990s and, increasingly, by social networking and video-sharing websites in the 2000s and 2010s. Through YouTube the US corporate giant Google has become a central facilitator in the spread of the Korean Wave

(Ono and Kwon, 2013). YouTube created a K-pop genre in the music category, the first to be created for a particular country. It reinforced the visuality of K-pop and greatly eased downloading, making possible inexpensive broad audience consumption with an easy-to-use search engine and an interlink with Google. Major South Korean companies such as SM Entertainment and YG Entertainment opened and operated YouTube channels. YouTube allowed users to post comments and build virtual fan communities.

The economic value, domestic and international, of the Korean Wave was expected to increase from $10 billion in 2012 to $57 billion in 2020 (Kim, 2002). As production has increased Korean dependence on imports has diminished, with domestic films capturing 64% of the domestic market in 2006. But this dropped to 52% by 2011 in the wake of South Korea's 2006 free trade agreement with the USA. Major export products have included:

- *TV dramas* (accounting for $252 million in export earnings in 2011) such as *Winter Sonata* (2002), *Jewel in the Palace* (2003) and *Boys Over Flowers* (2009). Principal export markets for these dramas in 2004 were Taiwan (20.5%), Japan (19%), China (19%), and Hong Kong (3%).
- *K-Pop Music*, whose export value reached $177 million in 2011, this being described by Kim (2013: 8) as a "deliberately planned industry targeting international audiences from the start" and marketed through digital communication networks. K-pop stars' musical-visual presentations for the Western market often conform to the "dominant notions of Asian-ness in their racial and sexual identities and try too hard" (Kim, 2013: 21).
- *Korean films*, whose export value reached $76 million in 2005 but then began to decline rapidly, staging a modest recovery to $15.8 million in 2011. Jin (2013) observes that the top 10 domestic Korean films each year are mostly commercial and hybrid, increasingly shifting from dramas to commercially successful Hollywood genre movies that respond to economic imperatives rather than dealing with serious social issues or national values, and are less concerned with ordinary people's lives and struggles. Yin (2013: 155) concludes that "Hollywood films as global standards reign supreme, while a local cinema primarily tries to copy or follow what Hollywood has done." A great deal of South Korean cultural produce therefore has been described as hybridized or pastiche versions of Hollywood or western commercialized media culture. Indeed Korean popular culture is not really Korean but a hybrid mix of influences whose purpose is to sell internationally. Kim (2013) cites criticisms of Korean movies that they are simply versions of Hollywood

blockbusters, focusing on violence and sexuality, although many Korean filmmakers have "blended Hollywood styles and genres with characteristically Korean stories and themes" (Kim, 2013: 11).

- *Online games*, are by far the greatest economic success story of the Korean Wave, and by far the most global (with significant penetration of North America and Europe as well as Asia) in so far as cultural products are concerned (although the success of Korean telecommunications and electronics companies, notably that of Samsung, is far greater), reaching $2.1 billion in 2011. Online gaming accounted for 97.6% of Korean gaming industry exports in 2010: rather than competing with the established console industry, South Korea concentrated on online gaming, notably the massively multiplayer online role-playing games (MMORPGS) and casual games. Many MMORPGS, notes Jin (2013: 156), are based on traditional fantasy themes, while others utilize hybrid themes and genres that "merge fantasy components with those of sword and sorcery and science fiction ... Several online games have relied on Western storylines; however, publishers and developers have melded them with Korean mentalities in producing games ... Local game corporations have also strategically adopted borderless storytelling and backgrounds to attract Western gamers as well as game users in their country." Jin further concludes (2013: 161) that "hybridization does not always lead to equal cultural exchange ... meaning the global flow of cultural products remains uneven and markedly one-sided in favor of Western popular culture and cultural products. Many foreign-based corporations have invested in the Korean game market while Korean developers have opened development studios, employing local developers, in Europe and the USA to help them penetrate American and European markets."

Nye and Kim (2013: 39) describe the Korean Wave as a "pronounced example of a crossover of culture and economy, and the commercialization of culture through nation branding, taking a neoliberal capitalist approach in the era of globalization." Its idols are often chosen as "commodity representatives of Korean brands, helping Korean trademarks to become more fashionable, cool image products through constant product placement and idol promotion."

It is uncertain, even unlikely, that Korean Wave products increase understanding of South Korea, its actual conditions and socio-political issues, or do much to counter hegemonic stereotypes, given that these products even reinforce these stereotypes in a bid for international consumption. Exportation does not necessarily enhance reciprocal flows (e.g. of cultural products from neighboring East Asian nations). Kim (2013a: 39) notes that it is overwhelmingly Korean and Japanese popular cultures that have entered the rest of East Asia, with little flow in the reverse direction. Impacts have not always been as significant or as positive as government and corporate policies have intended. Kim cites instances of Japanese and Taiwanese protests against "excessive" broadcasting of South Korean television dramas (whose regional success was partly boosted by their low prices relative to those of Japanese products). Despite YouTube's success with Psy's Gangnam Style music video in 2012, which reached a billion views within six months of posting, K-pop success has been less than overwhelming in the prized US market (Jung, 2013) and K-pop singers have been unable to overcome the "entanglements of race and sexuality in the popular imagination" (Jung, 2013: 107).

THE SOFT POWER MODEL

The term "soft power" has a broad application and media are generally regarded as a significant sphere for the exercise of soft power. The term was coined by Joseph Nye (1991) and has much in common with what Jowett and O'Donnell (2011) identify as "facilitative propaganda," in reference to actions that are intended to be of value to others but also have as their fundamental purpose the creation of a generalized good feeling towards a country, institution or person. This good feeling becomes a resource that may be leveraged for specific purposes in the short- or long-term future.

Nye is a former dean of the John F. Kennedy School of Government at Harvard, and a co-founder with Robert Keohane in 1977 of the International Relations theory of neoliberalism. Among many prestigious positions, he was chairman of the National Intelligence Council, 1993–1994. While his interest in and preference for peaceful solutions to international conflict would mark him as a liberal, his thinking is in many ways orthodox, not to say Conservative. His vision as to what is good or bad in the world is shaped significantly by what is in the interests of the USA. His concept of soft power has been referenced by world leaders, including Chinese premier Hu Jintao and US Defense Secretary Robert Gates. It has also been seized upon in some areas of international media studies. It presents an acceptable and diplomatic way of talking about international media relations without the negative labeling that is associated with the term "propaganda."

Nye sees soft power as a way of "getting others to want the outcomes you want" without coercion or bribery, and as a form of influence that can be exerted by all actors in international affairs including states, NGOs and international institutions. It is a way of "setting the agenda" for others as to what is important and what should be done about it. It belongs to discourses in political science on the asymmetrical and complex interdependence between nations (perhaps more nuanced but also more deceptive than the term "imperialism"). It has to do, fundamentally, with the strategic molding of international perceptions of (a) one's culture as a way of life that is attractive, (b) one's political values that are equally attractive, often relating to ideas of democracy, human rights and individual opportunities, and (c) foreign policies.

Use of the term excites the suspicion that this is simply a fashionable code for propaganda or for what the US military dubs "perception management." Some of the theory's key concepts, such as that of international perception, are highly volatile and difficult to measure or can only be measured by fairly crude polling methodologies. Whatever can be concluded from such measurements is limited, given that different sectors of an aggregate population can be attracted or repelled by different things. As a tool of government, soft power is hardly precise, since its effects cannot be controlled with certainty. Furthermore it is often difficult to disassociate soft power from hard power. Can it be any surprise that the leading protagonists of soft power are rated (by Monacle) with the UK in first place, and the USA in second? The widespread exercise of soft power mainly appears characteristic of nations that have acquired considerable coercive strength and who may calculate that their policies will appear more palatable in the absence of reminders of that strength.

In this book I have been wary of the concept of soft power. It encompasses much more than merely the media, for one thing. For another, much of my attention has focused on media complicity with the hard power of US imperialism, the media essentially acting as soft power advocates of hard power policies. Since the logic of US imperialism has evolved towards a form of leadership of the global system of economic neoliberalism and on behalf of the plutocratic and giant corporate interests that the system represents, to talk of soft power is to engage in a form of euphemistic discourse which is part of the propaganda strategy of which soft power is a part. Of somewhat greater interest is the adoption of discourses of soft power by nations that are growing in their overall global clout yet for whom the exercise or threat of hard power is impractical or inadvisable.

THE SOFT POWER MODEL (XINHUA, NATIONAL NEWS AGENCY OF CHINA)

The concept of soft power was used both by Chinese premier Hu Jintao, when he told the Chinese Communist Party in 2007 that China needed to enhance its soft power, and by Russian president Vladimir Putin, who urged Russian diplomats to apply soft power more extensively (Nye, 2013;

Shambaugh, 2013). China's concerns often have to do with whatever its leadership considers to be disparaging or damaging coverage of China by western media, and with its interest in developing positive brand recognition for global Chinese enterprises.

Much discussion in the western world about Chinese soft power does not dwell much on the media. As Nye argues, the broader context of historical and current international relations is more important than specific strategic initiatives. China's soft power initiatives tend to be top-down, Nye notes, whereas America's, by contrast, tend to be the products of civil society, not government. China's initiatives, Shambaugh (2013) suggests, better represent "public diplomacy" – an instrument that is wielded by governments, as opposed to soft power which largely originates from society. The two concepts are closely interrelated. They include, from 2004, the establishment of Confucius Institutes around the world, and hosting the 2008 Beijing Olympics, the 2009 Shanghai Expo, and the establishment of the China Public Diplomacy Association in 2013. For the Chinese government, says Shambaugh (2013: 211) national image is something to be marketed via the media rather than built by society or promoted via diplomacy. It is one thing to stage events but it is another to ensure that they are attractively covered, packaged and distributed for global media consumption. The media dimension of soft power was boosted by central government investment of $6.6 billion in the overseas expansion of some of China's foremost media institutions including: Central China Television (CCTV) which launched CNTV, an online television service; China Radio International (CRI); Xinhua, the Chinese national news agency, which set up the China Xinhua News Network or CNC; and US editions of *People's Daily*, *China Daily* which also introduced *Africa Weekly*, and *China Daily*'s subsidiary *Global Times* (Keck, 2013).

These may be regarded as recent manifestations of an ancient tradition that goes back at least as far as Confucius, who advocated the power of "moral influence" by government, a principle also lauded by military strategist Sun Tzu who regarded such influence as the path to social security and victory (Laskai, 2013). What kind of soft power is it that China can disseminate? Advocates variously concentrate on culture, politics and economic development. Zhou Mingwei, director general of China's Foreign Languages Press, recommends that China focus on three "core images" – ancient China, modern China, and peaceful China (Shambaugh, 2013: 211). Most Chinese analysts agree that soft power is about culture. There are different schools as to how culture is related to soft power. Professor Men Honghua stresses four core Chinese values of peace and harmony, morality, etiquette and benevolence. In the political realm, Yu Xintian represents the "propaganda as culture" approach, advocating a contemporary ideology of "socialism with Chinese characteristics." Yan Xuetong believes that China's political system is possibly the key to Chinese soft power, but this is either a system that must still be developed, as some believe, or one that combines authoritarianism with a mixed state/market economic model, a model that might be attractive to many developing countries. Others believe that China needs to build up a new culture. Still others believe that China's development experience, the "China Model," is at the heart of its soft power.

There is widespread consensus that China experiences a "soft power deficit" which Ding Gang (a Chinese journalist quoted by Shambaugh, 2013: 215) attributes to mediocre product quality, low brand recognition, poor global advertising, no exportable religion, a poor commercial reputation, academic bribery to attain degrees abroad, and non-universal China-specific popular culture. Huang Renwei locates the causes in China's culture, the lack of democracy, and remnants of feudalism which have limited political development. China's strong sense of nationalism is also an impediment. Its traditional methods of popular international communication, in which great emphasis is invested in slogans, do not appear to work well in other parts of the world.

For Nye and other critics of China's soft power, state-directed, top-down initiatives tend to be perceived as classic propaganda, lacking in credibility, especially when set against parallel but countervailing developments which in this case include the jailing of Nobel Peace Laureate Liu Xiaobo, and regular efforts to censor the Internet by shutting down Internet cafes, banning websites, and preventing access to popular western sites such as Facebook or Twitter. In some cases these measures appear designed to crush dissent and impede the exposure of corruption. China is sometimes seen as a latecomer to a game that has long been dominated by the USA – which has had plenty of time to prime global perspectives towards China, including the perception that Chinese growth represents a threat (Dynon, 2013). Negative news about China, including heavy pollution, a disregard for human rights, official corruption, and suppression of dissent, can drown out the good messages (Moss, 2013).

On the other hand, China's enormous market power may increasingly be influencing foreign investors to "kowtow" or subordinate themselves to Chinese regulations. Such investors include Hollywood movie makers who are increasingly prepared to shape movie content to suit Chinese sensitivities as well as interests, in return for market access, a phenomenon that Dynon (2013) argues can be found across artistic, commercial and political spheres.

Chinese soft power initiatives might have had more success in the developing than in the developed world, as in development projects related to agriculture, public facilities, infrastructure and industrial facilities, the provision of goods and materials, technical cooperation, HR development cooperation, Chinese medical teams, emergency humanitarian aid, overseas volunteer programs, and debt relief (Shambaugh, 2013: 203). Brautigam (2009) notes that Africans approve of assistance rendered by a developing country to other developing countries, a strategy that China has nurtured from the 1950s. In addition to major building projects and diplomatic visits, aid takes the form of educational programs, the teaching of Chinese, and scholarships for African students to study in China (King, 2013). Similar initiatives have been undertaken in Latin America, Eastern Europe, and parts of Asia.

China's national news agency, Xinhua, employed 10,000 staffers and journalists around the world by the 2000s, of whom 6,000 were based overseas (400 to 1,000 of them journalists – a modest but increasing proportion of them locally recruited). It maintained 117–150 overseas bureaus in 2013, with the ambition of reaching 180–200 by 2020. The agency supplied 62,000 domestic media outlets and 12,000 overseas clients in 2006 (Xin, 2012). Shambaugh (2013) refers to 80,000 paying institutional subscribers in total.

Xinhua enhanced its African presence during the first decade of the twenty-first century (Xin, 2009), setting up new bureaus (to a total of 23 by the 2000s) developing a news portfolio targeted at African readers, exchanging or selling news wires to African media, and providing technical equipment, support and training – even providing help to Ethiopia in blocking websites, television and radio signals. Its distribution is often free (especially in countries strategically important to China) or cheap – relative to western agencies such as AP, Reuters and AFP. Xinhua began charging African media in the late 1990s to early 2000s. When it does charge, subscriptions tend to be in the low five figures where its western rivals might charge six (Fish and Dokoupil, 2010). There is some cooperation with Western agencies: AFP and European Pressphoto Agency sell Xinhua images abroad. English language newspapers in Africa make liberal use of Xinhua copy. Kenyan media in Nairobi, the country's major media center, were reported by Xin (2009) to be enthusiastic users of Xinhua, CCTV and CNC World. Xinhua partnered with the country's flagship paper, the *Daily Nation*. On the down side Xinhua could be criticized for negative coverage of China's enemies, its support for some of the world's most dubious regimes (a reflection of Chinese non-interventionist policy), and for being the voice of the Chinese Communist Party. China's state media are mandated to represent the views of their government (Yuen-Ying, 2010).

Xin (2012) notes that in the 1990s Xinhua's insider critics decried the lack of in-depth analysis of African issues, claiming that the agency was too narrow in its selection of topics, mostly concentrating on politics and bilateral relations. More attention was given to economic issues from the late 1990s. In the 2000s the agency has tried to report on African problems in a non-judgmental, "friendly way," looking for lessons learned and attempting to respond to negative stories in the western media about China's presence in Africa. Critics find too little audio-visual supplementation and too much hard news, along with a tendency to neglect West Africa.

Xinhua tends to provide first-hand reporting from areas where western media have little presence, but otherwise its news services are heavily reliant on local media sources and international agencies. Although the agency has struggled to enhance speed, accuracy, objectivity, and editorial autonomy in competition with western agencies, there is a common perception, claims Xin (2012), that it has some way to travel before achieving an equivalent level of performance. Salaries for foreign correspondents are closer to the domestic salaries paid to Xinhua journalists in China than to international level salaries paid to western agency journalists. Journalists tend to complain of being overworked. While Xinhua provides more news about Africa than do the western news agencies, it tends to be more positive. Overall, most news on Xinhua foreign news wires is about the USA (there are 30 Xinhua journalists in New York), Europe (13 journalists in London), and China's neighbors (70 journalists in Hong Kong).

Hong Kong is the agency's Asia-Pacific Regional Bureau and the region has another 21 bureaus here, serving 1,300 subscribers of whom 15% are based in Hong Kong. Hong Kong is also home to four business entities associated with Xinhua. At the peak of the agency's drift towards commercialization in the 1990s there were about 40 such entities. These were drastically pruned in the early 2000s when the agency weeded out non-performing units and attacked corruption. About 50% of the news is produced from first-hand sources within the region and aimed at mainstream media outlets and websites, government departments, advisory organizations, and think-tanks.

In 2010 Xinhua launched an English-language television version, CNC World (China Xinhua News Network Corp.), reaching Europe, the Middle East and North Africa by 2011. Also in 2011 it moved its US headquarters to the top floor of a 44-floor skyscraper in Times Square and took out a six-year lease for a giant 60 x 40 foot advertising sign in the Square that can cost between $300,000 and $400,000 monthly. Xinhua also launched the business weekly *Economy and Nation*. It has become more dependent on commercially generated revenue in recent decades, generating $1.7 billion revenues in 2012 of which government clients accounted for 15 to 20% (Shanghai bureau chief Liang Zhiyong, 2013, in a personal interview). It has also branched out into video, web and audio streaming. Its top goal in 2013, according to Shambaugh, was to become a world-class, modern media conglomerate.

CONCLUSION

In this chapter I have focused principally on those manifestations of media imperialism that take the form of asymmetrical cross-boundary media relations. Many current examples relate back to imperial relations established from the seventeenth century onwards by European and North American powers. Such imperial powers host a disproportionate number of the world's global, international or transnational media conglomerates. In the case of Britain these included Reuters, until it was acquired by a North American media conglomerate to form Thomson Reuters, and the BBC. They also tend to manifest unequal media relations between former imperial centers and their previous colonies: examples include the continuing presence of British media in the Republic of Ireland, and of Russian language media in many republics of the former Soviet Union. Relations of media imperialism may also develop in contexts of geographically and culturally contiguous strong-versus-weak media markets, as represented in the case of Australia's dominating presence in the media markets of New Zealand. This form of media imperialism can morph into a form of pan-regionalism in which influential centers of media production tend to source a large proportion of all media productions that are targeted to the pan-regional audience, as in the case of the Arab world. A similar incidence is offered in East Asia where the Korean Wave figures among several significant centers of pan-regional influence. Finally I have considered the philosophy and practice of "soft power." This may be considered a more pro-active form of contemporary media influence, one that might be equally relevant to the next chapter whose focus is on aspects of resistance to the media imperialism of others. The approach characterizes Chinese media policy, and I have looked at its application by Chinese global media ventures such as Xinhua, CNC and CCTV.

10 Media Resisting Imperialism

WEAPONS OF RESISTANCE TO THE BRITISH EMPIRE

It is in the very nature of imperialism that it exploits, intensifies and perpetuates deeply unequal, although mutually dependent, relationships between the imperialist and the imperialized. Imperial power resides principally in three things, namely superior material wealth, the threat of coercive force, and an ideological system of justification that secures the support of most members of the imperial class and a good many of the oppressed, especially their coopted leadership. The inequality is experienced by many of the oppressed as an invasive, aggressive and heinous usurpation even when it may appear the better of several evils (e.g. the threat of invasion by a rival empire). It invites either overt retaliation or brooding resistance. The colonial relations of the British empire in the nineteenth century are particularly relevant in this context because they coincided with the emergence and flowering of most forms of mass communication that are associated with modernity, namely the press (and various technologies of printing, from large scale to small), telegraph, telephone, wireless, film, television, and phonograph.

These weapons are sometimes available to both imperialists and oppressed classes. In America, clumsy British attempts to control the press (e.g. the 1765 Stamp Act, which none of the colonies obeyed), "broadsides" and other pamphlets by American radicals contributed significantly to the success of the movement for American independence. Relatively high rates of literacy in the colonies then prevailed (e.g. 70% of white men and 40% of white women in New England) and there were more newspapers in the colonies than there were in Britain. Some 200 newspapers appeared between 1690 and 1820 although most did not survive. One that did was Benjamin Franklin's *Pennsylvania Gazette*, founded in 1728. It was relatively uncontroversial, but Benjamin's brother James founded the *New England Courant* in 1721 and on occasions this challenged religious and political authorities. Peter Zenger, publisher of the *New York Weekly Journal,* successfully defended himself against charges of sedition in 1735: no other colonial court trial of a printer for seditious libel has come to light (Emery, 1984). Pamphlets "helped to circulate arguments and perspectives which became the rhetorical foundation for the revolution and institutions of governments" (Bailyn, 1965).

BRITISH INDIA

Imperial state control over the media is variable. The British allowed an appreciable measure of discretion, although freedoms tolerated in any one period might quickly be rescinded in the event of civil disobedience. In British India, the Censor Act introduced by Governor-General Lord Wellesley in 1799 introduced prior censorship, but this was lifted by one of Wellesley's successors, the Marquess of Hastings, in 1818, likely reflecting the popular ideology of the press as a "fourth estate," and the progressive influence of missionaries in India. The Licensing Regulation Act of 1823, by contrast, established the government's right to cancel a newspaper's license. This in turn was abolished by Charles Metcalfe in 1835, but reintroduced by Viscount Canning in 1857. The Vernacular Press Act of 1878 awarded magistrates authority to require publishers to pay a security guarantee as assurance against breach of peace and security. This was repealed in 1881. The Newspapers Act of 1908 permitted magistrates to take judicial action against editors responsible for the publication of articles deemed likely to stir rebellion, and the Press Act of 1910 allowed the government to demand security from any newspaper. These measures were repealed by the Press Law of 1922 but reinstated by the India Press Ordinance of 1930 in response to the Civil Disobedience Movement (Natarajan, 1962).

Vigorous activity in the arena of press law can be indicative of control but also of resistance. A low estimate is that between 1907 and 1947 approximately 2,000 Indian newspapers were censored (some of them repeatedly) and that between 8,000 and 10,000 were seized (Kamra, 2009). Bayly (2000) indicates that relative tolerance towards the foundation and operation of local media was inspired in part by the advantages to the imperial state of having locally-generated, reliable sources of intelligence, sometimes printed in indigenous languages, about the lives and concerns of the governed. Indigenous or local leaders learned to negotiate the discretions they were allowed, nurturing media that were alternative to the media of the imperial class and that sometimes supported longer-term goals of greater political freedom, if not independence, although many were simply commercial propositions.

There are many examples of indigenous leaders throughout colonial possessions in Asia, Africa and South America who were as much journalists as they were politicians during the struggle for independence (Boyd-Barrett, 1977b). They sometimes used media not simply or even primarily as tools for political claims or even independence (which would inevitably attract unwelcome attention from the authorities), but as vehicles for the shaping of distinctive cultural and national identities, which might attract less negative attention. With independence once achieved, however, many such leaders sought control over the media to shore up their domestic authority.

Papers joined by disaffected expatriates could also be sources of opposition, as were Anglo-Indian newspapers that reported and commented on issues that divided the ruling classes, creating fissures that might provoke more widespread dissent. Although trained as a lawyer, the formation of Mahatma Gandhi was as much journalistic as legal. In 1903 in Natal, South Africa, he edited the weekly *Indian Opinion* in English, Tamil and Gujarati as well as *Young India* and *Harijan*. In 1922 he was charged with spreading disaffection through seditious articles. *Indian Opinion* was a vehicle for the venting of Indian grievances. In 1930s India, he launched *Harijan*, *Harijanbandhu* and *Haryansevak* in English, Gujarati and Hindi languages, using these as platforms to protest untouchability and poverty (Hoffmeyr, 2013).

The efforts of indigenous leaders were supplemented by expatriates whose experiences of colonialism radicalized them to oppose their state of origin. The first typographic newspaper of India (preceded over many hundreds of years by other forms of news communication) was the *Bengal Gazette* launched by James Hickey in 1780. The paper dared to attack both the general-governor of Bengal, Warren Hastings, and the Chief Justice. The first Bengali language weekly was *Digdarshan*, founded in 1818 by John Marshman, an Englishman, and other language papers followed. An expatriate Londoner, Robert Knight, became principal founder and first editor of the daily *Times of India*, which he helped form by combining four other newspapers in the 1850s and which he owned from 1860 to 1868. Knight was critical of what he considered the mismanagement and greed of British authorities and of the army whose lack of discipline and poor leadership he blamed for the Sepoy Mutiny of 1857–1858. He later founded the *Calcutta Statesman* in 1875 which he used to advocate for Indian causes and to counter the influence of Calcutta's Anglo-Indian dailies. He was particularly biting in his criticism of the British invasion of Afghanistan in 1878, and of the empire's lack of concern for famines that it had helped create on the northern frontier (Hirschmann, 2008).

NEWS AGENCIES AS RESISTANCE: TANJUG, NWICO, AND IPS

The modern international news market has developed from the early to mid-nineteenth century. An increasingly commercial, mass market news-paper press sought to impress its readers and generate revenue by demonstrat-ing its capacity for both domestic (national) and international or global news coverage. Only a privileged few newspapers have ever been able to sustain substantial worldwide networks of their own correspondents. Others have learned to share their international news correspondents and, more particularly, to depend on the services of international news agencies which develop a "wholesale" news operation, gathering news from many countries and selling this news on a commercial basis to "retail" clients, individual newspapers and others. This model has been easily extended over time to embrace radio, television and increasingly today online media (Boyd-Barrett, 1980; 2010b).

Throughout this entire period the international news business has shown high concentration, privileging the western world (notably the USA, Britain, France) and the perspectives of western media across the main sub-divisions of this market which are general news (principally for print and broadcast news media); television news (for television media); and financial, economic and commodity news (for banks, brokers, corporations). The nineteenth-century market was dominated by a cartel whose principal members, in alphabetical order, included Havas (forerunner of today's AFP, and head-quartered in Paris); Reuters, headquartered in London; and Wolff, head-quartered in Berlin. There were a few significant secondary agencies, including Continental, which served the territories of the Austro-Hungarian empire; then there was the leading US news agency, AP. These were obliged to integrate with the Reuters' dominated cartel. Other news agencies were mainly government approved or controlled national agencies largely dependent on the major agencies – with whom they frequently had exclu-sive ties – for their international news and to whom they supplied their national news in part exchange (Boyd-Barrett, 1980).

By the mid-twentieth century the cartel had dissolved, but western dominance continued. The principal players were now AFP, headquartered in Paris; AP and United Press International (UPI), both headquartered in New York; and Reuters, headquartered in London. Some major secondary agencies with significant international activity included TASS of the Soviet Union, Xinhua of China, dpa of West Germany, and EFE of Spain (Boyd-Barrett, 1980). By the early twenty-first century the line-up was AFP in Paris; AP in New York; Bloomberg, in New York; and Thomson-Reuters (its news division still headquartered in London, but otherwise now a Canadian corporation). Major secondary agencies included Xinhua of China, Interfax and ITAR-TASS of Russia, and Germany's dpa. Havas/ AFP, AP and Reuters have remained influential throughout almost the entire period. From its earliest days Reuters provided financial news to investment communities, but by the 1970s it had come to depend mainly on such subscribers for its sophisticated and now computerized financial news services, especially in such fields as currency exchange. After 1980 it faced increasingly severe competition from a new market entrant, Bloomberg, paving the way to its eventual takeover by Thomson to form Thomson-Reuters in 2008. Bloomberg is a financial news agency that also supplies general news.

For several decades, AP and Reuters have both operated television news services – APTN and Reuters Television, respectively – and these dominate the global market for worldwide "wholesale" television news for broadcasters, in collaboration with the Eurovision exchange of news between major national public service broadcasters. The news services of these major international news agencies entail the maintenance of news bureaus in most countries and territories of the world, gathering news and forwarding it to regional or global centers for regional or global distribution to agency clients. These news services comprise principally "hard" or "spot" news heavily characterized by major political, economic, military and sports news and news of major environmental and similar catastrophes (Boyd-Barrett, 1980; 1998a).

There have always been potential rivals to these major international news services. Their incentives have sometimes been political, as when a major power has sought to distance itself from a dependence on news supplied by agencies based in foreign powers. Such was the case of Russia in the nineteenth century when it found it difficult to shake itself free from its dependence on international news services of the cartel, channeled through the German agency Wolff (Rantanen, 1990). They have also been ideological, as in the case of the agencies founded in Communist Russia (up to 1991) and in its earlier years China. Russia's TASS has been supplanted by the Russian state news agency ITAR TASS. China's Xinhua has expanded internationally; it tends to give greater attention in its news services to the affairs of developing economies than is typically the case of the western news agencies (Xin, 2012).

A handful of western-based "alternative" agencies have contested the news agendas of the major agencies. Inter Press Service (IPS) was founded as a journalist-owned cooperative in 1964 by an independent Italian journalist, Robert Savio, and Argentine student Pablo Piacentini. Although headquartered in Italy its focus has always been on the global South. It began by serving media in South America, but then spread worldwide. It seeks to provide "journalism and communication for global change," involving news and other services that focus on development, gender and human rights issues. It specializes in analytical, background coverage rather than hard news, and aims to provide alternative perspectives and local voices. In 1994 it became a non-profit, international NGO organized around five autonomous regional centers within an umbrella IPS association. Half of its revenues come from donor grants and the rest are earned from sales of news services and project funding. In the 2000s the agency counted 417 journalists of whom 70% were based in countries of the South, providing 270,000 words of news a week in 27 languages, covering 150 countries, read by 200 million readers daily (Joye, 2010).

In the 1970s, international organizations such as the Non-Aligned Movement and UNESCO initiated a series of debates about the relevance of the international media and media inequalities to the prospects for the political, economic and cultural development of emergent economies. The role of news agencies figured prominently in these debates. IPS had been in existence for long enough to offer itself as a model for change. An even longer-established player was the national news agency of what was then Yugoslavia. Tanjug still exists today as the national news agency of Serbia, its global influence much diminished by the break-up of Yugoslavia and the secessionist wars that accompanied it. Its prior history is of great relevance in the history of goal-directed resistance to the media hegemony of imperial powers (Vukasovich and Boyd-Barrett, 2012).

For close on 70 years Tanjug, the national news agency of Yugoslavia and brainchild of Josep Broz Tito, President of the Socialist Federal Republic of Yugoslavia (1943–1980) – who was also first Secretary General of the Non-Aligned Movement (1961–1964) – played a major and nonconformist role in the global marketplace of information and coverage of history-making, breaking news events. At least up to 1990, Tanjug had a strong claim to representation of the perspectives of the non-aligned world.

Even from the perspective of conventional principles of western journalistic practice, Tanjug played a pivotal role by being the first to break news of events such as the last day in office of the first legally elected prime minister of the Congo, Patrice Lumumba, before his assassination in 1961; the US "Bay of Pigs" invasion of Cuba that same year; the US-aided military coup d'état against Chile's Popular Unity government and its democratically elected president, Salvador Allende, in 1973; the US bombardment of Tripoli in 1986; and the overthrow of the Communist regime of Nicolae Ceauşescu in Romania in 1989 (Vukasovich and Boyd-Barrett, 2012).

Tanjug's work foreshadowed by over 20 years the 1970s debates leading to UNESCO-endorsed calls for a New World Information and Communication Order (NWICO). Tito articulated the need for a non-aligned news agency perspective in 1955 (six years before the foundation in Belgrade, in 1961, of the Non-Aligned Movement). He later established Tanjug as the coordinating agency of the Non-Aligned News Agency Pool (NANAP) which today continues to exist as the Non-Aligned News Network (NNN) centered in Kuala Lumpur. Despite differences in size between Tanjug and the major international agencies, Tanjug invested significant effort in the gathering and distribution of original foreign news. Between 1944 and 1993, it maintained 237 international correspondents in 22 European countries, 15 Asian countries, 6 South American countries, 14 African countries, the USA and Australia) (Avramović, 1993). Unlike some other alternative news agencies such as Inter Press Service (established in 1964) and the features service Gemini News (1966–1988, now Panos), that have striven to represent the interests of the developing or emerging economies, Tanjug sought to represent countries of the Non-Aligned Movement specifically, and among these it had sympathetic purchase on the perspectives and struggles of the socialist countries (Vukasovich and Boyd-Barrett, 2012).

UNESCO's International Programme for the Development of Communication (IPDC), established in the wake of the 1980 McBride report (UNESCO, 1980), assisted in the formation or strengthening of national news agencies in non-aligned countries through such means as tariff concessions, journalism training and equipment supply. Agencies frustrated by their continuing dependence on Reuters, AFP, AP and UPI, voiced their complaints at UNESCO and NAM-sponsored events throughout the 1960s and 1970s (Boyd-Barrett and Thussu, 1992). They helped ignite advocacy for NWICO as a necessary prerequisite to a New Economic Order (NEO). Long before the NWICO debates, Tanjug had raised the question as to why news agencies of newly independent countries would expect to be well served by a global information environment controlled by corporations of the ex-imperial powers.

The genesis for what eventually became NANAP was inaugurated in 1954 when President Tito of Yugoslavia and Prime Minister Nehru of India issued a joint statement on 23 December outlining the policy of non-alignment (Stanković, 1967). The fourth of what would come to be known as the Non-Aligned Movement Summits (in Algiers, 1973) proved pivotal in establishing the issue of information and communication in the conversation on global economic imbalances (Crain, 2009). Definitions of domination were expanded to include cultural and social imperialism, establishing the threat of ideological domination to the developing world (Lakshmi, 1993).

In January of 1975, news agencies in 12 NAM member countries agreed to establish the Non-Aligned News Agencies Pool (NANAP), often simply referred to as "the pool," to serve as a method for the multilateral exchange of information (Ivačić, 1978b). Tanjug became the news agency leader in coordinating the collection and redistribution of news and information among non-aligned movement member countries (Crain, 2009). National news agencies throughout the NAM sent their journalists for training at Tanjug. NANAP, often referenced as an *outcome* of the NWICO debates, was in fact a *contributor* to them, and a primary model for cooperation between developing country news agencies, owing its gestation to the inspiration of Tanjug in the preceding two decades. Tanjug had played a remarkable, principled and often misunderstood role in the development of a distinct Third World press (Vukasovich and Boyd-Barrett, 2012). But the weak NANAP structure that succeeded NWICO (see Boyd-Barrett and Thussu, 1992), struggled to attain significant client use and resources.

NEWS AGENCIES: INTERFAX, POLITICAL AND ECONOMIC NEWS AGENCY OF RUSSIA

The general history of news agencies in Russia chronicles a swing, in pre-Soviet times, from media dependence on external, non-Russian news agencies for provision of news of the world beyond Russia, to the construction of a state-controlled, centralized, but global news-gathering machinery during the Soviet period. In the post-Soviet period, this yielded to a system of news-gathering that was considerably more self-sufficient than in pre-Soviet times and more diverse than in Soviet times.

Interfax is significant in this context for four principal reasons: (1) as a private, independent and commercially-operated news agency it has overtaken the State financed agencies, ITAR-TASS and RIA-Novosti, as the leading domestic news supplier about Russia and the Former Soviet Union (FSU) both for Russia and the FSU and for the rest of the world; (2) as the foremost economic and financial news agency of Russia and the FSU it has retained market share against the penetration of the global behemoths of the financial information industry Bloomberg and Thomson-Reuters; (3) it has contributed to the building of an informational infrastructure that is essential for modern capitalism and hence functions as a key lynchpin in the still-developing incorporation of Russia and the FSU into the neoliberal system of global capitalism, itself a powerful manifestation of soft power; and (4) it has achieved these things in part through a series of strategic alliances with major players in the global economic and financial information services industry (Boyd-Barrett, 2014).

Interfax founder and chairman Mikhail Komissar recollects (Interfax, 2009: p.11) how at Radio Moscow (within whose structure the new agency began, and where Komissar was editor-in-chief of foreign broadcasting) journalists had learned to adapt information for an international audience. They had long had exposure to the reports of foreign news agencies such as Reuters, AFP, AP, EFE and others, and knew how to adapt classic standards of speed, accuracy, independence, impartiality and reliability to their own reporting.

Komissar considered that a key, founding objective of Interfax was to explain, in language free of state obfuscation and ideology, and accessible for foreign and in particular western audiences, the confusing but momentous developments that were occurring in the Soviet Union in the late 1980s. Its coverage attracted high praise from leading western media. Once fully-fledged as a totally independent news agency, with all the associated costs that such a status entailed, Komissar learned to appreciate that the revenue potential from a limited number of media clients (many of whom had previously grown accustomed to receiving news agency services free of charge from state agencies) was limited. He looked to the business models of other agencies, noting that AP was a not-for-profit member cooperative, AFP was dependent on government clients for a significant share of its revenues, and that both Reuters and Bloomberg earned the vast majority of their sizable revenues from the sale of financial, economic and related information products and services to the financial community of banks, brokers, multinational corporations and the like.

The agency evolved through five major phases or categories of activity involving the supply of: (1) news (general, political) – this established the Interfax brand identity as it negotiated the perilous waters of reporting on the transition to a market economy, the attempted coup against Gorbachev, the dissolution of the Soviet Union and, later, the Chechnyan wars; (2) market data (prices of bonds and stocks, etc.); (3) fundamentals (information about companies, involving the construction of giant data-bases based on state-required disclosures, notably SPARK and SCAN, covering companies in Russia and the FSU as well as media reporting of them, and involving partnerships with Dun & Bradstreet, Business Wire among others); (4) credit risk (rating of companies in terms of their credit-worthiness), involving a partnership with Moody's; and (5) marketing (including investor relations and assessing the credit worthiness of business partners and clients, involving partnerships with Experian and Thomson among others) (Boyd-Barrett, 2014).

From the very beginning of its venture into economic and financial news services, Interfax was instrumental in introducing a new, market-oriented language for discussion about and reporting of what was "business," and what was "economic." Senior executives Gerasimov and Pogorely recount (Interfax, 2009: 50–2) that in the early 1990s one of the main challenges was the "huge deficit of news that was worthy of the term "business news," since very few domestic sources had been trained to think about such matters from the perspective of a market economy. "Why do you want to know that for?" might be the retort of a Soviet factory director presented with a question from a journalist asking about investment, projects or operating results. Essential basics such as currency values (whether rubles, foreign currency rubles, transferable rubles, each having different official and unofficial exchange rates) could not be easily or meaningfully established for conversion into foreign currencies.

Initiating a reputation for innovative products in these domains, Interfax issued a weekly publication from early 1991 on foreign trade, then added a daily English-language bulletin called *Soviet Business Report*, and again, in the second half of that year, introduced specialized publications on oil and gas, agriculture and the banking sector. A specialized news service on telecommunications followed in 1998. Almost every issue of the early bulletins carried essential and important economic news that only a short time before had been classified. Today Interfax clients for business and financial services receive real-time data and latest news from the Russian, Ukrainian and major international trading floors, as well as analytical forecasts, consensus forecasts and commentaries on financial markets. In 2010 Interfax claimed that more than 30,000 stock market players received Interfax news, from major banks to private investors (Boyd-Barrett, 2014).

Interfax was the first to systematically identify a national need for economic information services in the Russian Federation. From the beginning the agency had adopted perspectives on the world that were much closer to the Gorbachev camp than to that of the so-called communist "conservatives." The agency consciously aligned its business model with the needs of the emerging capitalist order, in two closely interrelated ways: the construction of an informational infrastructure and, proceeding cautiously, developing products to meet the news needs of, and about, each industry /market sector by industry/market sector. This represented a refining of the corporate mind-set towards a more acute appreciation of what was needed to help support the continued growth and strength of the new economy, later exemplified by the perception that credit-rating services would be an appropriate, needed and lucrative new area of activity.

GLOBAL BROADCASTERS: AL JAZEERA TO TELESUR

Most nations established national news agencies as essential signifiers of "nationhood." Agencies nurtured a public consciousness of "nation" throughout their respective territories in a syntagmatic construction of a world whose most important constituent parts were nations. That construction was projected to other countries through partnerships with the international agencies. Functioning similarly today, an increasing number of 24/7 television stations have emerged from national foundations yet with aspirations to international and global influence. Whether or not market-driven, the motivation usually has to do with the promotion, internationally or worldwide, of the interests of the local "nation." Models of ownership and control of both traditional wire services and new 24/7 stations represent similar configurations of non-profit media cooperative; market-driven media cooperative (open or closed to new members); government owned or controlled; intergovernmental; public non-profit ownership; journalist-owned and controlled; private ownership by one or more media corporations, and so on. The overall shape and feel of these organizations is generally western, even when not actually based in the West (Boyd-Barrett and Boyd-Barrett, 2010; Cushion and Lewis, 2010).

Hegemony of powerful news agencies has frequently generated resistance. From early on in the news business, we find examples of hegemonic, subaltern and counter-hegemonic agencies. The global cartel established initially through a series of agreements between Reuters, Havas and Wolf parceled out territorial markets between these core members, partly but not exclusively on the basis of imperial interest. Within each of these territories, a privileged but unequal relationship was established between the respective core or hegemonic agency and local, generally national (subaltern) agencies. Subaltern agencies fed local news on an exclusive basis to the core agencies and in turn (and on payment of a fee) they received the global news service of their respective hegemon. Subaltern agencies were granted exclusive ownership of the hegemon's news service within their local markets and this went out alongside each subaltern's local service to an exclusive membership list. Counter-hegemonic news agencies emerged, constraining this system in a variety of ways. Local media who were denied access to the local subaltern service of national and global news were motivated to join with other clients, perhaps in partnership with counter-hegemonic global agencies, to establish rival services (Boyd-Barrett and Boyd-Barrett, 2010).

The 24/7 news system of the early 2000s is less structured, but there is still a hierarchy. BBC World and CNN operate on a more influential scale

say, RT (Russia), Deutsche Welle (DW) or France24. Owned by British
US media conglomerates respectively, BBC and CNN eschew direct
government involvement, operate internationally, and are market driven.
They operate their own considerable news-gathering structures. Most subaltern 24/7 stations depend significantly on the international television footage streamed to them by APTN and Reuters TV.

The appearance of a counter-hegemon in Al Jazeera is noteworthy, though
not on the same scale of market threat that AP represented for the European
cartel in the 1900s. Such a threat may yet appear in the form of a Chinese
counter-hegemonic structure based principally on CCTV and Xinhua. CCTV
provides a less commercial or tabloid and more intellectual international
news service than many. China's policy of non-interventionism, however,
requires it to eschew critical editorializing of the RT variety in favor of an
Anglo-American model that frames news within a recognizably westernized
24/7 template. This allowed CCTV to discuss the "prospects for democracy"
in the Ukraine, following the 2014 western-backed coup in Kiev, while ignoring the absence of democracy in China and the democracy that had pertained
in the Ukraine prior to the coup.

Although counter-hegemons such as Al Jazeera boast about their independence from the hegemons, they are oftentimes subject to the political
and economic interests of their sponsors and by their boosterism of the
"sacred," – that is, the news terrain that counter-hegemons believe their
opponents have willfully neglected.

Launched on July 24, 2005, Telesur is a regional channel for Latin
America, financed principally by the Venezuelan government. Other shareholders include the governments of Argentina, Bolivia, Cuba, Ecuador,
Nicaragua and Paraguay. Its protagonists regard TeleSUR as a Pan-
American alternative to US-controlled cable news channels, an American
style Al Jazeera that promotes regional integration and mutual understanding by providing news from a uniquely Latin American perspective. Its news
agenda is determined by a Board of Directors, whose Advisory Council
includes well-known Latin-American, left-leaning intellectuals. Its official
website boasts an audience of millions spanning much of Latin America, the
USA, Europe, North Africa and part of the Middle East, and a news service
compiled from correspondents in 23 locations, including most major Latin
American cities, New York, Washington, Madrid and London. It broadcasts
primarily in Spanish, Portuguese, English and French. Comparable to Al
Jazeera in that it is identified with a region while seeking a broader
international audience, TeleSur is headquartered in Caracas. One study
found that Telesur constructs a news agenda quite distinct to that of two
other channels with which it was compared, namely CNN en Español

and a regional Columbian broadcaster NTN24 (Boyd-Barrett and Boyd-Barrett, 2010). TeleSur tapped a broader range of sources in its coverage of controversial, breaking South American news, and was friendlier to left-wing movements than almost any of its competitors. Its regional and global coverage reflected the priorities of the Venezuelan government.

Widely acclaimed for bringing a new voice to the world of global television news from its founding in 1996 in Qatar – a voice that subscribes to the basic norms of western journalism while reporting from Middle Eastern and Muslim perspectives – Al Jazeera's English-language channel, established in 2006, is noted for the contributions of many journalists recruited from western news services, most notably the BBC. The general style and tone sometimes resemble that of BBC World news, even while it devotes greater attention to countries of the south. Sir David Frost was an illustrious British recruit. Revenue includes advertising but comes principally from the Emir of Qatar. Qatar competes with the regional hegemon, Saudi Arabia, has significant economic interests in the Middle East, and hosts the US Central Command, whose regional headquarters was shifted from Saudi Arabia to Qatar's Al Udeid Air Base in 2009. Given this mixture and history, it is not possible to confidently assert that the channel is either independent or a state operation, although there are undoubtedly elements of both (Boyd-Barrett and Xie, 2008).

From being regarded with great suspicion by the Americans at the beginning of the "War on Terror" in the early 2000s – the USA bombed Al Jazeera bureaus in both Kabul and Baghdad – Al Jazeera has "mainstreamed." During the "Arab Spring" its reporting paid considerable attention to the "rebels," some of them associated with Al Qaeda, in Egypt (2011), Libya (2011) and Syria (from 2012). Mainstreaming is explicable in terms both of the interests of Qatar, and of the station's bid to gain acceptance on affluent western news markets, including the USA. By 2012 the agency had over 42 bureaus and 200 or more editorial staff.

Al Jazeera's Anglo-American or BBC approach to the global market has also been adopted by RT and several other international 24/7 operations. Previously called Russia Today, RT (established in 2005, with a total journalistic complement of about 100) is the offspring of a print, broadcasting and online features news agency – once described as a state news-analytical agency – RIA Novosti (originating as Sovinformburo, established in 1941), and presents global news from a perspective that is broadly sympathetic to Russia and often critical of the West. Its website claims a total clientele of 1,500 clients. These include many state organizations, whose prominence suggests that the agency is substantially subsidized by government along the lines of AFP.

France 24, established in 2006, is controlled by a partnership between publicly owned France Television (funded by license and advertising) and private Groupe TF1, but financed by the government to provide global news from a French perspective. According to its website it employs 260 journalists of its own and can draw on the journalism of its controlling television stations. Originally broadcasting in English, French and Arabic, President Sarkozy indicated in 2008 that he would like to see it reduced to only French language. Deutsche Welle Television (DW-TV), a public broadcaster established in 1992, is described on its website as "Germany's international broadcaster," charged with promoting Germany and providing a global news service from a European perspective.

The mightiest sources of resistance to western narratives tend to be financed by states and are mouthpieces of state interest. Examples include the Chinese news agency Xinhua and Xinhua's television arm CNC, as well as CCTV, the primary state broadcaster of China. These present a broadly favorable image of China, as one might expect, one that is astonishingly bereft of detailed coverage of Chinese politics. Their overseas coverage has been surprisingly bland and cosmetically westernized, although concentrating more on countries of the South than western rivals. It tends to be more positive in tone, not just about China but about countries of the South generally. In addition to their online presence, both CCTV (2012) and Al Jazeera (2013) have established US channels, although audiences for both are very modest as of 2014.

MOVIES AS RESISTANCE: CHINA AND INDIA

Just as some national and regional news agencies positioned themselves as the suppliers of news agendas that are alternative to those of the major western-based news agencies, so the global spread of US entertainment products has not infrequently inspired local initiatives in the name of resistance to the cultural hegemon.

Resistance to Hollywood has special resonance given the high visibility and iconic power of the very concept of Hollywood and its history, inspiring sobriquets such as "Bollywood," and "Nollywood" to describe film industries such as those of India (especially Mumbai) and Nigeria (especially Lagos) that have long come to rival Hollywood in terms of production, though not yet at least, in terms of revenues. At the time of writing in 2013, however, it is actually the cinema of China that arouses most interest in western movie circles because of the relatively high revenues that are already earned by Hollywood products in China, and the potential for much higher future earnings as the number of screens in China multiplies. The growth of domestic Chinese film production is of special relevance. In 2013 domestic productions in China accounted for well over 50% of Chinese box office revenue, albeit in a context in which the state imposed a severe cap on the number of Hollywood releases it permitted each year.

China

The total anticipated value of expenditure on media and entertainment in China in 2011, including both consumer and advertiser expenditure, was $109bn (Landreth, 2012), ranking China in third place behind the USA (number one, at $464bn) and Japan (number two, at $193 bn) (Lunden, 2012).

China rates only modestly as a global film producer. Global sales of Chinese movies, with a few notable exceptions, are mainly limited to the Chinese diaspora. Nevertheless, the Chinese market is large and increasingly wealthy. China represents a potential future challenge to Hollywood's traditional dominance but also, paradoxically, as an attractive immediate and long-term source of revenue for Hollywood distributors.

In 2011 China overtook Japan as the largest foreign market for US films. The number of screens in China reached 10,700 that year, and was expected to reach 18,000 by 2017. Growth has included large chains of urban multiplexes equipped for 3-D and other large format movies which command higher box office revenues. China itself is becoming a more significant filmmaker. Of the 315 movies released at Chinese cinemas in 2012, 231 were domestic. China accounted for 8% of the global film market in 2012.

Chinese box office revenue in 2012 was $2.7 billion, a significant jump from $2 billion in 2011 and a continuation of the double digit increases that it exhibited in the 2000s. Box office was expected to total anywhere between $5.5 and $10 billion by 2017 (Wang, 2013). This would put China on track to level with Hollywood before 2020. Hollywood's rate of growth is much below that of China's. In 2004–2009 Hollywood's total North American movie revenues (theater, DVD, streaming, etc.) fell by over 5% while international sales increased by 99% (KiPNews.org, 2011).

Growth of Chinese box office revenues also represents an opportunity for Hollywood movies and for co-productions in China. Imported movies accounted for 52% of the Chinese box office in 2012 (the first time in four years that they had accounted for the majority of earnings). The most successful US movie in China to date has been *Avatar* (2010), which grossed $225 million on the Chinese market (Fritz, 2013). Related earnings come from theme parks (Shanghai Disneyland is scheduled to open in 2015). Hollywood may earn as much as $3.4 billion at the Chinese box office by

2017, plus a further $1 billion from co-productions. Some Hollywood movies do better in China than in the USA; examples here include Ang Lee's *Life of Pi* and the 3D version of *Titanic* (Kaufman, 2012). Most such discussions do not consider box office revenues as a proportion of total earnings that movies make from rentals, DVD sales, PayTV, streaming, product promotion, copyright royalties and licenses, etc.

Resistance against cultural imports worldwide is frequently buttressed by local laws and regulations that interrupt or divert what would otherwise be the "free flow" of the market. This is especially the case in China, which for many decades has maintained quotas on the number of foreign movies that may be exhibited and whose state company, the China Film Group (CFG), exercises overweening power in the importation of movies for theatrical release, regulating co-productions, and scheduling and controlling the proportion of box office revenues that US distributors may accrue in the form either of flat fees or – more attractive to Hollywood – set percentages of the gross.

In a possible bid to stem the success of US movies in China (which peaked at 52% of the box office in 2012, when US blockbusters led the Chinese box office for 23 weeks [Cieply, 2013]), the CFG imposed month-long "blackouts." Foreign movies could not be released in blackout periods. Additionally, the CFG scheduled US blockbusters to compete with another on the same release dates, something that Hollywood filmmakers are generally anxious to avoid. In a 2012 agreement with the MPAA, CFG raised the quota for foreign movies from 20 to 34 and increased the proportion of ticket sales that Hollywood distributors could recoup (to as high as around 40% for co-productions).

State power cannot in itself control demand, and the CFG also benefits from its considerable share of the box office receipts earned by Hollywood movies (Cieply and Barboza, 2012). Following the 2008 success of Hollywood's *Kung Fu Panda* (which grossed $26 million in China), China's largest animation center, the National Animation Industry Park (NAIP), launched five features in 2011. Yet all of these flopped while, in that same year, *Kung Fu Panda 2* earned $93 billion. NAIP's lack of success might have been due to deficiencies in plotting and production technique, and a strategy of only targeting children. Since the time of Disney, Hollywood has leveraged the fact that the biggest grossing children's movies are those that also entertain the parents who bring their children to the movie theaters (Yang, 2013).

The rise of China as the world's second most valuable movie market after the USA has pressurized Hollywood to do whatever it can to get its movies seen in China and also to shape Hollywood movie content to ensure its acceptability to Chinese censors of the State Administration of Radio, Film and Television (SARFT) as well as appeal to Chinese audiences. Rumors of inappropriate influence on Chinese officials, in possible violation of the Foreign Corrupt Practices Act, are reinforced by a perception of the obvious benefits to Hollywood of Chinese manufacturer interest in paying for product placements in both Chinese and Western movies (Landreth, 2012). Such advertisers include Shuhua Milk for dairy products, Meters/Bonwe for clothing, Lenovo and TCL for computers and electronics, and Semir for clothing (Horn, 2011). The primary target audience is the Chinese consumer who may be seduced by the association of Chinese products with the prestige and modernism of the global as represented in Hollywood productions. Release of movies cannot be guaranteed in advance of SARFT approval, so the pressure is intense for those producers who have agreed to product placements to make sure that their films are well-regarded by SARFT (Zeitchik and Landreth, 2012).

Pressure to access the Chinese market has other consequences for content. Zeitchik and Landreth (2012) report that Chinese "bad guys" in Hollywood movies are vanishing just as, before them, Japanese "bad guys" disappeared as studios appeased powerful interests in what had previously been the number one national market for Hollywood exports and is now number two. Likewise, to improve the potential for success of co-productions it is helpful to include a number of positive, Chinese elements, featuring Chinese actors and Chinese products. Hollywood studios also sometimes give SARFT censors a preview of movies or scripts (Cieply and Barnes, 2013).

A popular if challenging method of circumventing the quota on foreign movie releases is that of Hollywood co-productions with Chinese studios or distributors. These do not count against the quotas. They also benefit from a more generous share of box office receipts (around 40% as opposed to the 20% that may be earned from quota films for which revenue sharing, as opposed to a flat fee, has been approved). Co-productions must be approved by the China Film Co-Production Company, a unit of the CFG (Cieply and Barboza, 2012). There are also partnerships such as 21st Century Fox's 20% ownership of China's Bona Film Group that make movies for both the Chinese (in Mandarin or Cantonese, or both) as well as the global market. Fox International Productions makes local language movies in China. CFG has partnered with Thomas Tull's US Legendary East Studio, maker of the *Dark Knight* Batman series, for the creation of Chinese movies. Additionally, special versions of US blockbusters are sometimes made for China with their own distinctive trailers. Australia's Village Roadshow Pictures Asia produced its first Chinese-language film (Mandarin and Cantonese) with *Journey to the West: Conquer the Dragons* in 2012, and plans to make other Chinese-language films solely for China (Florcruz, 2013).

China's domestic film industry has blossomed, appropriately symbolized by the opening in 2012 of the Qingdao studios with their capacity for the production of 200 movies a year. For the first six months of 2013, with the help of some market manipulation by CFG, Chinese movies performed much better than foreign ones at the box office (Li, 2013). This was in part due to the timely shift of Chinese productions from big budget historical costume dramas to smaller-scale, low-to-mid budget movies reflecting contemporary aspects of life in China (Xu, 2013). This might have suited the extension of the theater market to mid-sized and smaller cities of China and the continuing development of new multiplexes. Independent film producers, and a growth in the number of companies (e.g. Broadway Cinematheque Moma) that support art house cinema, have assisted, as has the dedication of CCTV Channel 6 to domestic productions (Jaffe, 2013). These must still attain approval of the Chinese censors. However this sector of the industry is also one that is prone to periodic official clamp-downs (Watts, 2013) which have targeted independent film-makers, film schools and forums.

China's film-makers have become increasingly ambitious to achieve success in the West, although the most successful global release to date is still the classic *Crouching Tiger, Hidden Dragon* (Cieply, 2013) which earned $128m at the North American box office in 2000. Follow-up attempts to match this success (including *Hero*) were not nearly so successful, suggesting that for China as for India the prospects of consistent penetration of the world's wealthiest media markets (other than their own) are still relatively unpromising.

Possibly the most important and immediate route for China to secure a strong international presence in moving image entertainment is in television. Because of the size of its domestic market, China is already the most prolific producer of television series (15,000 episodes in 2013). From 2015, China's regulators require that in response to near saturation of the domestic market, television producers may only show their programs on two television networks, a reduction from four. There was excited discussion at the 2014 Shanghai television festival about how producers would need to boost television exports. Strong demand was identified for costume dramas, food documentaries, dating programs, documentaries about modern life in China, in-law dramas. Southeast Asia was the major market, but West Asia and Africa were also identified as areas suitable for immediate growth (Xinhua, 2014).

India

Over many decades, India has produced more films each year than any other country. The first full-length Indian feature film was released in 1913,

and the first chain of Indian cinemas began in 1902. In 2011 India produced close on 1,300 feature films. In terms of the average number of feature films produced annually between 2005–2009 India ranked top with
1,178, followed by Nigeria (1093), the USA (555), Japan (409), China
(380), France (228), Russia (227), Germany (179) Spain (164), Italy (124),
South Korea (118), and the UK (117). No other country produced more
than 100 films a year (UNESCO, 2012).

The Indian market is modest in size when compared with China's, and
overseas sales are principally for the Indian diaspora. Hybrid productions
such as *Slumdog Millionaire* notwithstanding, the classic features of
Bollywood entertainment, especially the "Masala" genre, are strong on spectacle, color, drama and dance, but not on character and plot development.
These characteristics impede distribution beyond the diaspora. Likewise,
prospects for the internationalization of Chinese film are restricted by highly
specific cultural features. The Indian diaspora of some 25 million is a good
deal smaller than that of China's 50 million, although concentrated in some
important media markets including Britain. Growth was restricted for many
years prior to 2000 by regulations that made film-making ineligible for bank
credit or private equity, with the result that the field attracted very high interest lenders, some associated with gangsters and politicians.

Indian film has not, so far, presented itself to Hollywood either as much of
a potential threat as China, nor as exciting a promise of profit. In 2011 both
countries had a similar number of screens (10,000 to 11,000), but the Indian
market is much more fragmented in terms of languages and production centers, and Indian audiences are accustomed to paying less at the box office.
Some of the strongest opportunities for co-production lie in television (worth
$5.5 billion in 2009), most notably in the case of News Corporation's STAR
network. Many popular reality shows on Indian television pay royalties to
Hollywood: including *Big Boss* which has 114 million viewers in India and
100 million outside and is the result of a partnership between US Viacom and
local station Network 18; *Master Chef India* and *Perfect Bride*, which are
produced by STAR; and *Who Wants to be a Millionaire*, *Indian Idol* and *Maa
Exchange*, which play on Sony channels. The Indian company Reliance
Entertainment owns 50% of the US studio DreamWorks.

Both countries have invested in multiplexes. In 2009, these represented
only 2% of screens in India but captured one third of the revenues for
Bollywood productions and one half of the revenues for Hollywood productions. The total value of the Indian film market (box office) in 2012 was
$1.4 billion as against China's $2.7 billion but growth prospects for China
were more enticing (an anticipated $5 billion by 2016 for China as against
$3 billion for India).

The most important center of production of Indian movies is Mumbai, the home of "Bollywood." Yet Mumbai certifies almost as many foreign as it does domestic features. Close to three quarters of the foreign celluloid features in India are Hollywood productions (184 out of 244 foreign movies) and close to 90% of video features (1,593 out of 1758), although Indian movies attract around 95% of the total box office revenues. In 2011 the Indian government certified 1,255 Indian celluloid, 862 video, and 45 digital features. Additionally it certified 244 foreign celluloid, 1,758 video, and 24 digital features. In the video category, therefore, foreign imports, mainly Hollywood's, far outnumber Indian productions.

Of the Indian features the majority were filmed in Hindi (206) (most popular in the North), Telugu (192) and Tamil (185). Other languages of production included Bengali (home of "Tollywood") (122), Oriya (38), Malayalam (195), Marathi (107), Kannada (138) and English (6). A relatively small number of features (147) were dubbed from one regional language to another. More foreign movies are being dubbed, sometimes into more than one regional language. Most feature films were certified in Mumbai (462, of which 227 were foreign), Chennai (202, of which 16 were foreign), Hyderabad (164, all Indian), Bangalore (159, all Indian), and Kolkata (118, all Indian)(Government of India, 2011).

CONCLUSION

The theme of communications resistance to empire is as old as empire itself. Its most typical forms are attempts to challenge imperial rule from within colonies through the establishment of vernacular media or the cooption of settler or imperial media, and the challenge in post-colonial contexts to continuing play of media products originating from the powerful, "ex-imperial" powers. In this chapter I have considered instances of the use of media by the independence movement in India, and gone on to analyze resistance to western-based international media systems. In the domain of news agencies I discussed the role of Tanjug, the news agency of Yugoslavia and for several decades the voice for the Non-Aligned Movement in partial challenge to the market dominance of the western-based news agencies. Tanjug's influence helped shape the contours of the NWICO debates and made it a natural contender for the role of coordinating agency of the Non-aligned Movement's news agencies' pool. I also considered the role in Russia of the financial and political news agency Interfax as a counterweight to the market strength of Thomson-Reuters and Bloomberg. I then considered the strength of centers of movie production that challenge

Hollywood market dominance, such as Chinese cinema and the cinemas of India (including Bollywood) that can serve to consolidate national media culture and the imaginative new constructions of national identity, which in turn may become resources for the nurture of later forms of resistance.

I have not focused specifically on the role of social media as instruments of resistance. Their functionality is likely to be just as great if not greater for imperialists as for revolutionaries. Social media are not social movements in themselves. Authorities can and do use them for surveillance, disinformation and counter-revolutionary organization. Social media are run generally by large, for-profit corporations that collude with governments. The latter have the power to shut them down. The excitement about social media during the protests against the Iranian elections of 2009, and throughout the so-called "Arab Spring" of 2010–2011 was not justified by the results of those episodes. Social organization increasingly requires tactical skill in the deployment of social media but success depends on many other important variables.

11 | Conclusion

NEW DIRECTIONS FOR THE STUDY OF MEDIA AND EMPIRE

My main endeavor has been to re-introduce and re-valorize the concept of media imperialism. I have acknowledged many of the criticisms that older approaches to media imperialism have attracted – even though I do not agree with all of these – as well as many of the more recent and insightful approaches to our understanding of international, transnational and transcultural media communications. I recognize that since the 1970s the world has changed significantly, in terms both of international relations and of what constitutes media and communications. When I first wrote about media imperialism in the 1970s the term "globalization" was not yet current and the age of personal computing was still distant for most. These considerations notwithstanding, I consider that investigations into media imperialism were not followed through at that time as they deserved.

I adduce several reasons. NWICO predictably failed to achieve substantial change in global communications inequalities, although it provided some encouragement to governments for restricting foreign ownership, imposing import quotas, and strengthening national news agencies. The centrality of the UN and of UN agencies as sources of social change began to fade in favor of older bilateral and regional arrangements spearheaded by the most prosperous nations. The collapse of the Soviet Union and the capitalist transformation of China temporarily seemed to pull the carpet out from under older anti-capitalist and pro-socialist critiques. Left-inclined scholars reverted to the seemingly less provocative languages of "public sphere," and "discourse." Neo-liberal waves of deregulation, privatization, commercialization, concentration and commodification, in communications as in other spheres, promised and in some cases actually did help to deliver substantial economic advances for whole societies as well as for many of their peoples, particularly in what came to be called the BRIC nations. Naturally these processes were far from smooth or durable and for some they were most decidedly deceptive, while the intensity of economic growth accelerated the onset of extremely worrying trends of egregious social inequality, environmental degradation, species and resource depletion, and climate change. Yet few things have been as astonishing or transformational as technology innovation in the domain of communications, and the digital revolution is likely still to be in its infancy.

In the 1970s the world was still undergoing decolonization, and with it therefore, the promise of an end to empires, a promise that was repeated up to and throughout the disintegration of the Soviet Union and the hope of an end to many of the world's conflicts that had been exacerbated by the Cold War. By the 1990s it was apparent that while nineteenth-century style empires had disappeared, new or re-discovered forms of empire had taken their place even as the residues of the nineteenth century remained, along with many of the contentious issues of inequality, artificial borders, and ethnic and tribal conflicts to which they had helped give birth. Through these mists the contours of a "free trade" global capitalist system emerged more clearly, regulated largely on behalf of corporations through international bodies such as the World Trade Organization, and disproportionately responsive to the interests of the more powerful economies. "Hold-outs," countries which resisted co-option into this system – especially if they possessed oil, gas or precious raw materials – were subjected by western elites and mainstream media to demonization and vilification, often as prelude to military threat or attack, and regime change, on a variety of generally false pretexts. The importance of mainstream media as vehicles of state and corporate (or corporate state) propaganda, even in the so-called democracies, could no longer be ignored. Repeated instances of uncritical media support to state propaganda in the contexts of such conflicts as those of Afghanistan, Iraq, Libya, Syria and Iran have gravely discredited older scholarly discourses and narratives about the functioning of the press.

I have therefore wanted to re-address issues of empire and the wide range of relationships between media and empire formation, maintenance and decline. In doing so I have concluded that there was never just one single theory of media imperialism, any more than there was ever just one form of imperialism, but that rather there is a complex array of different ways in which media and communications relate to phenomena of empire, from support to resistance. There are therefore many theories of media imperialism, within the compass of a field of study that we may call the study of media and empire. Some of these theories focus specifically on the media as institutional agents and beneficiaries of processes of capital accumulation that are inseparable from broader processes of imperialism. Others focus more on the ways in which forms of imperialism, their narratives, actors, conflicts and processes, are represented by and played out through informational and entertainment media. There is certainly scope, too, for the modification of the original concept, perhaps moving more in the direction of "mediatized imperialism" as an approach that highlights the extent to which the actions of human beings in a material world are shaped reflexively by the media and are in turn constantly re-represented and re-interpreted to shape the material world. A significant motivation behind my approach has been the urge to recover, acknowledge, and in some small way seek atonement for the immense and ineffable cruelties of imperial adventure, the facilitative role of communications and both the knowing and unknowing depths of complicity of mainstream media in exalting, omitting, forgetting, diminishing. I am as much interested in media imperialism as a phenomenon that plays out within the domestic markets of imperial powers as I am in its role in colonized markets, because the cluelessness of domestic populations is central to the endurance of imperial power. I have focused particularly on the imperial and neo-imperial ambitions of the USA which inherited the mantle of superpower from Great Britain in the years leading up to and especially in the years immediately following World War Two. After the disintegration of the Soviet Union, and before the acceleration of Chinese capitalism the USA became the sole superpower. It was a rare, perhaps a unique moment in human history, one that the USA might have used to introduce a new model, a new culture of governance. Regrettably that opportunity was quickly wasted. Preferred was a foreign policy whose underlying logic is one of global domination at the hands of intensely networked corporate and plutocratic elites operating through a small number of regulatory bodies and military alliances under US leadership. This ruling structure still corresponds to a hierarchy in the relative power of different nation states while at the same time morphing into a globalized class structure that is to some extent independent of nation states.

Many scholars and analysts believe that such logic is unsustainable, that the real structure of the world has become flatter and more pluralist. In this book I have resisted that conclusion. In the realm of media and communications as in military weaponry and expenditure I have tried to draw attention to the very considerable lead that the USA still enjoys over most other countries of the world in most domains. I do not know whether or for how long this state of affairs will continue. Our era is in many important ways unprecedented, not least in the sophistication of surveillance and military might, and it is not impossible that a threshold has been passed that opens up the real possibility of a single global apparatus of both coercive and hegemonic power, notwithstanding the considerable and persistent actual and potential scope for conflict between rival centers of power. Many sources attest to the emergence of unprecedented degrees of inequality on this planet, accompanied by equally unprecedented concentrations of wealth and power that are wholly inimical to any meaningful claim to democratic process. As political processes become further and further removed from the material interests of the majorities of people, we will inevitably see more and more dependence on the media to create narratives and nurture ideologies whose purpose is to "normalize" and "naturalize" this state of affairs of inequality and oppression, and as equally we will also witness the formation by media of the counter-propagandas of those who are willing to contest the dominant power. At the very least, I do not believe that the age of empires or of Empire has passed. I anticipate that communications infrastructures, communications industries of information, entertainment and data – including their weaponized manifestations in robotic, drone, and cyber warfare – and symbolic representations will continue to be critical to both the exercise of power and resistance to it, both materially and ideologically.

Bibliography

Agence France Presse (AFP)(2013) IAEA, Iran talks fail again as US hikes pressure, *Channel News Asia*, available at www.channelnewsasia.com/news/world/iaea-iran-talks-fail-again-as-us-hikes-p/676504.html (last accessed 18 May 2013).

Agence France Presse (AFP) (2010) Nigeria's Nollywood eclipsing Hollywood in Africa, *Independent*, available at www.independent.co.uk/arts-entertainment/films/nigerias-nollywood-eclipsing hollywood-in-africa-1974087.html (last accessed 15 May 2013).

Alford, M. (2011) Why not a propaganda model for Hollywood? In P. Hammond (ed.), *Screens of Terror*. London: Arima.

Al Jazeera (2009) The Iranian political system, *Al Jazeera*, available at www.aljazeera.com/news/middleeast/2009/06/200961111422655588.html (last accessed 21 April 2013).

Almiron, N. (2010) *Journalism in Crisis: Corporate Media and Financialization*. New York: Hampton Press.

Amnesty International (2012) *Libya: Rule of Law or Rule of Militias?* London: Amnesty International.

Anon (2011) *This is Nollywood,* available at www.thisisnollywood.com/

Appadurai, A. (1992) *Modernity at Large: Cultural Dimension of Globalization* (Public Worlds). Minnesota: University of Minnesota Press.

Arkin, W. (2002, 10 March) Secret plan outlines the unthinkable, *Los Angeles Times*, available at http://articles.latimes.com/2002/mar/10/opinion/op-arkin (last accessed 24 January 2014).

Arsenault, A. and Castells, M. (2008) The structure and dynamics of global multi-media business networks, *International Journal of Communication*, 2: 707–48.

Associated Press (2013, 3 Sept) The Russian president says he hasn't excluded possibility of backing a U.N. resolution on punitive military strikes, Amnesty International (2011), *The Battle for Libya: Killings, Disappearances and Torture.* London: Amnesty International.

Associated Press (2011, 21 Feb) Elections in Libya's Misrata show a splintered nation, *CTV News*, available at www.ctvnews.ca/elections-in-libya-s-misrata-show-a-splintered-nation-1.771455 (last accessed 24 January 2014).

Associated Press (2005, 30 May) Wolfowitz comments revive doubts over Iraq's WMD, *USA Today*, www.usatoday.com/news/world/iraq/2003-05-30-wolfowitz-iraq_x.htm (last accessed 12 July 2012).

Associated Press (2005, 8 Sept) Powell calls pre-Iraq U.N. speech a "blot" on his record, *USA Today*, available at www.usatoday.com/news/washington/2005-09-08-powell-Iraq_x.htm (last accessed 12 July 2012).

Associated Press (2003, 12 March) Iran can't build nuke without tripping alarm bells, US says. *The Times of Israel*, available at www.timesofisrael.com/iran-cant-build-nuke-without-tripping-alarm-bells-us-says/ (last accessed 18 May 2013).

Avramović, M. (ed.) (1993) *Tanjug Pola Veka*. Belgrade: Novinska Agencija Tanjug.

Bai, M. (2012, 22 Feb) Scott Ritter's other war, *New York Times*, p. MM38.

Bacchi, U. (2013, 9 Sept) Syria: Assad not responsible for Ghouta gas attack, says freed hostage Pierre Piccinin, *International Business Times*, available at www.ibtimes.co.uk/syria-chemical-attack-assad-rebels-blame-hostage-504735 (last accessed 24 January 2014).

Bailyn, B. (ed.)(1965) *Pamphlets of the American Revolution, 1750–1776*. Cambridge, MA: Harvard University Press.

Bajoria, J. and Pan, E. (2010, 5 Nov) The U.S.-India nuclear deal, *Council for Foreign Relations*, available at www.cfr.org/india/us-india-nuclear-deal/p9663 (last accessed 7 May 2013).

Baker, R. (2012, 4 April) How war reporting in Syria makes a larger conflict inevitable, *Who What Why*, available at whowhatwhy.com/2012/04/02/how-war-reporting-in-syria-makes-a-larger-conflict-inevitable/ (last accessed 25 January 2013).

Baker, R. (2011, 15 June) More questions about the Libyan sex atrocity reporting. Who what why Factchecks the media, *WhoWhatWhy*, available at whowhatwhy.com/2011/06/15/whowhatwhy-factchecks-the-media-more-questions-about-the-libyan-sex-atrocity-reporting (last accessed 3 January 2013).

Balaghi, S. (2013) A brief history of 20th-Century Iran, *Greyonline*, available at www.nyu.edu/greyart/exhibits/iran/briefhistory/ (last accessed 21 April 2013).

Bamford, J. (2005) *A Pretext for War: 9/11, Iraq and the Abuse of America's Intelligence Agencies*. New York: Anchor.

Barstow, D. (2008, 20 April) Behind TV analysts, Pentagon's hidden hand, *New York Times*, available at www.nytimes.com/2008/04/20/us/20generals.html?pagewanted=all

Bayly, C.A. (2000) *Empire and Information: Intelligence Gathering and Social Communication in India, 1780–1870*. London: Cambridge University Press.

BBC (2006, 10 March) Secret sale of UK plutonium to Israel, *Newsnight*.

Bennett, L., Lawrence, R. and Livingstone, S. (2008) *When the Press Fails: Political Power and the News Media from Iraq to Katrina*. Chicago: University of Chicago Press.

Bergman, R. (2012, 29 Jan) Will Israel attack Iran?, *New York Times*, available at www.nytimes.com/2012/01/29/magazine/will-israel-attack-iran.html?pagewanted=all&_r=0 (last accessed 26 April 2013).

Bisturek, R. (2013, 14 Sept) Turkey indicts six jihadists for alleged attempts to acquire chemicals with intent to produce sarin, *Information Clearing House*, available at www.informationclearinghouse.info/article36228.htm (last accessed 24 January 2014).

Blitzer (2012, 11 July) The situation room (transcripts), *CNN*, available at transcripts.cnn.com/TRANSCRIPTS/1207/11/sitroom.01.html (last accessed 3 May 2012).

Bloodhound (2007a, 17 Sept) Special Report: ABC-Debate scandal, unanswered and unasked questions, *Bloodhound*, available at http://mediabloodhound.typepad.com/weblog/2007/09/special-report-.html (last accessed 10 April 2013).

Bloodhound (2007b, 26 Sept) Special Report: NPR goes easy on ABC News spokesman in debat affair, *Bloodhound*, available at http://mediabloodhound.typepad.com/weblog/2007/09/special-repor-1.html (last accessed 10 April 2013).

Blum, W. (2012a, 3 Oct) Syria: The story thus far, *The Anti-Empire Report*, available at http://killinghope.org/bblum6/aer109.html (last accessed 25 January 2013).

Blum, W. (2012b, 7 April) Putting Syria into some perspective, *World Socialist Web Site*, available at www.informationclearinghouse.info/article31017.htm (last accessed 25 January 2013).

Blum, W. (2004) *Killing Hope: U.S. Military and CIA Interventions since World War II*, revised edition. Monroe, ME: Common Courage Press.

Borger, J. (2012, 22 March) Nuclear watchdog chief accused of pro-western bias over Iran, *The Guardian*, available at www.theguardian.com/world/2012/mar/22/nuclear-watchdog-iran-iaea (last accessed 24 January 2014).

Borger, J. (2010, 30 Nov) Nuclear Wikileaks: cables show cosy US relationship with IAEA chief, *The Guardian*, available at www.theguardian.com/world/2012/mar/22/nuclear-watchdog-iran-iaea (last accessed 24 January 2014).

Borger, J. (1999, 3 March) UN "kept in dark" about US spying in Iraq, *The Guardian*, available at www.theguardian.com/world/1999/mar/03/iraq.julianborger (last accessed 24 January 2014).

Bowles, W. (2013, 30 Aug) US-Israeli false flag gas attack unravels: commit a war crime to cover up a war crime?, *Information Clearing House*, available at www.informationclearinghouse.info/article36028.htm (last accessed 24 January 2014).

Bowles, W. (2012, 17 Feb) Syria and the media: "Activists say …", *Information Clearing House*, available at www.informationclearinghouse.info/article30562.htm (last accessed 25 January 2013).

Bowles, W. (2011, 23 March) Libya's "Operation Odyssey Dawn": Kosovo Revisited. *Global Research*, available at http://www.globalresearch.ca/libya-s-operation-odyssey-dawn-kosovo-revisited/23880 (last accessed 11 June 2014).

Boyd-Barrett, C. and Boyd-Barrett, O. (2010) 24/7 news as counter-hegemonic soft power in Latin America. In S. Cushion and J. Lewis (eds), *The Rise of 24-Hour News Television*. New York: Peter Lang.

Boyd-Barrett, O. (2014) *Interfax: Breaking Into Global News*. Lancaster: Carnegie Publishing House.

Boyd-Barrett, O. (2010a) Recovering agency for the propaganda model: the implications for reporting war and peace. In R. Keeble (ed.), *Peace Journalism, War and Conflict Resolution*. London: Peter Lang.

Boyd-Barrett, O. (ed.) (2010b) *News Agencies in the Turbulent Era of the Internet*. Barcelona: Generalitat de Catalunya: Col.leccio Lexikon.

Boyd-Barrett, O. (2007) Positioning the news audience as idiot. In S. Maltby and R. Keeble (eds), *Communicating War: Memory, Military and Media*. Bury St. Edmunds: Arima. pp. 90–102.

Boyd-Barrett, 0. (2006) Cyberspace, globalization and empire, *Global Media and Communication*, 2 (1): 21–42.

Boyd-Barrett, O. (2004) Judith Miller, the *New York Times*, and the propaganda model, *Journalism Studies*, 5 (4).

Boyd-Barrett, O. (2003) Doubt foreclosed: U.S. mainstream media and the attacks of 9–11. In N. Chitty, R. Rush and M. Semati (eds), *Studies in Terrorism*. Penang: Journal of International Communication/Southbound Press, pp. 35–54.

Boyd-Barrett, O. (1998a) The globalization of news. In O. Boyd-Barrett and T. Rantanen (eds), *The Globalization of News*. London: Sage.

Boyd-Barrett, O. (1998b) Media imperialism reformulated. In D.K. Thussu (ed.), *Electronic Empires*. London: Edward Arnold.

Boyd-Barrett, O. (1982) Cultural dependence and mass media. In M. Gurevitch, J. Curran and J. Woollacott (eds), *Culture, Society and the Media*. London: Macmillan.

Boyd-Barrett, O. (1980) *The International News Agencies*. London: Constable.

Boyd-Barrett, O. (1977a) Media imperialism: towards an international framework for the analysis of media systems. In M.Gurevitch, J.Curran and J. Woollacott (eds), *Mass Communication and Society*. London: Edward Arnold, pp.116–35.

Boyd-Barrett, O. (1977b) Mass communication in cross-cultural contexts. In *Mass Communication and Society* (Unit 5 of DE353). Milton Keynes: Open University Press.

Boyd-Barrett, O., Herrera, D. and Bauman, J. (2010) *Hollywood and the CIA*. London: Routledge.

Boyd-Barrett, O. and Thussu, D. (1992) *Contra-flow in Global News: International and Regional News Exchange Mechanisms*. Luton: John Libbey.

Boyd-Barrett, O. and Xie, S. (2008) (2008) Al-Jazeera, Phoenix Satellite Television and the return of the state: case studies in market liberalization, public sphere and media imperialism. *International Journal of Communication*, 2: 206–224

Bramhall, S. (2012, 14 Feb) The covert US war against Syria, *Salon.com*, http://open.salon.com/blog/stuartbramhall/2012/02/14/the_covert_us_war_against_syria

Brautigam, D. (2009) *The Dragon's Gift: The Real Story of China in Africa*. New York: Oxford University Press.

Broad, W.J., Markoff, J. and Sanger, D. (2011, 15 Jan) Israel tests on worm called crucial in Iran nuclear delay, *New York Times*, available at www.nytimes.com/2011/01/16/world/middleeast/16stuxnet.html?pagewanted=all (last accessed 24 January 2014).

Brown, S. (1937) *Press in Ireland: A Survey and a Guide*. Dublin: Brown and Nolan.

Brzezinski, Z. (1997) *The Grand Chessboard: American Primacy and its Geostrategic Imperatives*. New York: Basic Books.

Bunker, R.J. (2011) Grand strategic overview: epochal change and new realities for the United States, *Small Wars and Insurgencies*, 22: 5.

Butt, Y. (2012, 12 Dec) Flawed graph weakens case against Iran nuclear program, *Christian Science Monitor*, available at www.csmonitor.com/Commentary/Opinion/2012/1205/Flawed-graph-weakens-case-against-Iran-nuclear-program-video (last accessed 18 April 2013).

Butt, Y. and Dalnoki-Veress, F. (2012, 28 Nov) DIY graphic design, *Bulletin of the Atomic Scientists*, available at www.thebulletin.org/web-edition/op-eds/diy-graphic-design (last accessed 18 April 2012).

Byrce, J. (1901) *Studies in History and Jurisprudence*. New York: Oxford University Press.

Byrne, A. (2012, 5 Jan) A mistaken case of Syrian regime change, *Asian Times*, available at www.atimes.com/atimes/Middle_East/NA05Ak03.html (last accessed 25 January 2013).

Cain, R. (2012) Chinese revenues for US films has doubled in five months, *Chinafilmbiz*, available at http://chinafilmbiz.wordpress.com/2012/05/04/chinese-box-office-for-u-s-films-has-doubled-in-five-months/ (last accessed 22 August 2012).

Cartalucci, T. (2013, 27 Aug) Reuters: US to strike Syria before UN evidence collected and the real meaning of "limited strikes", *Landdestroyer*, available at http://landdestroyer.blogspot.com/2013/08/reuters-us-to-strike-syria-before-un.html (last accessed 24 January 2014).

Cartalucci, T. (2012a, 25 July) BBC covers up war crimes, misleads over Syrian security operations, *Land Destroyer Report*, available at http://landdestroyer.blogspot.com/2012/07/bbc-rides-with-al-qaeda-in-aleppo-syria.html (last accessed 25 January 2013).

Cartalucci, T. (2012b, 29 May) West's Houla Syria narrative crumbles, expels Syrian diplomats anyway. *Information Clearing House*, available at www.informationclearinghouse.info/article31449.htm (last accessed 25 January 2013).

Cartalucci, T. (2012c, 19 March) Syrian rebels are foreign-backed terrorists: latest terrorist attack in Damascus illustrates illegitimacy of both Syria's rebels and the UN/Nato backing them, *Landdestroyer*, available at http://landdestroyer.blogspot.com/2012/03/syrian-rebels-are-foreign-backed.html

Cartalucci, T. (2011) CIA Coup-College recycled revolutionary "props", *Infowars.com*, available at www.infowars.com/cia-coup-college-recycled-revolutionary-props/ (last accessed 24 January 2014).

Castells, M. (2000) *The Rise of the Network Society* (The Information Age: Economy, Society and Culture, Volume 1), 2nd edition. New York: Wiley.

Centre for Iranian Studies (2006) *Understanding Iran's Assembly of Experts*, Centre for Iranian Studies, Durham University, available at www.dur.ac.uk/resources/iranian.studies/Policy%20Brief%201.pdf (last accessed 21 April 2013).

Chamberlain, J. (2013, 3 June) Nuclear states defy treaty, up stockpiles, watchdog warns, *Common Dreams*, available at www.commondreams.org/headline/2013/06/03-1 (last accessed 12 September 2013).

Chan, J. -Y.-H. and Fung, A. (2011) Structural hybridization in film and television production, *Visual Anthropology*, 24 (1–2).

Channel 4 (2011) How Murdoch ran Britain, *Dispatches*.

Chomsky, N. (1998a) *Deterring Democracy*. New York: Vintage.

Chomsky, N. (1998b) *What Uncle Sam Really Wants*. London: Pluto.

Chulov, M. and Pidd, H. (2011, 15 Feb) Defector admits to WMD lies that triggered Iraq war, *The Guardian*, available at www.guardian.co.uk/world/2011/feb/15/defector-admits-wmd-lies-iraq-war (last accessed (17 Dec 2012).

Cieply, M. (2013a, 6 Nov) China wants its movies to be big in the US too, *New York Times*, available at www.nytimes.com/2013/11/07/business/media/china-wants-its-movies-to-be-big-in-the-us-too.html (last accessed 14 November 2013).

Cieply, M. (2013b, 21 April) Heroes proving mortal in China, *New York Times*, p. A1.

Cieply, M. and Barboza, D. (2012, 29 April) In China, foreign films meet a powerful gatekeeper, *New York Times*, available at www.nytimes.com/2012/04/30/business/media/china-film-group-acts-as-a-powerful-gatekeeper.html?_r=0 (last accessed 14 November 2013).

Cieply, M. and Barnes, B. (2013, 14 Jan) To get movies into China, Hollywood gives censors a preview, *New York Times*, available at www.nytimes.com/2013/01/15/business/media/in-hollywood-movies-for-china-bureaucrats-want-a-say.html

Clark, C. and Jimenez, M. (2012, 13 April) Leaders rethink the war on drugs at Summit of the Americas, *The Globe and Mail*, available at www.theglobeandmail.

com/news/politics/leaders-rethink-the-war-on-drugs-at-summit-of-the-americas/article2402426 (last accessed 18 July 2012).

Clark, W. (2007, 3 Oct) Executive order NRDP, *ForaTV*, available at www.youtube.com/watch?feature=player_detailpage&v=6DzG-AFZR0s

Cockburn, A. and St. Clair, J. (1999) *Whiteout: The CIA, Drugs and the Press*. New York: Verso.

Cockburn, P. (2013, 3 Jan) Cockburn continues exposure of lies about Syria, *Larouche.pac*,available at http://larouchepac.com/node/25028 (last accessed 25 January 2013).

Cogan, J. (2010, 30 Aug) Evidence that Afghan leaders are on CIA payroll, *World Socialist Web Site*, available at www.wsws.org/articles/2010/aug2010/ciaa-a30.shtml (last accessed 27 July 2012).

Cohen, J. and Solomon, N. (1994, 7 July) 30-year anniversary: Tonkin Gulf lie launched Vietnam War, *FAIR.org*, available at http://fair.org/media-beat-column/30-year-anniversary-tonkin-gulf-lie-launched-vietnam-war (last accessed 6 December 2013).

Common Dreams Staff (2012, 18 April) Israel's Deputy Prime Minister admits Ahmadinejad never said Israel should be "Wiped off the face of the map," *Common Dreams*, available at www.commondreams.org/headline/2012/04/18–2 (last accessed 1 May 2013).

Cook, T. (1998) *Governing with the News: The News Media as a Political Institution*. Chicago: The University of Chicago Press.

Cordesman, A. (2000, 7 Feb) Iran and nuclear weapons: a working draft, *Centre for Strategic and International Studies*.

Crain, M (2009, November) *Telling Their Own Story: The Transformation of the Non-Aligned News Agencies Pool, 1975–2005*. Paper presented at the annual meeting of the NCA 95th Annual Convention, Chicago Hilton & Towers, Chicago, Retrieved from http://www.allacademic.com/meta/p366025_index.html

Cromwell, D. (2012, 18 July Libyan elections – burying the Amnesty Report, *MediaLens.org*, available at www.medialens.org/index.php?option=com_content&view=article&id=690:libyan-elections-burying-the-amnesty-report&catid=25:alerts-2012&Itemid=9 (last accessed 24 January 2014).

Croteau, D. and Hoynes, W. (2005) *The Business of Media: Corporate Media and the Public Interest*. Thousand Oaks, CA: Sage.

Curtin, M. and Shah, H. (2010) *Reorienting Global Communication: Indian and Chinese Media Beyond Borders*. Chicago: University of Illinois Press.

Curtis, A. (2012, 6 Oct) He's behind you: how Colonel Gaddafi and the Western establishment created a pantomime world, *Information Clearing House*, available at www.informationclearinghouse.info/article32851.htm (last accessed 13 January 2013).

Curtis, A. (2006) *The Power of Nightmares,* BBC.

Curtis, A. (2002) *A Century of the Self*, BBC.

Cushion, S. and Lewis, J. (eds) (2010) *The Rise of 24-Hour News Television: Global Perspectives*. New York: Peter Lang.

Davies, N. (2012, 29 Oct) Armed rebels and Middle-Eastern power plays: how the U.S. is helping to kill peace in Syria, *AlterNet*, available at www.alternet.org/world/armed-rebels-and-middle-eastern-power-plays-how-us-helping-kill-peace-syria (last accessed 25 January 2013).

Democracy Now (2013, 5 Sept) Iran-Contra Redux? Prince Bandar heads secret Saudi-CIA effort to aid Syrian rebels, topple Assad, *Democracy Now,* available at www.democracynow.org/2013/9/6/iran_contra_redux_prince_bandar_heads (last accessed 24 January 2014).

Dighe, R. (n.d.) Business support for Prohibition and its repeal. *Rockarch.org*, available at http://www.rockarch.org/publications/resrep/dighe.pdf (last accessed 17 June, 2014).

Dimaggio, A. (2009) *When Media goes to War: Hegemonic Discourse, Public Opinion, and the Limits of Dissent.* New York: Monthly Review Press.

Ditz, J. (2013a, 28 Aug) Iran has more or less same stockpile it had in May, *Antiwar. com,* available at http://news.antiwar.com/2013/08/28/new-iaea-data-iran-still-not-close-to-israels-red-line (last accessed 12 September 2013).

Ditz, J. (2013b, 28 Aug) US: Assad to blame for chemical attack even if he didn't do it insists Commander in Chief responsible for anything that happens, *Antiwar. com*, available at http://news.antiwar.com/2013/08/28/us-assad-to-blame-for-chemical-attack-even-if-he-didnt-do-it (last accessed 24 January 2014).

Ditz, J. (2013c, 19 Aug) Diplomats: Iran may be stepping up civilian use, *Antiwar. com*, available at http://news.antiwar.com/2013/08/19/irans-civilian-use-of-uranium-frustrates-hawks (last accessed 12 September 2013).

Ditz, J. (2013d, 18 June) Russian FM: Iran prepared to stop 20% uranium enrichment, *Antiwar.com*, available at http://news.antiwar.com/2013/06/18/russian-fm-iran-prepared-to-stop-20-percent-uranium-enrichment (last accessed 12 September 2013).

Ditz, J. (2013e, 3 June) IAEA chief frets searching Iran site finding nothing, *Antiwar. com*, available at http://news.antiwar.com/2013/06/03/iaea-chief-frets-searching-iran-site-finding-nothing (last accessed 12 September 2013).

Ditz, J. (2010, 8 Feb) AP article fuels Iran war hysteria, *Antiwar.com*, available at http://news.antiwar.com/2010/02/08/ap-article-fuels-iran-war-hysteria/ (last accessed 23 April 2013).

Ditz, J. (2009, 15 Nov) CIA funneling hundreds of millions of dollars to Pakistani spy agency: roughly a third of secretive spy group's budget comes from CIA, *Antiwar. com*, available at http://news.antiwar.com/2009/11/15/cia-funneling-hundreds-of-millions-of-dollars-to-pakistani-spy-agency/ (last accessed 27 July 2012).

Diuk, N. (2004, 4 Dec) In Ukraine, homegrown freedom, *Washington Post*, p. A23.

Dixon, H. (2011, 4 Oct) Guantanamo's detox man, *Reuters.com*, available at http://blogs.reuters.com/hugo-dixon/tag/guantanamo-bay (last accessed 16 July 2012).

Dombey, N. (2009, 22 Dec) This is no smoking gun, nor Iranian bomb: nothing in the published "Intelligence Documents" shows Iran is close to having nuclear weapons, *The Guardian*, available at www.theguardian.com/commentisfree/2009/dec/22/no-iran-nuclear-bomb-trigger (last accessed 24 January 2014).

Dozier, K. and Apuzzo, M. (2013, 28 Aug) AP sources: intelligence on weapons no "slam dunk," AP, available at http://bigstory.ap.org/article/ap-sources-intelligence-weapons-no-slam-dunk (last accessed 24 January 2014).

Draitser, E. (2013, 3 Sept) Debunking Obama's chemical weapons case against the Syrian government, *Global Research*, available at www.globalresearch.ca/so-called-intelligence-debunking-the-u-s-government-assessment-of-the-syrian-governments-use-of-chemical-weapons-on-august-21-2013/5347359 (last accessed 24 January 2014).

Dubai Press Club (2012) *Arab Media Outlook: Forecasts and Analysis of Traditional and Digital Media in the Arab World* 4th edition. Dubai: Dubai Press Club.

Dynon, N. (2013, 19 June) Soft power: A U.S.-China battleground, *The Diplomat*, available at http://thediplomat.com/china-power/soft-power-a-u-s-china-battleground/ (last accessed 6 November 2013).

Edwards, D. (2013, 13 June) "Limited but persuasive" evidence: Syria, sarin, Libya, lies, *MediaLens.org*, available http://medialens.org/index.php/alerts/alert-archive/alerts-2013/735-limited-but-persuasive-evidence-syria-sarin-libya-lies.html (last accessed 24 January 2014).

Edwards, D. (2012) Won't get fooled again? Hyping Syria's WMD "threat," *Global Research*, available at www.globalresearch.ca/wont-get-fooled-again-hyping-syrias-wmd-threat/5315387 (last accessed 25 January 2013).

Eisenstein, E. L. (1979) *The Printing Press as an Agent of Change: Communications and Cultural Transformations in Early-Modern Europe*. Cambridge: Cambridge University Press.

Emery, E. (1984) *The Press and America: An Interpretive History of the Mass Media*. Upper Saddle River, NJ: Prentice-Hall.

Entertainment Software Association (2013) Essential factors about the computer and video game industry, *Entertainment Software Association*, available at www.theesa.com/ (last accessed 21 November 2013).

Entman, R.M. (2003) *Projections of Power: Framing News, Public Opinion, and US Foreign Policy*. Chicago: University of Chicago Press.

Ervand, A. (2008) *A History of Modern Iran*. Cambridge: Cambridge University Press.

Escobar, P. (2012, 4 Aug) Syrian blood etches a new line in the sand, *Voltairenet.org*, available at www.voltairenet.org/article175260.html (last accessed 25 January 2013).

FAIR (2013a, 15 May) Iraq then, Syria now?, *New York Times*, sarin and skepticism, *FAIR.org*, available at http://fair.org/take-action/action-alerts/iraq-then-syria-now (last accessed 24 January 2014).

FAIR (2013b, 6 May) Syria skepticism: chemical claims should be investigated, not used as pretext for war, *FAIR.org*, available at http://fair.org/take-action/media-advisories/syria-skepticism (last accessed 24 January 2014).

FAIR (2012, 6 Jan) NYT misleads readers on Iran crisis: paper disappears some inaccurate reporting, *FAIR.org*, available at http://fair.org/take-action/action-alerts/nyt-misleads-readers-on-iran-crisis/ (last accessed 26 April 2013).

FAIR (2011a, 29 Mar) Public TV's Libya limits, *FAIR.org*, available at http://fair.org/take-action/action-alerts/public-tvs-libya-limits, (last accessed 3 January 2013).

FAIR (2011b, 23 May) Libya and the La Fenton, B. (2003, 16 Sept) Macmillan backed Syria assassination plot, *The Guardian*, available at www.guardian.co.uk/politics/2003/sep/27/uk.syria1 (last accessed 24 January 2014).

FAIR (2002, 1 Oct) What a difference four years makes: why U.N. inspectors left Iraq – then and now, *FAIR.org*, available at http://fair.org/extra-online-articles/what-a-difference-four-years-makes (last accessed 31 December 2012).

Ferguson, C.D. and Potter, W.C. (2006, 12 Sept) Lining up to enrich uranium, *International Herald Tribune*, available at www. Iht.com/articles/2006/09/12/opinion/edfurguson.php (last accessed 12 April 2013).

Fifth Estate (1992, Dec) *To Sell a War* (TV). Toronto: Canadian Broadcasting Corporation.

Filkins, D. (2010, 1 March) Despite doubt, Karzai brother retains power, *New York Times,* available at www.nytimes.com/2010/03/31/world/asia/31karzai. html?ref=dexterfilkins&gwh=19 5708F2C58CC728CFC0EAF0944CB3B (last accessed 27 July 2012).

Filkins, D. and Marchetti (2010, 25 Aug) Karzai aide in corruption inquiry is tied to CIA, *New York Times*, available at www.nytimes.com/2010/08/26/world/ asia/26kabul.html?ref=dexterfilkins (last accessed 27 July 2012).

Fish, I. and Dokoupil, T. (2010, 3 Sept) All the propaganda that's fit to print, *The Daily Planet,* available at www.thedailyplanet.com/index.php?option=com_content& view=article&id=3555:all-the-propaganda-thats-fit-to-print &catid=52:industry-links&Itemid=282 (last accessed 24 January 2014).

Fisk, R. (2013, 28 April) Syria and sarin gas: US claims have a very familiar ring: reports of the Assad regime's use of chemical weapons are part of a retold drama riddled with plot, *The Independent,* available at www.independent.co.uk/news/ world/middle-east/syria-and-sarin-gas-us-claims-have-a-very-familiar-ring-8591214. html (last accessed24 January 2014).

Florcruz, M. (2013, 4 April) Hollywood eyes China audiences in latest movie trailers, *Salon.com,* available at www.salon.com/2013/04/04/hollywood_eyes_ chinese_audiences_in_latest_movie_trailers_partner (last accessed 24 January 2014).

Frank, T. (2001) *One Market Under God: Extreme Capitalism, Market Populism and the End of Democracy.* New York: Anchor.

Fritz, B. (2012, 2 Jan) Imports top local films as China box office grows 28% in 2012, *Los Angeles Times*, available at http://articles.latimes.com/2013/jan/02/entertainment/ la-et-ct-china-box-office-20130102 (last accessed 14 November 2013).

Fritz, B., Horn, J. and Pierson, D. (2012, 28 Aug) In China, Hollywood blockbusters face off on same days, *Los Angeles Times*, available at http://articles.latimes. com/2012/aug/28/entertainment/la-et-ct-china-movies-20120828 (last accessed 14 November 2013).

Frontline (2004) *The Ghosts of Rwanda* (TV). Washington: Public Broadcasting Service.

Gaist, T. (2013, 8 May) US shrugs off Syrian opposition's chemical weapons use, presses for war, *World Socialist Web Site*, available at www.wsws.org/en/articles/2013/05/08/ syri-m08.html (last accessed 24 January 2014).

Galeano, E. and Gibbs, D.N. (2004) Pretexts and US foreign policy: the war on terrorism in historical perspective, *New Political Scientist*, 26:3, Sept, available at http://dgibbs.faculty.arizona.edu/sites/dgibbs.faculty.arizona.edu/files/pretexts_0. pdf (last accessed 12 July 2012).

Galeano, J. (2003) *Las Venas Abiertas de América Latina*, 2nd edition, Madrid: Siglo.

GAO (2008, Oct) United States Government Accountability Office, *PLAN COLOMBIA: Drug Reduction Goals Were Not Fully Met, But Security Has Improved: US Agencies Need More Detailed Plans for Reducing Assistance,* GAO, available at www.gao.gov/new.items/d0971.pdf (p. 17) (last accessed 24 January 2014).

Gaudiosi, J. (2012, 18 July) New reports forecast global video game industry will reach $82 billion by 2017, *Forbes.com*, available at www.forbes.com/sites/johngaudiosi/2012/07/18/new-reports-forecasts-global-video-game-industry-will-reach-82-billion-by-2017/ (last accessed 21 November 2013).

Gavlak, D. and Ababneh, Y. (2013, 29 Aug) Syrians in Ghouta claim Saudi-supplied rebels behind chemical attack, *Mint Press*, available at www.mintpressnews.com/witnesses-of-gas-attack-say-saudis-supplied-rebels-with-chemical-weapons/168135 (last accessed 24 January 2014).

Ghosh, B. (2009, 28 Oct) A brief history of CIA assets, *Time*, available at www.time.com/time/specials/packages/article/0,28804,1933053_1933052_1933042,00.html (last accessed 17 December 2012).

Gibbs, D.N. (2004) Pretexts and US foreign policy: the War on Terrorism in historical perspective, *New Political Scientist*, 26:3, Sept, available at http://dgibbs.faculty.arizona.edu/sites/dgibbs.faculty.arizona.edu/files/pretexts_0.pdf, (last accessed July 12, 2012).

Giraldi, P. (2013, 7 May) CIA pays the Potentate, *The American Conservative*, available at www.theamericanconservative.com/articles/cia-pays-the-potentate (last accessed 23 May 2013).

Glaser, J. (2013, 13 Feb) UN report: Iran is diverting uranium for peaceful purposes, *Antiwar.com*, available at http://news.antiwar.com/2013/02/20/un-report-iran-is-diverting-uranium-for-peaceful-purposes/ (last accessed 18 May 2013).

Glaser, J. (2012a, 12 Dec) Gitmo judge bans any mention of defendants' detention, torture, *Antiwar.com* (last accessed 16 December 2012).

Glaser, J. (2012b, 1 Aug) The power of propaganda on Iran, and how it works, *Antiwar.com*, http://antiwar.com/blog/2012/08/01/the-power-of-war-propaganda-on-iran-and-how-it-works

Glaser, J. (2012c, 25 April) Foreign oil companies vie for Libyan oil as a new government takes shape, *Antiwar.org*, available at http://news.antiwar.com/2012/04/25/foreign-oil-corporations-vie-for-libya-as-new-government-takes-shape (last accessed 4 January 2013).

Global Commission on Drug Policy (2011) War on drugs, available at www.globalcommissionondrugs.org/wp-content/themes/gcdp_v1/pdf/Global_Commission_Report_English.pdf (last accessed 24 January 2014).

Goff, S. (2003) The blurring of the lines: US overt and covert assistance in Colombia. In *International Action Center, War in Colombia: Made in the USA,* New York.

Gonzalez, J. (2002) *Harvest of Empire: A History of Latinos in America.* New York: Penguin.

Gordon, M., Schmitt, E. and Arango, T. (2012, 1 Dec) Flow of arms to Syria through Iraq persists, to U.S. dismay, *New York Times*, available at www.nytimes.com/2012/12/02/world/middleeast/us-is-stumbling-in-effort-to-cut-syria-arms-flow.html?pagewanted=all (last accessed 27 April 2013).

Government of India, Central Board of Film Certification (2012) *Annual Report 2011,* available at http://cbfcindia.gov.in/CbfcWeb/fckeditor/editor/images/Uploadedfiles/file/Publications/ANNUAL_2011.pdf

Gowans, S. (2012, 2 Oct) What's left? Syria's uprising in context, available at http://gowans.wordpress.com/2012/02/10/syrias-uprising-in-context/

Greenwald, G. (2012a, 29 Nov) AP's dangerous Iran hoax demands an accounting and explanation, *The Guardian*, available at www.guardian.co.uk/commentis-free/2012/nov/29/ap-iran-nuclear-program-graph-explanation (last accessed 18 April 2013).

Greenwald, G. (2012b, 28 Nov) AP believed it found evidence of Iran's work on nuclear weapons, *The Guardian*, available at www.guardian.co.uk/commentis-free/2012/nov/28/ap-iran-nuclear-bomb (last accessed 18 April 2013).

Greenwald, G. (2012c, 9 Nov) CNN claims Iran shot at a US drone, revealing mind-set, *The Guardian*, available at www.guardian.co.uk/commentisfree/2012/nov/08/cnn-iran-drones-gulf (last accessed 27 April 2013).

Greenwald, G. (2012d, 20 July) The US and Israel blame Iran for the suicide attack in Bulgaria, but offer no evidence for the accusation, *Salon.com*, available at www.salon.com/2012/07/20/journalism_v_propaganda/ (last accessed 27 April 2013).

Greenwald, G. (2012e, 29 Feb) Gen. McCaffrey privately briefs NBC execs on war with Iran, *Salon.com*, available at www.salon.com/2012/02/28/gen_mccaffrey_privately_briefs_nbc_execs_on_war_with_iran/ (last accessed 2 April 2013).

Greenwald, G. (2011, 26 Sept) What media coverage omits about U.S. hikers released by Iran, *Salon.com*, available at www.salon.com/2011/09/26/iran_105/ (last accessed 25 April 2013).

Greenwald, G. (2010, 31 March) "Reporting" on Iran should seem familiar, *Salon.com*, available at www.salon.com/2010/03/31/iran_55/ (last accessed 23 April 2013).

Gregory, A. (2012, 25 Feb) Insinuation as war propaganda, *The Beacon*, available at http://blog.independent.org/2012/02/23/insinuation-as-war-propaganda/ (last accessed 25 April 2013).

Grey, B. (2012, 31 Jan) The New York Times and the drive to war against Iran, *World Socialist Web Site*, available at www.wsws.org/en/articles/2012/01/pers-j31.html (last accessed 26 April 2013).

Griffin, D.R. (2009) *Osama Bin Laden: Dead or Alive?* Northampton: Oliver Branch.

Griffin, D.R. (2008) *New Pearl Harbor Revisited: 9/11, the Cover-up and the Exposé.* Northampton: Oliver Branch.

Griffin, D.R. (2004) *The New Pearl Harbor: Disturbing Questions about the Bush Administration and 9–11.* Northampton: Olive Branch.

Grigg, W.N. (2011) The War Party's atrocity porn, *Lew Rockwell*, available at www.lewrockwell.com/grigg/grigg-w/97.html (last accessed 1 January 2013).

Habermas, J. (1991) *The Structural Transformation of the Public Sphere.* Cambridge, MA: MIT Press. Available at http://articles.latimes.com/2011/jul/14/entertainment/la-et-word-20110714 (last accessed 14 November 2013).

Halliday, J. and Cumings, B. (1988) *Korea: The Unknown War.* London: Viking.

Hallin, D. (1989) *The Uncensored War: The Media and Vietnam.* Berkeley: The University of California Press.

Hardt, M. and Negri, A. (2001) *Empire.* Boston: Harvard University Press.

Hayes, T. (1990, 3 Sept) The oilfield lying below the Iraq-Kuwait dispute, *New York Times*, available at www.nytimes.com/1990/09/03/world/confrontation-in-the-gulf-the-oilfield-lying-below-the-iraq-kuwait-dispute.html (last accessed 24 January 2014).

Hazelton, J. (2011, Nov) Hollywood's cultural revolution, *CNBC Business*, available at www.cnbcmagazine.com/story/hollywoods-cultural-revolution/1493/1/ (last accessed 22 August 2012).

Herman, E. and Bodhead, F. (1984) *Demonstration Elections*. Kuala Lumpur: South End.

Herman, E. and Chomsky, N. (2002 [1988]) *Manufacturing Consent: The Political Economy of the Mass Media*. New York: Pantheon.

Herman, E. and McChesney, R. (1998) *The Global Media: The Missionaries of Global Capitalism*. London: Cassell.

Herman, E. and Peterson, D. (2010, 22 Jan) The Oliver Kamm school of falsification: imperial truth-enforcement, British branch. *MRzine*, available at http://mrzine.monthlyreview.org/2010/hp220110.html (last accessed 23April 2013).

Herman E. and Peterson, D. (2009, 28 July) Iran: riding the "Green Wave" at the campaign for peace and democracy and beyond, *Media Lens*, available at www.medialens.org/index.php/alerts/alert-archive/2009/575-iran-riding-the-qgreen-waveq-at-the-campaign-for-peace-and-democracy-and-beyond-part-1.html (last accessed 21 April 2013).

Hersh, S. (2008, 7 July) Preparing the battlefield: the Bush administration steps up its secret moves against Iran, *The New Yorker*, available at www.newyorker.com/reporting/2008/07/07/080707fa_fact_hersh (last accessed 21 April 2013).

Hibbs, M. (2012, 10 Dec) Intel inside: has the IAEA's information become politicized?, *Foreign Policy*, available at www.foreignpolicy.com/articles/2012/12/10/intel_inside (available at 18 April 2013).

Hirschmann, E. (2008) *Robert Knight: Reforming Editor in Victorian India*. London: Oxford University Press.

Hoffmeyr, I. (2013) *Gandhi's Printing Press*. Cambridge, MA: Harvard University Press.

Horn, J. (2011,14 July) Red China: will it play in Peoria and Shanghai?, *Los Angeles Times*, available at www.latimes.com/business/la-fi-china-movies-sg,0,6826195.storygallery (last accessed 24 January 2014).

Horton, S. (2011a, 23 July) AP Iran scare piece proves itself wrong, *Antiwar.com*, available at http://antiwar.com/blog/2011/07/23/ap-iran-scare-piece-proves-itself-wrong/ (last accessed 18 April 2013).

Horton, S. (2011b, 23 July) NYT scare piece just lies, innuendo, *Antiwar.com*, available at http://antiwar.com/blog/2011/07/23/nyt-iran-scare-piece-just-lies-innuendo/ (last accessed 25 April 2013).

Hosenball, M. (2009, 16 Sept) Intelligence agencies say no new nukes in Iran, *Newsweek*, available at www.newsweek.com/id/215529 (last accessed 21 April 2013).

IbisWorld Industry Report Q Press8711-GL (2012) Global movie production and distribution, clients, *ibisworld.com*, available at www.ibisworld.com/industry/global/global-movie-production-distribution.html (last accessed 24 January 2014).

IDATE (2010*) TV 2010: Market Facts and Trends*. Montpellier, Fr.: IDATE.

IFPI (2012) *Recording Industry in Numbers*. London: IFPI.

Innis, H. (2007, first published 1950) *Empire and Communication*. Toronto: Dundurn.

Innocent, M. (2012, 31 July) 20 years and counting, *The Nation Institute*, available at nationalinterest.org/profile/malou-innocent (last accessed 31 July 2012).

Interfax (2009) *Your Interfax: Information Bulletin for Subscribers. Twentieth Anniversary Edition*. Moscow: Interfax.

International Television Expert Group (2010) *Global TV 2010 – Markets, Trends, Facts and Figures (2008–2013) ITEG*, available at www.international-television.org/tv_market_data/world-tv-market-2010.html (last accessed 10 December 2012).

Iwabuchi, K. (2013) Korean Wave and inter-Asian referencing. In Y. Kim (ed.), *The Korean Wave: Korean Media Go Global*. London: Routledge, pp. 43–57.

Jacobs, A. (2012, 16 Aug) Pursuing soft power, China puts stamp on Africa's news, *New York Times*, available at www.nytimes.com/2012/08/17/world/africa/chinas-news-media-make-inroads-in-africa.html?pagewanted=all&_r=0 (last accessed 24 January 2014).

Jaffe, G. (2012, 9 Dec) China's indie filmmakers and the way of the dragon seal, *Los Angeles Times*, available at http://articles.latimes.com/2012/dec/09/entertainment/la-ca-mn-china-indie-films-20121209 (last accessed 14 November 2013).

Jahn, G. (2013, 17 April) APNewsBreak: diplomats: Iran ups nuke technology, *Journalgazette.net*, available at www.journalgazette.net/article/20130417/API/1304170666 (last accessed 18 April 2013).

Jahn, G. (2012a, 30 Nov) Supposed Iranian nuke graph off: UN still worried, *Huffington Post*, available at www.huffingtonpost.com/huff-wires/20121130/iran-nuclear/?utm_hp_ref=world&ir=world (last accessed 18 April 2013).

Jahn, G. (2012b, 28 Nov) AP Exclusive: graph suggests Iran working on bomb, *Salon.com*, available at www.salon.com/2012/11/27/ap_exclusive_graph_suggests_iran_working_on_bomb/ (last accessed 18 April 2013).

Jahn, G. (2011, 22 July) AP Exclusive: Iran prez said pushing for nukes, *Yahoo.com*, available at http://news.yahoo.com/ap-exclusive-iran-prez-said-pushing-nukes-120313424.html (last accessed 18 April 2013).

Jayasekera (2013, 10 May) Top Indian official threatens Pakistan with nuclear annihilation, *World Socialist Web Site*, available at www.wsws.org/en/articles/2013/05/10/shay-m10.html (last accessed 10 May 2013).

Jenkins, S. (2012, 12 April) The 'War on Terror' is corrupting all it touches, *The Guardian*, available at www.theguardian.com/commentisfree/2012/apr/12/war-on-terror-corrupting (last accessed 24 January 2014).

Jensen, C. (2001) Review of the printing revolution in early modern Europe. *LORE: Rhetoric, Writing, Culture*. San Diego State University, available at http://www-rohan.sdsu.edu/dept/drwswebb/lore/1_3/jensen_eisen.htm (last accessed 17 June 2014).

Jin, D. (2013) Hybridization of Korean popular culture. In Y. Kim (ed.), *The Korean Wave: Korean Media Go Global*. London: Routledge, pp. 148–164.

Johnson, C. (2004) *Blowback: The Costs and Consequences of American Empire*, 2nd edition. New York: Holt Paperbacks.

Johnson, L. (2001, 17 Jan) Sanctions hurt children more than Saddam, *CommonDreams.com*, available at www.commondreams.org/views01/0117-06.htm (last accessed 21 July 2012).

Joye, S. (2010) Journalism for global change: reflections on the alternative news agency Inter Press Service. In O. Boyd-Barrett (ed.) *News Agencies in the Turbulent Era of the Internet*. Barcelona: Generalitat de Catalunya: Col.leccio Lexikon.

Jowett, G. and O'Donnell, V. (2011) *Propaganda and Persuasion*. 5th Edition. Thousand Oaks, CA: Sage.

Jung, E. (2013) K-pop female idols in the West. In Y. Kim (ed.), *The Korean Wave: Korean Media Go Global*. London: Routledge, pp. 106–119.

Kahin, G. (1986) *Intervention: How America Became Involved in Vietnam*. New York: Knopf.

Kamm, O. (2009, 14 Dec) Explosive deceit: the exposure of Iran's programme to test an essential component of a nuclear weapon confirm a pattern of duplicity by a bellicose regime, *The Times*.

Kamra, S. (2009) The "Vox Populi" or the infernal propaganda machine, and judicial force in colonial India, *Cultural Critique*, 72: 164–202.

Kang, J., Hayes, P., Bin, L., Suzuki, T. and Tanter, R. (2005, 1 Jan) South Korea's nuclear surprise, *Bulletin of the Atomic Scientists*, available at http://goliath. ecnext.com/coms2/gi_0199–3549782/South-Korea-s-nuclear-surprise.html

Karsh, E. (2002) *The Iran-Iraq War 1980–1988*. London: Osprey.

Kasper, D. (Writer)(1992) *The Panama Deception*, Rhino Home Video, DVD.

Kaufman, A. (2012, 16 Dec) "Life of Pi" is second Hollywood film to gross more in China than U.S., *Los Angeles Times*, available at http://articles.latimes.com/2012/ dec/16/entertainment/la-et-ct-life-of-pi-china-box-office-20121216 (last accessed 24 January 2014).

Keck, K. (2013, 7 Jan) Destined to fail: China's soft power push, *The Diplomat*, available at http://thediplomat.com/2013/01/07/destined-to-fail-chinas-soft-power-offensive/ (last accessed 6 November 2013).

Keeble, R. (2011, 28 April) If at first you don't succeed – four decades of US-UK attempts to topple Gaddafi, *www.MediaLens.org*, available at www.medialens.org/ index.php?option=com_content&view=article&id=620:if-at-first-you-dont-succeed-four-decades-of-us-uk-attempts-to-topple-gadaffi&catid=24:alerts-2011&Itemid=68 (last accessed 3 January 2013).

Kelley, R. (2012, 23 May) The IAEA and Parchin: do the claims add up?, *Stockholm International Peace Research Institute*, available at http://www.sipri.org/media/ expert-comments/the-iaea-and-parchin-do-the-claims-add-up (last accessed 6 May 2013).

Kellner, D. (2011) *Media Spectacle and Insurrection*. London: Bloomsbury Academic.

Kellner, D. (2003) *From 9/11 to Terror War: The Dangers of the Bush Legacy*. Boulder, CO: Rowman and Littlefield.

Kellner, D. (1992) *The Persian Gulf TV War*. Boulder, CO: Westview.

Keohane, R. and Nye, J. (1977) *Power and Interdependence: World Politics in Transition*, TBS (The Book Service).

Kiel, P. (2007, 11 Dec) Administration prevents former Gitmo prosecutor from testifying before Congress, *TPMmuckraker*, available at http://tpmmuckraker.talkingpoints-memo.com/2007/12/admin_prevents_former_gitmo_pr.php (last accessed 16 July 2012).

Kim, S. (2013) For the eyes of North Koreans? In Y. Kim (ed.), *The Korean Wave: Korean Media Go Global*. London: Routledge, pp. 93–105.

Kim, Y. (ed.)(2013a) *The Korean Wave: Korean Media Go Global*. London: Routledge.

Kim, Y. (2013b) Korean Wave pop culture in the global Internet age. In Y. Kim (ed.), *The Korean Wave: Korean Media Go Global*. London: Routledge. pp. 75–92.

King, E. (2014) *Obama, the Media, and Framing the U.S. Exit from Iraq and Afghanistan*. Farnham: Ashgate.

King, K. (2013) *China's Aid and Soft Power in Africa*. Rochester, NY: BOYE6.

Kinzer, S. (2007) *Overthrow: America's Century of Regime Change from Hawaii to Iraq*. New York: Times Books.

Kirgis, F. (2003) North Korea's withdrawal from the Nuclear Non-Proliferation Treaty, *ASIL Insights*, available at www.asil.org/insigh96.cfm (last accessed 3 May 2013).

Kirkpatrick, D. (2012, 26 Dec) First fighting Islamists, now the free market, *New York Times*, p. A10.

Klapper, J. (1960) *The Effects of Mass Communication*. New York: Free Press.

Klein, N. (2008) *Shock Doctrine*. New York: Picador.

Kraidy, M. (2005) *Hybridity: The Cultural Logic Of Globalization*. Philadelphia: Temple University Press.

Kreiger, D. (2005, 4 March) Saving the nuclear nonproliferation agreement, waging peace, *Nuclear Age Peace Foundation*, available at www.wagingpeace.org/articles/2005/03/00_krieger_saving-nuclear-agreement.htm (last accessed 3 May 2013).

Krugman, P. (2007, 29 Oct) Fearing fear itself, *New York Times*, available at www.nytimes.com/2007/10/29/opinion/29krugman.html?_r=0 (last accessed 27 April 2013).

Kuttner, R. (2007, 19 May) A conversation with Zbigniew Brzezinski, *The American Prospect*, available at http://prospect.org/article/conversation-zbigniew-brzezinski (last accessed 17 April 2013).

Lakshmi, K. (1993) *Communications Across the Borders: The U.S., the Non-Aligned, and the New Information Order*. New Delhi: Radiant Publishers.

Landey, J. (2008, 20 March) Bush erroneously says Iran announced desire for nuclear weapons, *McClatchy Newspapers*, available at www.mcclatchydc.com/2008/03/20/31114/bush-erroneously-says-iran-announced.html (last accessed 17 April 2013).

Landreth, J. (2012a, 25 April) Did Hollywood dirty its hands in China? Reaction to SEC inquiry, *Los Angeles Times*, available at http://latimesblogs.latimes.com/entertainmentnewsbuzz/2012/04/sec-inquiry-reaction-from-beijing-international-film-festival.html (last accessed 14 November 2013).

Landreth, J. (2012b, 21 April) Beijing's film festival opens amid China's movie industry boom, *Los Angeles Times*, available at http://articles.latimes.com/2012/apr/21/business/la-fi-ct-beijing-film-fest-20120421 (last accessed 14 November 2013).

Langner, R. (2011, Feb) Ralph Langner: Cracking Stuxnet, a 21st-century cyber weapon, *TED Ideas Worth Spreading*, available at www.ted.com/talks/ralph_langer_cracking_stuxnet_a_21st_century_cyberweapon.html (last accessed 12 April 2013).

Lantier, M. (2013, 26 Aug) John Kerry's "Colin Powell moment," *World Socialist Web Site*, available at http://www.wsws.org/en/articles/2013/08/27/pers-a27.html (last accessed 30 July 2014).

Laskai, L. (2013, 19 Aug) Soft power or ancient wisdom?, *The Diplomat*, available at http://thediplomat.com/china-power/soft-power-or-ancient-wisdom/ (last accessed 6 November 2013).

Lee, H. (2013) Cultural policy and the Korean Wave. In Y. Kim (ed.), *The Korean Wave: Korean Media Go Global*. London: Routledge, pp. 185–198.

Lendman, S. (2013, 25 Feb) IAEA report confirms Iran's peaceful nuclear program, available at http://sjlendman.blogspot.hk/2013/02/iaea-report-confirms-irans-peaceful.html (last accessed 18 May 2013).

Lendman, S. (2012, 28 Oct) Trafficking anti-Iranian propaganda, *Daily Censored*, available at www.dailycensored.com/trafficking-anti-iranian-propaganda/ (last accessed 27 April 2013).

Leverett, F. and Leverett, H. (2013) *Consequences of Western Intransigence in Nuclear Diplomacy with Iran,* available at www.aljazeera.com/indepth/opinion/2013/05/2013589151459212.html (last accessed 2013).

Li, G. (2013, 22 Aug) China's movie market booms with local content, *Reuters.com*, available at www.reuters.com/article/2013/08/22/film-china-idUSL4N0G720520130822 (last accessed 14 November 2013).

Lobe, J. (2013, 15 May) Nuclear Iran can be contained and deterred, says report, *Antiwar.com*, available at http://original.antiwar.com/lobe/2013/05/14/nuclear-iran-can-be-contained-and-deterred-says-report/ (last accessed 18 May 2013).

Lobe, J. (2008, 30 May) Murdoch goes after Condi, urges blockage against Iran, *Infowars.com*, available at www.infowars.com/murdoch-goes-after-condi-urges-blockade-against-iran/ (last accessed 17 April 2013).

Lunden, J. (2012, 11 June) PwC: entertainment & media spend was $1.6 trillion in 2011; will rise to $2.1T By 2016 With Digital Leading Growth, *Techcrunch.com* available at http://techcrunch.com/2012/06/11/pwc-entertainment-media-spend-was-1-6-trillion-in-2011-will-rise-to-2-1t-by-2016-with-digital-leading-growth/

Mackey, R. (2012, 17 April) Israeli minister agrees Ahmadinejad never said Israel "must be wiped off the map," *New York Times*, available at http://thelede.blogs.nytimes.com/2012/04/17/israeli-minister-agrees-ahmadinejad-never-said-israel-must-be-wiped-off-the-map/

Makinen, J. (2014) China's movie box office surges 27% to $3.6 billion in 2013, *Los Angeles Times*, available at www.latimes.com/business/la-fi-ct-china-box-office-20140102,0,5648771.story#ixzz2pGIF1PFN (last accessed 1 January 2014).

Marcus, J. (2012, 27 Feb) Analysis: how Israel might strike at Iran, *BBC News*: Middle East, available at www.bbc.co.uk/news/world-middle-east-17115643

Marsden, C. (2004, March 18) Britain: coroner rejects inquest into death of Dr. David Kelly. *World Socialist Web Site*, available at http://www.wsws.org/en/articles/2004/03/kell-m18.html (last accessed 17 June 2014).

Martin, M. (2013, 16 May) Activision's market share climbed to almost 20% in 2012, *Los Angeles Times*, available at www.gamesindustry.biz/articles/2013-05-16-activisions-market-share-climbed-to-almost-20-percent-in-2012 (last accessed 21 November 2013).

Martin, P. (2011, 30 March) American media silent on CIA ties to Libya rebel commander, *World Socialist Web Site*, available at http://wsws.org/en/articles/2011/03/hift-m30.html (last accessed 3 Janary 2013).

Martin Moreno, F. (2007) *Mexico Negro*. Mexico City: Santillana Ediciones Generales.

Maschke, G. (2009, 28 Dec) Typography casts additional doubt on authenticity of alleged Iranian "nuclear trigger" document, available at www.georgemaschke.net/2009/12/28/typographical-inconsistencies-cast-doubt-on-iranian-nuclear-trigger-document/ (last accessed 23 April 2013).

Mattelart, A. (2010) *The Globalization of Surveillance: The Origin of the Securitarian Order*. Cambridge: Polity.

Mattelart, A. (1979) *Multinational Corporations and the Control of Culture: The Ideological Apparatuses of Imperialism*. East Sussex: Harvester.

McChesney, R. (2004) *The Problem of the Media: U.S. Communication Politics in the 21st Century.* New York: Monthly Review Press.

McChesney, R. and Schiller, D. (2003) The political economy of international communications: foundations for the emerging global debate about media ownership and regulation, Programme Area: Technology and Society, *United Nations Research Institute for Social Development,* Paper No. 11.

McCoy, A. (2009) *Policing America's Empire.* Madison: University of Wisconsin Press.

McCoy, A. (2003) *The Politics of Heroin, CIA Complicity and the Global Drug Trade.* Chicago, IL: Chicago Review Press.

McDonnell, J. and Dilanian, K. (2011, 4 Sept) CIA once handed key Libya rebel figure to Kadafi, documents show, *Los Angeles Times,* available at http://articles.latimes.com/2011/sep/04/world/la-fg-libya-islamists-20110904 (last accessed 24 January 2014).

McGovern, R. (2013, 28 Aug) The broader stakes of Syrian crisis, *Information Clearing House,* available at www.informationclearinghouse.info/article36008.htm (last accessed 24 January 2014).

McGovern, R. (2010, 3 Dec) New York Times beats drums for war, *Real News,* available at www.therealnews.com/t2/index.php?option=com_content&task=view&id=31&Itemid=74&jumival=5945 (last accessed 25 April 2013).

McKinsey and Company (2013) *Global Media Report, 2013,* available at www.mckinsey.com/.../PDFs/Global_Media_Report_2013.ashx (last accessed 8 January 2014).

McLuhan, M. (1967) *The Medium is the Message: An Inventory of Effects with Quentin Fiore, produced by Jerome Agel,* first edition. New York: Random House.

McLuhan, M. (1964) *Understanding Media: The Extensions of Man,* first edition. New York: McGraw-Hill.

McLuhan, M. (1962) *The Gutenberg Galaxy: The Making of Typographic Man,* first edition. Toronto: University of Toronto Press.

Media Lens (2012a, 7 March) Bombing Osirak, burying UN Resolution 487 – an exchange with the BBC's Jonathan Marcus, *MediaLens.org,* available at www.medialens.org/index.php?option=com_content&view=article&id=671:bombing-osirak-burying-un-resolution-487-an-exchange-with-the-bbcs-jonathan-marcus&catid=25:alerts-2012&Itemid=69 (last accessed 26 April 2013).

Media Lens (2012b, 1 March) Iran – next in line for western "intervention"?, *MediaLens.org,* available at www.medialens.org/index.php/alerts/alert-archive/2012/668-iran-next-in-line-for-western-intervention.html (last accessed 26 April 2013).

MediaLens (2012c, 14 Feb) UN "travesty": resolutions of mass destruction, Part 1, *MediaLens.org,* available at http://newint.org/features/web-exclusive/2012/02/20/un-resolutions-of-mass-destruction-part-one/ (last accessed 25 January 2013).

Media Lens (2012d, 18 Jan) Selective outrage – Iran and Libya, *Media Lens,* available at www.medialens.org/index.php?option=com_content&view=article&id=661:selective-outrage-iran-and-libya&catid=25:alerts-2012&Itemid=69 (last accessed 26 April 2013).

MediaLens (2011a, 31 Oct) Targeting Syria – the "bad news" for the *Guardian,* *MediaLens.org,* available at www.medialens.org/index.php/alerts/alert-archive/2011/648-targeting-syria-the-bad-news-for-the-guardian.html (last accessed 25 January 2013).

MediaLens (2011b, 22 June) Three little words: Wikileaks, Libya, oil, *MediaLens. org*, available at www.MediaLens.org (last accessed 3 January 2012).

MediaLens (2011c, April) Targeting Syria – the "bad news" for the *Guardian*, *MediaLens.org*, available at www.medialens.org/index.php?option=com_content& view=article&id=648:targeting-syria-the-bad-news-for-the-guardian&catid= 24:alerts-2011&Itemid=68 (last accessed 24 January 2014).

MediaLens (2011d, 23 March) Wars of first resort, available at www.MediaLens. org

Media Lens (2010, 14 Jan) Media alert: nuclear deceit – The Times and Iran, *Medialens. com*, available at www.medialens.org/index.php/alerts/alert-archive/2010/39-nuclear-deceit-the-times-and-iran.html (last accessed 24 January 2014).

Media Lens (2008, 25 June) Selling the fireball – George Bush and Iran, *MediaLens. com*, available at www.medialens.org/index.php/alerts/alert-archive/2008/544-selling-the-fireball-george-bush-and-iran.html (last accessed 17 April 2013).

Media Lens (2007, 22 Feb) Iran in Iraq. *Dissident Voice*, available at http://www. dissidentvoice.org/Feb07/MediaLens22.htm

MediaLens (2002) Iraq and arms inspectors – the big lie, *MediaLens*, available at www. medialens.org/index.php?option=com_content&view=article&id=219:iraq-and-arms-inspectors-the-big-lie-part-1&catid=16:alerts-2002&Itemid=43 (last accessed 31 December 2012).

Media Matters (2012, 18 April) Broadcast news networks misrepresent intelligence on Iranian nuclear issues, *Media Matters.org*, available at http://mediamatters. org/blog/2012/04/18/report-broadcast-news-networks-misrepresent-int/184478 (last accessed 27 April 2013).

Melman, Y. and Raviv, D. (2012) *Spies Against Armageddon: Inside Israel's Secret Wars*. Beirut: Levant Books.

Mercereau, J. (2005) *The Changing Landscape of the Irish Press*, available at www. slideshare.net/jeannfm/british-newpapers-in-Ireland

Meyssan, T. (2012, 9 Aug) Perfecting the method of "color revolutions": Western leaders slip back into childhood, *Global Research*, available at www.global-research.ca/index.php?context=viewArticle&code=MEY20120807&arti-cleId=32261 (last accessed 9 August 2012).

Millien, R. (2010, 16 Dec) *The US$173.4B Global Intellectual Property Marketplace?*, available at http://dcipattorney.com/2010/12/the-us173-4b-global-intellectual-property-marketplace/ (last accessed 20 August 2012).

Mitchell, G. (2007, 4 Dec) Debunking Iran's nuclear program: another "intelli-gence failure" – on the part of the press? Editor and publisher, available at www.editorandpublisher.com/PrintArticle/Debunking-Iran-s-Nuclear-Program-Another-Intelligence-Failure-On-the-Part-of-the-Press- (last accessed 24 January 2014).

Moise, E.E. (1996) *Tonkin Gulf and the Escalation of the Vietnam War*. Chapel Hill: University of North Carolina Press.

Moon of Alabama (2013, 3 Jan) Engineering consent for an attack on Syria: lies, damned lies and UN statistics, *Counter Information*, available at http://alterin-fonews.blogspot.com/2013/01/engineering-consent-for-attack-on-syria.html (last accessed 25 January 2013).

Moreno, M.F. (2007) *Mexico Negro*. Mexico City: Alfaguara.

Morgenthau, H. (1965) *Politics Among Nations*. 3rd Edition New York: Knopf.

Morris, B. (2008, 18 July) Using bombs to stave off war, *New York Times,* available at www.nytimes.com/2008/07/18/opinion/18morris.html?pagewanted=all&_r=0 (last accessed 17 April 2013).

Mosco, V. (2009) *The Political Economy of Communication.* Thousand Oaks, CA: Sage.

Moss, T. (2013, 4 June) Soft power? China has plenty, available at http://thediplomat.com/2013/06/04/soft-power-china-has-plenty/?all=true (last accessed 6 November 2013).

Moyers, B. (1987) *The Secret Government: The Constitution in Crisis* (a PBS documentary).

MPAA (2013) *Theatrical Market Statistics 2012,* Motion Pictures Association of America, available at www.mpaa.org/Resources/3037b7a4-58a2-4109-8012-58fca3abdf1b.pdf (last accessed 14 November 2013).

Myllylahti, M. (2011) The New Zealand Media Ownership Report 2011. *Zealand Media Ownership Report,* JMAD, available at https://dev.aut.ac.nz/__data/assets/pdf_file/0009/234468/JMAD-Interim-Report-2011.pdf

Naiman, R. (2012, 20 April) The US and Iran are talking: why is the New York Times peddling Islamophobia?, *Huffington Post,* available at www.huffingtonpost.com/robert-naiman/the-us-and-iran-are-talki_b_1438080.html (last accessed 27 April 2013).

Nalapat, M.D. (2012, 14 June) Syria: NATO plans new Sykes-Picot, Middle East chaos, Information Clearing House, available at www.informationclearinghouse.info/article31586.htm (last accessed 25 January 2013).

Narwani, S. (2013, 28 April) Chemical weapons charade in Syria, *World Socialist Web Site,* available at www.wsws.org/en/articles/2013/12/16/pers-d16.html (last accessed 24 January 2014).

Narwani, S. and Mortada, R. (2013, 24 Sept) Questions plague UN Syria report: who was behind the East Ghouta chemical weapons attack?, *Global Media Research,* available at www.globalresearch.ca/questions-plague-un-syria-report-who-was-behind-the-east-ghouta-chemical-weapons-attack/5351337 (last accessed 14 October 2013).

Natarajan, S. (1962) *A History of the Press in India.* Delhi: Asia Publishing House.

National Science Board (2012) *Science and Engineering Indicators 2012.* Washington, DC: National Science Board. Chapter 6: Industry, Technology, and the Global Marketplace.

Naurackas, J. (2013, 2 Sept) Which Syrian chemical attack account is more credible?, *FAIR.org,* available at www.fair.org/blog/2013/09/01/which-syrian-chemical-attack-account-is-more-credible (last accessed 24 January 2014).

Neate, R. (2011, 14 Nov) Libya seeks UK firms to develop oil sector and construction industry, *The Guardian,* www.theguardian.com/business/2011/nov/15/libya-oil-industry-british-firms (last accessed24 January 2014).

Nelson, S. (2013, 5 Sept) Rep. Alan Grayson: Syria intelligence manipulated, *US News,* available at www.usnews.com/news/blogs/washington-whispers/2013/09/05/alan-grayson-syria-intelligence-manipulated (last accessed 24 January 2014).

Netmarketshare (2012) Market share statistics for internet technologies, *netmarketshare.com,* available at www.netmarketshare.com/ (last accessed 4 December 2012).

New York Times (2013, 30 April "Ghost money" and lots of it, *New York Times*, available at www.nytimes.com/2013/05/01/opinion/ghost-money-and-lots-of-it-in-afghanistan.html (last accessed 24 January 2014).

New York Times (2012, 9 Oct) Mexican drug trafficking (Mexico's drug war), *New York Times*, available at http://topics.nytimes.com/top/news/international/countriesandterritories/mexico/drug_trafficking/index.html (last accessed 17 December 2012).

Noam, E. (2009) *Media Ownership and Concentration in America*. New York: Oxford University Press.

Noble, S. (Director) *The Power Principle: I. Empire*. Metanoia Films, available at metanoia-films.org/the-power-principle/ (last accessed 14 December 2012).

Noble, S. (Director) *The Power Principle: II. Propaganda*. Metanoia Films, available at metanoia-films.org/the-power-principle/ (last accessed 14 December 2012).

Nordenstreng, K. and Varis, T. (1974) Television traffic – a one-way street? A survey and analysis of the international flow of television programme material, *Reports and Papers on Mass Communication*, No. 70. Paris: UNESCO.

Norton-Taylor, R. (1999, 8 Jan) Arms inspectors "shared Iraq data with five states", the *Guardian*, reprinted in *Media Lens*, available at www.medialens.org/index.php/alerts/alert-archive/2002/219-iraq-and-arms-inspectors-the-big-lie-part-1.html

Nye, J. (2013, 29 April) The power issue: what China and Russia don't get about soft power: foreign policy, *The Diplomat*, available at www.foreignpolicy.com/articles/2013/04/29/what_china_and_Russia_don_t_get_about_soft_power/ (last accessed 6 November 2013).

Nye, J. (2005) Soft power: the means to success in world politics, *Foreign Affairs*, available at www.foreignaffairs.com/articles/59732/g-john-ikenberry/soft-power-the-means-to-success-in-world-politics (last accessed 24 January 2014).

Nye, J. (1991) *Bound To Lead: The Changing Nature Of American Power*. New York: Basic Books.

Nye, J. and Kim, Y. (2013) Soft power and the Korean Wave. In Y. Kim (ed.), *The Korean Wave: Korean Media Go Global*. London: Routledge, pp. 31–42.

O'Carroll, L. (2013) Seymour Hersh on death of Osama bin Laden: "It's one big lie, not one word of it is true." *Raw Story*, available at www.redicecreations.com/article.php?id=27045 (last accessed 7 December 2013).

Ó Cathail, M. (2012, 18 July) Crying wolf over hyped Iranian missile threat, *Information Clearing House*, available at www.informationclearinghouse.info/article31918.htm (last accessed 27 April 2013).

Ó Colmáin, G. (2013, 25 Jan) France, Qatar, and the new world disorder, *Dissidentvoice.org*, available at http://dissidentvoice.org/2013/01/france-qatar-and-the-new-world-disorder/ (last accessed 26 January 2013).

Ocean Tomo, LLC, available at www.oceantomo.com/productsandservices/investments/intangible-market-value (last accessed 15 November 2010).

Ono, K.A. and Kwon, J. (2013) Re-worlding culture? In Y. Kim (ed.), *The Korean Wave: Korean Media Go Global*. London: Routledge, pp. 199–214.

Oreskovic, A. and Carsten, P. (2013, 13 Nov) Sina record revenues fuelled by Weibo, Alibaba. *Reuters.com*, available at http://mobile.reuters.com/article/technology-News/idUSBRE9AB19820131113?irpc=932 (last accessed 24 January 2014).

Orford, A. (2003) *Reading Humanitarian Intervention: Human Rights and the Use of Force in International Law*. Cambridge: Cambridge University Press.

Paley, D. (2012) Colombia and Mexico: drug war capitalism, *Against the Current*, July–August, also available at http://dawnpaley.files.wordpress.com/2012/07/dawn.pdf (last accessed 19 July 2012).

Panther, G. (2007, 14 July) More neocrazy media sycophancy, *Anti-War.com*, available at www.antiwar.com/prather/?articleid=11284 (last accessed 11 April 2013).

Parenti, M. (2009) Afghanistan, another untold story, *Michael Parenti Political Archive*, available at www.michaelparenti.org/afghanistan%20story%untold.html (last accessed 12 July 2012).

Parenti, M. (1995) *Against Empire*, revised edition. San Francisco, CA: City Lights.

Park, J. (2013) Negotiating identity and power in transnational cultural consumption. In Y. Kim (ed.), *The Korean Wave: Korean Media Go Global*. London: Routledge, pp. 120–134.

Parry, R. (2012) New York Times admits Lockerbie case flaws, *Consortiumnews.com*, available at http://consortiumnews.com/2012/05/21/nyt-admitconcedes-lockerbie-case-flaws (last accessed 3 January 2013).

Parry, R. (2009, 30 Sept) US press corps fails again on Iran, *Consortiumnews.com*, available at www.consortiumnews.com/2009/093009.html (last accessed 23 April 2013).

Paterson, T. (2002, 18 Dec) Leaked report says German and US firms supplied arms to Saddam, *The Independent* (UK) published in *Consortium News.com*, available at www.commondreams.org/headlines02/1218-06.htm (last accessed 24 January 2014).

Payan, T. (2006) *The Three U.S.-Mexico Border Wars*. Westport, CT: Praeger Security International.

Perez, B. (2014, 4 Jan) Stable growth for China's IT sector, *South China Morning Post*, Business, p.1.

Perkins, J. (2004) *Confessions of an Economic Hit Man*. New York: Plume.

Peterson, P. Foundation (2012, 12 April) The U.S. spent more on defense in 2011 than did the countries with the next 13 highest defense budgets combined, *Peter G. Peterson Foundation*, available at www.pgpf.org/Chart-Archive/0053_defense-comparison.aspx (last accessed 1 May 2013).

Peterson, S. (2011) Imminent Iran nuclear threat? A timeline of warnings since 1979, *Christian Science Monitor*, available at www.csmonitor.com/World/Middle-East/2011/1108/Imminent-Iran-nuclear-threat-A-timeline-of-warnings-since-1979/Earliest-warnings-1979-84 (last accessed 12 April 2013).

Petras, J. (2008, 25 May) Provocations as pretexts for imperial war: from Pearl Harbor to 9/11, *Global Research*, available at www.thirdworldtraveller.com/Petras_James/Imperial_War_Pretexts.html (last accessed 12 July 2012).

Pilger, J. (2010) *The War You Don't See* (DVD). London: Dartmouth Films.

Porter, G. (2014) *Manufactured Crisis: The Untold Story of the Iran Nuclear Scare*. Charlottsville, VA: Just World Books.

Porter, G. (2013, 30 July) Ex-envoy's account clarifies Iran's 2003 nuclear decision, *Inter Press Service*, www.ips.org (last accessed 12 September 2013).

Porter, G. (2012a, 13 Dec) Iranian bomb graph appears adapted from one on Internet, *Inter Press Service*, available at www.ipsnews.net/2012/12/iranian-bomb-graph-appears-adapted-from-one-on-internet/ (last accessed 18 April 2013).

Porter, G. (2012b, 30 Nov) Fake AP graph exposes Israeli fraud and IAEA credulity, *LobeLog.com*, available at www.lobelog.com/fake-ap-graph-exposes-israeli-fraud-and-iaea-credulity/ (last accessed 18 April 2013).

Porter, G. (2012c, 6 June) Bush blocked Iran disarmament deal, *ConsortiumNews. com*, available at http://consortiumnews.com/2012/06/06/bush-blocked-iran-nuke-deal/ (last accessed 17 April 2013).

Porter, G. (2012d, 29 Feb) How the media got the Parchin story wrong, *Lobelog. com*, available at www.lobelog.com/how-the-media-got-the-parchin-access-story-wrong/ (last accessed 26 April 2013).

Porter, G. (2010, 5 Jan) New revelations tear holes in Iran nuclear trigger story, *Inter Press Service*, available at http://ipsnorthamerica.net/news.php?idnews=2769 (last accessed 12 September 2013).

Porter, G. (2009, 28 Dec) U.S. intelligence found Iran nuke document was forged, *Inter Press Service*, available at www.ipsnews.net/2009/12/politics-us-intelligence-found-iran-nuke-document-was-forged/ (last accessed 24 January 2014).

Postman, N. (1994) *The Disappearance of Childhood*. Vintage: Random House.

Prather, G. (2007, 24 July) Scott Horton interviews Dr. Gordon Prather, *Antiwar. com Radio*, available at www.youtube.com/watch?v=HHByLEWJ4es (last accessed 3 May 2013).

Project for the New American Century (2000) *Rebuilding America's Defenses: Strategies, Forces and Resources for a New Century*, Washington, DC: PNAC.

Qadir, R. (2011, 22 Feb) How the "NYT" swallowed the Stuxnet worm, *Mondoweiss*, available at http://mondoweiss.net/2011/02/how-the-nyt-swallowed-the-stuxnet-worm.html (last accessed 25 April 2013).

Raimondo, J. (2011, 11 Oct) Iranian terror plot: fake, fake, fake, *Antiwar.com*, available at http://original.antiwar.com/justin/2011/10/11/iranian-terror-plot-fake-fake-fake/ (last accessed 25 April 2013).

Raimondo, J. (2008, 22 Nov) Stop Hillary!, *Antiwar.com*, available at http://original. antiwar.com/justin/2008/11/21/stop-hillary/ (last accessed 19 April 2013).

Rantanen, T. (1990) *Foreign News in Imperial Russia: The Relationship Between International and Russian News Agencies, 1856–1914*. Helsinki: Annales Academiae Scientiarum Fennicae.

Real News Network (2013, 29 Nov) Why would Saudi Arabia support the 9/11 conspirators, why would the US govt. cover it up?, Paul Jay interview with Senator Bob Graham, *The Real News,* available at http://therealnews.com/t2/index.php?option=com_content&task=view&id=31&Itemid=74&jumival=11120 (last accessed 7 December 2013).

Reuter, P.H. (1988) *Sealing the Borders: The Effects of Increased Military Participation in Drug Interdiction*. Santa Monica, CA: RAND.

Reuters (2012, 8 Aug) U.S. still believes Iran not on verge of nuclear weapon, *Reuters.com*, available at www.reuters.com/article/2012/08/09/us-israel-iran-usa-idUSBRE8781GS20120809 (last accessed 10 May 2013).

Ricks, T. (2006) *Fiasco: The American Military Adventure in Iraq*. New York: Penguin.

Risen, J. (2012a, 3 June) Intrigue in Karzai family as an Afghan era closes, *New York Times*, available at www.nytimes.com/2012/06/04/world/asia/karzai-family-moves-to-protect-its-privilege.html?ref=jamesrisen (last accessed 27 July 2012).

Risen, J. (2012b, 14 April) Seeking nuclear insight in fog of the Ayatollah's utterances, *New York Times*, available at www.nytimes.com/2012/04/14/world/middleeast/seeking-nuclear-insight-in-fog-of-the-ayatollahs-utterances.html?pagewanted=all (last accessed 27 April 2013).

Risen, J. (2010, 11 Dec) Propping up a drug lord, then arresting him, *New York Times*, available at www.nytimes.com/2010/12/12/world/asia/12drugs.html?_r=1&pagewanted=all (last accessed 27 July 2012).

Risen, J. (2008, 4 Oct) Reports link Karzai's brother to Afghanistan heroin trade, *New York Times*, available at www.nytimes.com/2008/10/05/world/asia/05afghan.html?pagewanted=all (last accessed 27 July 2012).

Ritter, S. (2009, 27 Sept) Keeping Iran honest, the *Guardian*, available at www.guardian.co.uk/commentisfree/cifamerica/2009/sep/25/iran-secret-nuclear-plant-inspections (last accessed 21 April 2013).

Ritter, S. (2008, 26 June) The nuclear expert who never was, *Truthdig*, available at www.truthdig.com/report/item/20080626_the_nuclear_expert_who_never_was (last accessed 24 January 2014).

Ritter, S. (2006) *Target Iran*. New York: Nation Books.

Ritter, S. and Pitt, W.R. (2002) *War on Iraq*. New York: Profile Books.

Robertson, R. (1992) *Globalization: Social Theory and Global Culture* (published in association with *Theory, Culture & Society*). Sage: London.

Rodericks, D. (2008, 2 Dec) Legalizing drugs: the money argument, *Baltimore Sun*, available at http://articles.baltimoresun.com/2008-12-02/news/0812010121_1_argument-war-on-drugs-two-things (last accessed 24 January 2014).

Rosen, D. (2012, 10 May) The new Hollywood, *Filmmaker*, available at www.filmmakermagazine.com/news/2012/05/the-new-hollywood/ (last accessed 22 August 2012).

Rosenberg, B. (2008) News media ownership in New Zealand, *CAFCA publications*, available at https://dev.aut.ac.nz/__data/assets/pdf_file/0009/234468-Interim-Report-2011.pdf

Rosenberg, M. (2013, 28 April) With bags of cash, C.I.A. seeks influence in Afghanistan, *New York Times*, available at http://mobile.nytimes.com/2013/04/29/world/asia/cia-delivers-cash-to-afghan-leaders-office.html (last accessed 23 May 2013).

Rosenthal, J. (2012, 24 July) German intelligence: "al-Qaeda" all over Syria. *Information Clearing House*, available at www.informationclearinghouse.info/article31974.htm (last accessed 25 January 2013).

Rozen, L. (2007, 14 Sept) Subject to debate: did ABC know about its expert's sourcing problem?, *Mother Jones*, available at www.reuters.com/article/2012/08/09/us-israel-iran-usa-idUSBRE8781GS20120809

RT (2013, 6 Sept) Footage of chemical attack in Syria is fraud, *RT*, available at http://rt.com/op-edge/mother-chemical-attack-footage-fraud-509 (last accessed 24 January 2014).

Rühle, H. (2010, 7 May) Nuclear proliferation in Latin America: is Brazil developing the bomb?, *Spiegel Online International*, available at www.spiegel.de/international/world/nuclear-proliferation-in-latin-america-is-brazil-developing-the-bomb-a-693336.html (last accessed 24 January 2014).

Rydell, C.P. (1994) *Controlling Cocaine: Supply Versus Demand Progress*. Santa Monica, CA: RAND.

Sahimi, M. (2009, 18 March) A new Judith Miller for Iran hawks?, *Antiwar.com*, available at www.antiwar.com/orig/sahimi.php?articleid=14420 (last accessed 19 April 2013).

Said, E. (1994) *Culture and Imperialism*. New York: Vintage.

Said, E. (1979) *Orientalism*. New York: Vintage.

Salbuchi, A. (2012, 11 April) *Libya: So It Was All About Oil After All*. Moscow: *RT.*

Salt, J. (2012, 3 July) Straight talking: the Syrian cauldron, *Information Clearing House,* available at www.informationclearinghouse.info/article31766.htm, (available at 25 January 2013).

Sanders, R. (2012, 9 Jan) How to start a war: the American use of war pretext incidents, *Global Research*, available at globalresearch.ca/how-to-start-a-war-the-american-use-of-war-pretext-incidents/28554 (last accessed 6 December 2013).

Sanders, R. (2002) How to start a war: the American use of war pretext incidents 1848–1989, *Mindfully.org*, available at www.mindfully.org/Reform/2002/How-To-Start-A-WarMay02.htm (last accessed 13 September 2012).

Sanger, D. and Schmitt, E. (2013, 4 Sept) Allies' intelligence differs on details, but still points to Assad forces, *New York Times,* available at www.nytimes.com/2013/09/04/world/middleeast/allies-intelligence-on-syria-all-points-to-assad-forces.html?_r=0 (last accessed 24 January 2014).

Satter, D. (2014) The last gasp of empire: Russia's attempts to control the media in the former Soviet republics, *Center for International Media Assistance*, available at http://cima.ned.org/publications/last-gasp-empire-russias-attempts-control-media-former-soviet-republics#sthash.tAfX2PCF.dpuf (last accessed 18 January 2014).

Schiller, H. (1992, original 1969) *Mass Communications and American Empire,* second edition, updated (Critical Studies in Communication & in the Cultural Industries). Boulder, CO: Westview Press.

Schofield, M. (2014, 16 Jan) New analysis of rocket used in Syria chemical attack undercuts U.S. claims, *Star-Telegram*, available at www.star-telegram.com/2014/01/15/5488779/new-analysis-of-rocket-used-in.html (last accessed 20 January 2014).

Scott, H. (2004) 200 years of U.S. imperialism: Haiti under siege, *International Socialist Review, 35*, May/June.

Scott, P.D. (2007) *The Road to 9/11: Wealth, Empire and the Future of America.* Berkeley: University of California Press.

Scott, P.D. and Marshall, J. (1998) *Cocaine Politics: Drugs, Armies and the CIA in Central America.* Berkeley: University of California Press.

Seibel, M. and Allam, H. (2013) To some, US case for Syrian gas attack, strike has too many holes, *McClatchy*, available at www.mcclatchydc.com/2013/09/02/201027/to-some-us-case-for-syrian-gas.html (last accessed 24 January 2014).

Seper, J. (1999, 3 May) KLA finances fight with heroin sales: terror group is linked to crime netework, *Washington Times*, A1.

Shah, A. (2004, 24 April) The Bush doctrine of pre-emptive strikes; a global pax Americana. *Global Issues*, available at http://www.globalissues.org/article/450/the-bush-doctrine-of-pre-emptive-strikes-a-global-pax-americana (last accessed 11 June, 2014)

Shambaugh, D. (2013) *China Goes Global: The Partial Power*. New York: Oxford University Press.

Sharpe, G. (1983) *Making Europe Unconquerable: The Potential of Civilian-based Deterrence and Defense* New York: HarperCollins.

Shirazi, N. (2013a, 10 May) Muck and Meir: prolific analyst botches facts to vindicate failed Iran sanctions policy, *Campaign Against Sanctions and Military Intervention in Iran*, available at www.campaigniran.org/casmii/index.php?q=node/13234 (last accessed 11 May 2013).

Shirazi, N. (2013b, 19 April) Is anybody listening? U.S. Intel chief says Iran isn't building nukes, *Information Clearing House*, available at www.informationclearinghouse.info/article34672.htm (last accessed 21 April 2013).

Shirazi, N. (2012, 27 Nov) Graphoganda! Or how I learned to stop worrying and love George Jahn's embarrassing nonsense, *WideasleepinAmerica,* available at www.wideasleepinamerica.com/2012/11/graphoganda-or-how-i-learned-to-stop. html (last accessed 18 April 2013).

Shoemaker, P. and Reese S. (1995) *Mediating the Message: Theories of Influences on Mass Media Content.* London: Longman Trade/Caroline House.

Siff, E.Y. (1999) *Why the Senate Slept: The Gulf of Tonkin Resolution and the Beginning of America's Vietnam War.* Westport, CT: Praeger.

Silverstein, R. (2012, 29 Nov) The Mossad and the Iranian graph that never was, *Tikun Olam,* available at www.richardsilverstein.com/2012/11/29/the-mossad-and-the-iranian-graph-that-never-was/ (last accessed 18 April 2013).

Sinclair, J. (1999) *Latin American Television: A Global View.* New York: Oxford University Press.

Sinclair, J., Jacka, E. and Cunningham, S. (1996) *New Patterns in Global Television: Peripheral Vision.* London: Oxford University Press.

Sinclair, J. and Straubhaar, J. (2013) *Latin American Television Industries.* London: British Film Institute/Palgrave.

Skelton, C. (2012, 13 July) The Syrian opposition: who's doing the talking?, *The Guardian,* available at www.guardian.co.uk/commentisfree/2012/jul/12/syrian-opposition-doing-the-talking (last accessed 25 January 2013).

Slater, G. (2011) The value of expanding the Information Technology Agreement: an industry standpoint, *World Trade Organization,* available at www.wto.org/english/ tratop_e/inftec.../speaker12slater.pdf (last accessed 20 August 2012).

Smith, R. (2011, 6 July) Pakistan's nuclear-bomb maker says North Korea paid bribes for know-how, *The Washington Post,* available at http://articles.washingtonpost. com/2011-07-06/world/35238319_1_abdul-qadeer-khan-plutonium-weapons-nuclear-weapons (last accessed 17 December 2012).

Snyder, M. (2013, 30 Aug) *Who Benefits from a War between the United States and Syria? The Economic Collapse,* available at http://theeconomiccollapseblog.com/ archives/who-benefits-from-a-war-between-the-united-states-and-syria (last accessed 24 January 2014).

Solomon, N. (2006, 25 September) Media tall tales for the next war. *Media Beat,* available at http://www.coldtype.net/Assets.06/MediaBeat%2006/MB.33.06.pdf (last accessed 11 June 2014).

Sotloff, S. (2011, 24 Oct) Salafis applying a rigid form of Islam in more and more communities, *Time Magazine,* available at www.time.com/time/world/article/0,8599,2104578,00html3ixzz1jv CpebRe (last accessed 4 January 2013).

Sparks, C. (2007) *Globalization, Development and the Mass Media* (Media Culture & Society). London: Sage.

Stanković, S (1967) *Tito and "Non-Alignment." Radio Free Europe.* Retrieved from http://www.osaarchivum.org/files/holdings/300/8/3/text/133-5-9.shtml

Starr, B. (2012, 11 Nov) Iran fires at U.S. drone, *CNN,* available at http://security.blogs. cnn.com/2012/11/08/first-on-cnn-iranian-jets-fire-on-u-s-drone/, (last accessed 3 May 2013).

Starr, S. (2012, Nov) Costs and consequences of the Fukushima Daiichi disaste, *Physicians for Social Responsibility* (PSR), available at www.psr.org/environment-

and-health/environmental-health-policy-institute/responses/costs-and-consequences-of-fukushima.html (last accessed 9 May 2013).

Stein, J. (2010, 30 Sept) CIA hired Karzai brother before 9/11, Woodward says, *The Washington Post*, available at http://voices.washingtonpost.com/spy-talk/2010/09/cia_hired_karzai_brother_befor.html (last accessed 27 July 2012).

Stinnett, R. (2001) *Day of Deceit: The Truth about FDR and Pearl Harbor*. New York: Free Press.

Stockholm International Peace Research Institute (SIPRI) (2012) *SIPRI Yearbook 2012*. New York: Oxford University Press.

Stone, O. and Kuznick, P. (2012) *The Untold History of the United States*. New York: Gallery Books.

Straubhaar, J. (2007) *World Television: From Global to Local*. Thousand Oaks, CA: Sage.

Straubhaar, J. (1991) Beyond media imperialism: asymmetrical interdependence and cultural proximity, *Critical Studies in Mass Communication*, 8: 39–59.

Sung, S. (2013) "Digitization and online cultures of the Korean Wave." In Y. Kim (ed.), *The Korean Wave: Korean Media Go Global*. London: Routledge. pp. 135–147.

Symonds, P. (2009, 6 Oct) New York Times recycles fabrications about Iran's nuclear programs, *World Socialist Web Site*, available at https://wsws.org/en/articles/2009/10/iran-o06.html (last accessed 22 April 2013).

Szalvai (2009) *Emerging Forms of Globalization Dialectics: Interlocalization as a New Praxis of Power and Culture in Commercial Media and Development*, PhD Dissertation. Bowling Green State University, Ohio.

Telhami, S. and Kull, S. (2011, 9 Sept) *The American Public on the 9/11 Decade: A Study of American Public Opinion*. Program on International Policy Attitudes, University of Maryland, available at www.sadat.umd.edu/911Anniversary_Sep11_rpt.pdf (last accessed 1 May 2013).

Television Bureau of Advertising (2012) *TV Basics*. TVB.org, available at http://www.tvb.org/media/file/TV_Basics.pdf (last accessed 11 June 2014).

Thomas P., Cloherty J., and Dubbins A. (2011, 29 March) Records show 56 safety violations at U.S. nuclear power plants in past 4 years, *ABC World News*, available at http://abcnews.go.com/Politics/us-nuclear-power-plants-safe/story?id=13246490#.UWl4lbVTBT4 (last accessed 13 April 2013).

Thomas, P.N. (2010) *Political Economy of Communications in India: The Good, the Bad and the Ugly*. New Delhi: Sage.

Thrall, T. (2000) *War in the Media Age*. New York: Hampton.

Thussu, D. (2008) *News as Entertainment: Rise of Global Infotainment*. London: Sage.

Thussu, D. (2006) *International Communication*. London: Sage.

Timmerman, K.R. (1991) *The Death Lobby: How the West Armed Iraq*. New York: Houghton Mifflin.

Tinuoye, K. (2012, 27 Jan) Welcome to "Nollywood": Nigerian film industry entices Hollywood stars, *The Grio*, available at http://thegrio.com/2012/01/27/welcome-to-nollywood-nigerian-film-industry-entices-hollywood-stars/ (last accessed 22 August 2012).

Tisdall, S. (2007, 21 May) Iran's secret plan for summer offensive to force US out of Iraq, the *Guardian*, available at www.guardian.co.uk/world/2007/may/22/iraq.topstories3 (last accessed 21 April 2013).

Tomlinson, H. and Boyes, R. (2012, 20 Feb) Defiant Iran cuts off oil to Britain, *The Times*, available at www.google.com/search?q=Tomlinson+and+Boyes%2C+Defiant+Iran&aq=f&oq=Tomlinson+and+Boyes%2C+Defiant+Iran&aqs=chrome.0.57j0j62.10735j0&sourceid=chrome&ie=UTF-8 (last accessed 26 April 2013).

Tugend, A. (2003, May) Pundits for hire, *American Journalism Review*, available at http://ajrarchive.org/article.asp?id=2995 (last accessed 12 April 2014).

Tunstall, J. (2007) *The Media were American: U.S. Mass Media in Decline*. London: Oxford University Press.

Tunstall, J. (1977) *The Media are American*. London: Constable.

Turse, N. (2013, 13 May) Nuclear terror in the Middle East, *Huffington Post*, available at www.huffingtonpost.com/nick-turse/iran-nuclear-attack-study_b_3265921.html (last accessed 18 May 2013).

Turse, N. (2010, 9 Feb) America's shadowy base-world, *TomDispatch.com*, available at www.tomdispatch.com/archive/175204/nick_turse_america%27s_shadowy_baseworld (last accessed16 July 2012).

UNESCO (2012) *Cinema Statistics*, UNESCO Institute for Statistics, available at www.uis.unesco.org/culture/Pages/movie-statistics.aspx

UNESCO Media Services (2009, 5 May) *Nollywood Rivals Bollywood in Film/Video Production*, available at www.unesco.org/new/en/media-services/single-view/news/nollywood_rivals_bollywood_in_filmvideo_production/ (last accessed 22 August 2012).

UNESCO (1980) *Many Voices, One World. The McBride Report*. Paris: UNESCO.

Ungerman, G. and Brohy, A. (Producers)(2003) *Plan Colombia: Cashing in on the Drug War Failure*. DVD, Free Will Productions

Ungerman, G. and Brohy, A. (Producers)(2001) *Hidden Wars of Desert Storm*, DVD, Free Will Productions.

United Kingdom Cabinet Office (1961a) (PDF) *Atomic Activities in Israel*, 17 July 1961. JIC/1103/61.

United Kingdom Cabinet Office (1961b) (PDF) *Secret Atomic Activities in Israel*, 27 March 1961. JIC/519/61.

United States Census Bureau (2013) *Statistical Abstract of the United States: 2012*. Washington: US Government.

United States Department of Defense (2010, April) *Nuclear Posture Review Report*. United States Department of Defense, available at www.defense.gov/npr/docs/2010%20nuclear%20posture%20review%20report.pdf (last accessed 7 May 2013).

United States Government Accountability Office (2008, Oct) *PLAN COLOMBIA: Drug Reduction Goals Were Not Fully Met, but Security has Improved: US Agencies Need More Detailed Plans for Reducing Assistance*, available at www.gao.gov/new.items/d0971.pdf (last accessed 19 July 2012).

United States Government Printing Office (2005) *Comprehensive Report of the Special Adviser to the DCI on Iraq's WMD with Addendums (Duelfer Report)*. Washington, DC: USGPO.

United States International Trade Commission (1999) *Recent Trends in US Services Trade, 1999 Annual Report*. Washington: US Government.

Van Auken, B. (2013a, 30 Aug) Obama and media manufacture pretext for attack on Syria. *World Socialist Web Site*, available at www.wsws.org/en/articles/2013/08/30/pers-a30.html

Van Auken, B. (2013b, 1 June) Syrian opposition fighters arrested with chemical weapons, *World Socialist Web Site*, available at www.wsws.org/en/articles/2013/06/01/syri-j01.html (last accessed 24 January 2014).

Van Auken, B. (2011, 9 April) New York Times demands escalation, *World Socialist Web Site*, available at www.wsws.org/en/articles/2011/04/time-a09.html (last accessed 9 January 2013).

Van Auken, B. (2009, 30 Sept) Cheats and deceivers, *World Socialist Web Site*, available at www.wsws.org/en/articles/2009/09/pers-s30.html (last accessed 21 April 2013).

Video Games Blogger (2013, 18 Oct) Top 10 bestselling video games worldwide in Week 42, 2013, *Video Games Blogger*, available at www.videogamesblogger.com/2013/10/18/top-10-bestselling-video-games-worldwide-in-week-42-2013.htm#ixzz2lJTBH8tB

Video Games Sales Wiki (2013) Video game industry, *Video Games Sales*, available at http://vgsales.wikia.com/wiki/Video_game_industry

Villar, O. and Cottle, D. (2012) *Cocaine, Death Squads, and the War on Terror: US Imperialism and Class Struggle in Colombia*. New York: Monthly Review Press.

Vine, D. (2012) The Lily-Pad strategy: how the Pentagon is quietly transforming its overseas base empire and creating a dangerous new way of war, TomDispatch.com, available at www.tomdispatch.com/post/175568/tomgram%3A_david_vine%2C_u.s._empire_of_bases_grows/#more (last accessed 16 July 2012).

Vukasovich, C. (2012) The medium is the weapon: The enduring power of Balkan War (mis)coverage. Doctoral Dissertation, Bowling Green State University, Ohio.

Vukasovich, C. and Boyd-Barrett, O. (2012) Whatever happened to Tanjug? Re-loading memory for an understanding of the global news system, *International Communication Gazette*, 74: 693–710.

Walt, S. (2012, 11 March) Top ten media failures in the Iran war debate, *Foreign Policy*, available at http://walt.foreignpolicy.com/posts/2012/03/11/top_ten_media_failures_in_the_iran_war_debate (last accessed 27 April 2013).

Wang, B. (2013, 17 Oct) Variety and movie industry analysts agree China's movie box office heading to $5–$10 billion in 2017, *Next Big Future*, available at http://nextbigfuture.com/2013/10/variety-and-movie-industry-analysts.html (last accessed 14 November 2013).

Washington Post (2012, 22 Aug) Highlights of the Nuclear Posture Review, *The Washington Post*, available at www.washingtonpost.com/wp-dyn/content/graphic/2010/04/06/GR2010040604804.html (last accessed 24 January 2014).

Watts, L. (2013, 30 Aug) China cracks down on independent film, *Salon.com*, available at www.salon.com/2013/08/30/china_acts_to_chill_interest_in_independent_films/ (last accessed 14 November 2013).

Weaver, D.L., McCombs, M.E., and Shaw, D.L. (1997) *Communication and Democracy: Exploring the Intellectual Frontiers in Agenda-setting Theory* (Routledge Communication Series). New York: Routledge.

Webb, G. (1996) *Dark Alliance: The CIA, the Contras, and the Crack Cocaine Explosion*. New York: Seven Stories.

Webb, S. (2007, 19 June) Iran falling short of oil refining ambitions, *Reuters.com*, available at www.reuters.com/article/2007/06/19/us-iran-refinery-idUSL1490018620070619 (last accessed 13 April 2013).

Weber, M. (2012) *The Protestant Ethic and the Spirit of Capitalism*. Las Vegas, NV: CreateSpace Independent Publishing Platform.

Weiner, T. (1996) '93 report by C.I.A. tied Haiti agent to slaying, *New York Times*, available at www.nytimes.com/1996/10/13/world/93-report-by-cia-tied-haiti-agent-to-slaying.html (last accessed 6 December 2013).

Weisbrot (2009, 26 June) Was Iran's election stolen?, *Washington Post*, available at http://newsweek.washingtonpost.com/postglobal/needtoknow/2009/06/was_irans_election_stolen.html (last accessed 24 January 2014).

Weiss, M. (2009, 19 Sept) Israel spurns nuclear watchdog's call to open atomic sites to inspection, *Irish Times*, available at www.irishtimes.com/newspaper/world/2009/0919/1224254860406.html (last accessed 22 April 2013).

Will, G.F. (2009, 29 Oct) A reality check on drug use, *Washington Post*, A19.

Williams, R. (1958) *Culture and Society*. London: Chatto and Windus.

Wilson, R. (2005, March) Letters to the Editor, *The Atlantic Magazine*.

Wingfield-Hayes, R. (2013, 1 April) What happened to Japan's electronics giants?, *BBC*, available at www.bbc.co.uk/news/world-asia-21992700

Winseck, D. and Pike, R. (2007) Communication and Empire: Media, Markets and Globalization 1860–1930. Durham, NC: Duke University Press.

Wise, L. (2013, 30 Aug) Chemical weapons experts weigh in on Syria intelligence report, *McClatchy*, available at www.mcclatchydc.com/2013/08/30/200931/chemical-weapons-experts-weigh.html

Wittner, L. (2012, 23 April) The shame of nations, *Counterpunch*, available at www.counterpunch.org/2012/04/23/the-shame-of-nations/ (last accessed 16 July 2012).

Whitney, M. (2006, 17 January) The countdown to war with Iran. *Online Journal*, available at http://www.onlinejournal.com/artman/publish/article_425,shtml (last accessed 11 June 2014).

Wofstal, J. (1992, March) Iran hosts IAEA mission: Syria signs safeguard pact, *Arms Control Today*, 22: 28.

Woodard, B. (2010) *Obama's Wars*. New York: Simon and Shuster.

World Nuclear Association (2013, March) Uranium enrichment, *World Nuclear.org*, available at www.world-nuclear.org/info/Nuclear-Fuel-Cycle/Conversion-Enrichment-and-Fabrication/Uranium-Enrichment/ (last accessed 6 May 2013).

Xin, X. (2012) *How the Market is Changing China's News: The Case of Xinhua News Agency*. New York: Lexington.

Xin, X. (2009) Xinhua news agency in Africa, *Journal of African Media Studies*, 1(3): 363–77.

Xinhua (2014, June 14) Chinese TV producers covet overseas markets. *China Daily*, available at http://www.chinadaily.com.cn/business/2014-06/14/content_17587648.htm (last accessed 14 June 2014).

Xu, W. (2013, 5 Oct) Low budget films pack a wallop, *Shanghai News Daily*, available at http://shanghainewsdaily.com/low-budget-films-pack-a-wallop (last accessed 14 November 2013).

Yang, Y. (2013, 10 May) Big Panda v. Little Rabbit story, *China Daily*, available at http://usa.chinadaily.com.cn/weekly/2013-05/10/content_16489144.htm (last accessed 14 November 2013).

Yu, S. (2014, 14 Jan) China's online giants Alibaba and Tencent go head to head, *South China Morning Post*, available at www.scmp.com/business/china-business/article/1408024/chinas-online-giants-alibaba-and-tencent-go-head-to-head (last accessed 18 January 2014).

Yuen,-Ying, C. (2010, June) A scholar's view: the state media have an iron grip and grand plans, *Globalasia.org*, available at www.globalasia.org/Issue/Article Detail/329/a-scholars-view-the-state-media-have-an-iron-grip-and-grand-plans. html (last accessed 24 January 2014).

Zand, B. (2010, 6 Dec) Blinkered view of Iraq: diplomats were misled by Saddam's "cordial" manner, *Spiegel Online International*, available at www.spiegel.de/international/world/blinkered-view-of-iraq-diplomats-were-misled-by-saddam-s-cordial-manner-a-733153.html

Zeidler, S. and Grover, R. (2012, 29 June) China to launch Netflix-lie movie service, Reuters. com, available at http://in.reuters.com/article/2012/06/28/entertainment-us-hollywood-china-jiaflix-idINBRE85R19120120628

Zeitchik, S. and Landreth, J. (2012, 12 June) Hollywood gripped by pressure system from China, *Los Angeles Times*, available at http://articles.latimes.com/2012/jun/12/entertainment/la-et-china-censorship-20120612 (last accessed 14 November 2013).

Zinn, H. (2010) *A People's History of the United States*. New York: Harper.

Index